The American Crisis

Frederick William Dame

ISBN-13: **978-1500771133**

ISBN-10: **1500771139**

Library of Congress Control Number (LCCN): 2014915103

CreateSpace Independent Publishing Platform

North Charleston, SC

2014

Second edition 2015

The American Crisis

Frederick William Dame

TABLE OF CONTENTS

Letter To American Patriots

Dear American Patriots!

Between December 1776 and December 1783, I wrote nineteen chapters of what history refers to as *The American Crisis Papers*, which were signed *Common Sense*. For this work I have been honored with the sobriquet *Pamphleteer of the Revolution*. That historical period was a crisis par excellence in the forming stages of what was to become the Republic of the United States of America.

America is now in its second crisis, fueled by the illegal election of Barack Hussein Obama as the 44th President (but bogus President) of the United States of America and his support by a treasonous DemocRAT Party. Barack Hussein Obama, the personification of evil, and his moonstruck followers have created a new American Crisis with the goal of tearing asunder the *Constitution for the United States of America* and the country's republican form of government. The demons are in the process of destroying American wisdom and knowledge made law by America's Founding Fathers.

I unequivocally state that Barack Hussein Obama's goal is the total annihilation of the United States of America so that socialism-communism can be implemented. However, this is only one part of a two-pronged pincer movement to devastate our country. The second part is, that concurrent with our *Constitution*, Islamic sharia law will be introduced so that it will eventually supplant the American *Constitution*.

This is a humiliation and demoting of constitutionally guaranteed freedoms. America will be combated by a two-front ideological attack and the United States of America will cease to exist. Ultimately Americans will lose every legally guaranteed right that they hold dear.

Honored Patriots! You should not be surprised! Americans made a choice in 2008 and 2012. That choice yielded the great consequence of America's

ix

self-destruction because of the voting citizens' ignorance and their inability to understand hope and change.

In the American Colonial Revolution there was also a call for hope and change. The hope was that American Colonials would begin a new era in political governing after they had changed the political system from one of royal despotism under the British King George III, to one of a republic responsible to WE the People only in a constitutionally established framework.

In the 1920s, the 1930s, and the 1940s socialism-communism was considered the hope of the world. Famous people like the British mathematician and philosopher Bertrand Russell, Max Shachtman, candidate of the Workers Party for Mayor of New York City in 1944, and the socialist-communist leaning president Franklin Delano Roosevelt never tired in propagandizing for the socialism-communism paradise. The ruse is still continuing under the United Nations Climate Chief Christiana Figueres, who has stated that only communism can successfully fight climate change and global warming. The American ethnologist and anarchist David Graeber of the London School of Economics and Political Science argues a similar position. Methinks that the pro-socialism-communism snake oil sellers forget the fact that easily over 100,000,000 people – this is a very conservative estimation – have been killed by attempts to establish the greatest criminal system in the world in the twentieth century: socialism-communism.

Barack Hussein Obama's mantra of hope and change was definitely of a different sort. Obama's hope is that in addition to becoming an Islamic America, the country will become a socialist-communist state and that the system of a free market economy which has so productively produced wealth and success to those entrepreneurs who actively participate in such a free market economy is changed to the government-regulated careers of brainwashed individuals. This situation is what the DemocRAT Party has always wanted since the Civil War. The slaves were supposed to remain slaves. The politically misinformed, regardless of color, are to be the new

x

slaves to the big-government-handout system guaranteed by the DemocRAT Party.

Americans chose the evilness of Barack Hussein Obama in 2008 and 2012 without thinking about the consequences of their actions. Thus they elected to become disenfranchised from the fool-proof legacy of the Judeo-Christian teachings with the emphasis on moral obligations as envisioned by the Founding Fathers.

The DemocRAT Party has had a long history of undermining personal and ethical responsibility in a political system. One only need to take a cursory look at the junk, revisionist American civics, history, and sociology courses that have been taught and are still being taught and propagated in American schools, colleges, and universities since the end of World War II. A prime example of this intellectual junk is seen in the Common Core educational program, where two plus two is no longer four, or the argument that it does not make a difference if one's answers are wrong, but only that one is understood.

Logic, morals, ethics, Christianity, American history, American traditions and culture are no longer important according to the political usurpers that are the DemocRAT Party and the Barack Hussein Obama regime.

American Exceptionalism was planned from the beginning of the United States of America. Of course, this is in total contradiction to the collectivism of Marxist-big government, named with the innocent nomenclature *the administration of things*, which if not peacefully welcomed by the citizens, will be rammed down their collectivist weasands.

Remember that Barack Hussein Obama claims that *You didn't build that!* What the enemy media and the generally dumb citizen do not comprehend is that such a statement is the absolute refutation of the historical truths of the success of entrepreneurs and the free market economy. The statement is a denial of scientific fact and the propagandist of this deception, Barack Hussein Obama, is totally unqualified to lead the America people because everything he undertakes has the goal of shackling the individual to ignorance, Marxist teaching, and Islamic sharia law. The truth is that the foundational laws that created an atmosphere that allowed American Exceptionalism to develop and thrive are laws that permitted individuals to achieve their full political and economic potential. When the political leader contends the opposite, it is propagandizing a situation that is a falsity and the chief propagandist, Barack Hussein Obama, is a liar. American's constitutional fathers were not liars. They were believers in the Laws of Nature and established a legal framework that gave birth to American Exceptionalism.

The reality behind Barack Hussein Obama's hope and change is that all of the voters exist to be dumbed-down to the most primitive levels of intellect, if ever the word intellect can be used. This hope and change is aimed at the control of a high percentage of Americans virtually incapable of using any cognitive power of logic. This is proven by the fact that when Obama calls for change in the United States of America – the last great bastion of positive, free market economy and republican federal form of government – it has to be the dismantling of the complete economic system and form of government. That is the logic that Americans did not want to, or were unable to comprehend in 2008, 2012, and now!

Being free according to the Laws of Nature is an ever-continuing process. The Founding Fathers understood that this process will make the citizen enlightened. Yet it requires a political environment framed by moral laws coming from WE the People, not executive orders being dictated by a totalitarian, treasonous government. Modern-day Americans are in a bottomless pit of ignorance. They want big government to provide for them and forget that the bigger the government, the surer it is to take away their freedoms. In my day we patriotic revolutionaries fought against big government and for the natural laws and rights vested in WE the People.

My original *The American Crisis Papers* described the moments of truth America was facing in the Colonial Revolutionary Period in American history. The days of enlightened visionaries in my era gave America the foundation of freedom. The present days of Obama nightmares are taking those freedoms away. There is no rational wisdom in Obama's policies because he is not and will never be a seeker of Truth.

In January 2014, Frederick William Dame contacted me in time-warped Philadelphia and conveyed to me his concerns about the present condition of the United States of America. His logic is that there are very similar conditions in America today that were present in the Colonial America of my day. Mr. Dame asked me if I would give him permission to use *The American Crisis Papers* of 1776-1783 as a basis from which to convey his arguments that America is in a modern-day crisis. I am overjoyed that there is still a core patriotic feeling for the country of freedom that evolved out of the American Revolution. I consider it an honor to be of patriotic importance in the era of Barack Hussein Obama who is the ultimate insult to freedom-loving Americans.

With this letter I allow Frederick William Dame to freely use my original *American Crisis Papers* so that American patriotic citizens and those who have been brainwashed by the DemocRAT Party and Barack Hussein Obama will be able to realize the dangers of the totalitarianism of big government and creeping Islam, which the English orientalist George Sale, the translator of the Koran into English in 1734, described as "certainly one of the most convincing proofs that Mohammedism (sic) was no other than human invention, that it owed its progress and establishment almost entirely to the sword." May Americans use the wisdom in Mr. Dame's *American Crisis* to reverse this Satanical attack on free, God-fearing Americans.

In closing, I make the following statement concerning Barack Hussein Obama and cite the Roman philosopher, politician, lawyer, orator, political theorist, consul, and constitutionalist Marcus Tullius Cicero who says in *Orationes in Verrem*, Actio I, 3. 8:

"... *civium* ... *cruciatus multorumque innocentium sanguis istius supplicio luendus est!*

Stamus Contra Malum

Thomas Paine
The Pamphleteer of the Revolution
Time-warped Philadelphia, June in 1784

***

Note: Cicero writes *civium Romanorum cruciatus* … . (The freely applied translation of the above Latin quotation is: *The ordeal of (the) citizens and the blood of the innocent demand atonement by means of hanging this thug [Barack Hussein Obama]*.)

Frederick William Dame

The American Crisis

These Are The Times That Try American Patriots' Souls

A Call To Take Action

Number One

These are truly the times that try American Patriots' souls. The backboneless soldiers who do not honor their oaths to the *Constitution for the United States of America* and the non-patriotic peacock generals are, in this crisis, shrinking from the service of their country; but those that stand upright now, deserve the love and thanks of every patriotic man and woman in the United States of America. Tyranny, in the person of Barack Hussein Obama and his regime, like Hell, is not easily conquered; yet we have this consolation with us, that the harder the conflict, the more glorious the triumph of WE the People over this evil will be. What we obtain too cheap, we esteem too lightly: it is dearness only that gives everything its value. Heaven knows how to put a proper price upon its goods; and it would be strange indeed if so celestial an article as **freedom** guaranteed by the *Constitution for the United States of America* should not be highly rated. Obama, with an army of POLDS (Progressives, Obots, Liberals, Dumbed-downers, Socialists-Communists) to enforce his tyranny, has declared that he has a right with his self-executed directives and regulations (not only to **tax** with ObamaCare, the real name is the Affordable Care Act, which is neither affordable and Barack Hussein Obama does not care; but "to **bind** us in **all cases whatsoever**," and if being bound in that manner, is not slavery, then there is not such a thing as slavery upon earth. Even the expression is impious; for so unlimited a power can belong only to God and not to Barack Hussein Obama or any anti-American, corrupt, evil politician.

Whether hope and change that came with the appearance of Barack Hussein Obama on the American political scene was declared too soon, or delayed too long, I will not now enter into as an argument; my own simple opinion is, that had Obama been vetted by the sissy, lamestream

1

media at any time, it would have been much better. We did not make a proper vetting Barack Hussein Obama, neither could we, while we were in a brainwashed condition. The fault was all our own. We have none to blame but ourselves. But no great deal is lost yet. All that the so-called Congress has been doing these bygone four plus years, is rather a long Rip-Van-Winkle sleep without even one wink as a control function, which the spirit of the 1776ers would have quickly repulsed, and which time and a little patriotic resolution will soon recover. I have as little superstition in me as any man living, but my secret opinion has ever been, and still is, that God Almighty will not give up a people to Obama's destruction, or leave them unsupportedly to perish, who have so earnestly and so repeatedly sought to avoid the calamities of war, and protect themselves from aggressors by every decent method which wisdom could invent. Neither can I suppose that He has relinquished the government of the world, and given us up to the care of devils. I cannot see on what grounds the narcissist, self-appointed king and narcissist self-appointed queen, can look up to heaven for help against us. Obama is a common criminal, an unconvicted felon, a thief! His pretenses are not good!

'Tis surprising to see how rapidly a panic will sometimes run through a country. All nations and ages have been subject to them. We once trembled like an ague at the report of a Japanese attack on Pearl Harbor; and in the Cold War of the twentieth century the whole communist forces, after ravaging the entirety of Eastern Europe, were defeated like men petrified with fear; and this brave exploit was performed by a few broken forces collected and headed by Liberty. Would that heaven continue to inspire the Alaskan maid to spirit up her countrymen, and save her fair fellow sufferers from ravage and ravishment of the Obama regime! Panics, in some cases, have their uses; they produce as much good as hurt. Their duration is always short; the mind soon grows through them, and acquires a firmer habit than before. But their peculiar advantage is that they are the touchstones of both sincerity and hypocrisy, and bring things and men to light, which might otherwise have lain forever undiscovered. In fact, they have the same effect on secret traitors, which an imaginary apparition would have upon Obama POLDS. Panics sift out the hidden thoughts of humans, and hold them up in public to the world, whether the purchased media desires it or not. Many a disguised socialist, communist, and republican in name only has lately shown his head. WE the People shall penitentially solemnize with curses the day on Barack Hussein Obama and his thugs arrived in Washington, D. C.

As I was once a proud member of the troops, and marched with them to protect the United States of America, I am well acquainted with many circumstances, which those who live at a distance know but little or nothing of. Our military situation has become exceedingly cramped, with Obama's rules of engagement that support the enemy and Obama-nominated idiot United Nations ambassadors, and absolutely dumb national security advisors, as well as a do-nothing Secretaries of State Hillary Clinton and John Kerry. Our military forces are now inconsiderable, being not one-fourth as great as they once were. We now have no strong army at hand to combat the Taliban in Afghanistan and Pakistan and Islamic terrorists throughout North Africa and the Middle East. Even in the United States dedicated law enforcement agencies are hampered in their jobs by the Attorney General Eric Holder, a major thug in the Obama regime. We cannot shut ourselves up and stand our defence due to Obama's non-leadership. Our weapon systems have been given away to America's enemies operating in Libya, Syria, and on the borders of Israel. The secret of United States Seal Team Six was divulged and members were placed in a situation where six of them were killed by Islamic Taliban in Afghanistan. Important members of our special operations troops have been removed from their positions, undergone military courts martial for defending America, and received prison terms. There are Muslim Brotherhood members and sympathizers in the White House. Obama supports jihadists in Africa and the Middle East. It must occur to every thinking American Patriot, whether in the armed forces or not, that these kind of politics are factual examples of Obama hate to be used for destructive purposes. They will last as long as the enemy Obama regime directs its hate against a particular object of American tradition and culture. Such is our present situation and condition.

Our first object is to secure the individual states against the enemy Obama regime. With logic and truth on our side Barack Hussein Obama and his POLDS will not win. We must bring other Americans, those who are patriotic and particularly those who are too emotionally and intellectually lazy, to reason. This is a formidable goal because the greater majority of the latter group have been dumbed down and thoroughly brainwashed. Though our numbers are greatly inferior to our enemy, the enemy will nevertheless commit great errors in their endeavors and break the law. WE the People must see to it that the law is enforced, which will undoubtedly mean that WE the People will have to remove those who are not enforcing OUR laws. But if WE believe the power of Hell to be limited, WE must likewise believe that their leader from Hell and his POLDS are under some providential control. WE the People shall not retreat. WE the People shall bear the burden with a patriotic and martial spirit. All of our wishes are centered in one, which is, that the country will come to reason and drive the enemy Obama and his regime out of Washington and into oblivion. WE the People must appear to full advantage in difficulties and in action. There is a natural firmness in some minds which cannot be unlocked by trifles, but which, when unlocked, discovers a cabinet of fortitude; and I reckon it among those kind of public blessings, which we do not immediately see, that God hath blessed US the People with uninterrupted patriotism and drive, and has given US a mind that flourishes.

I shall conclude this essay with some miscellaneous remarks on the state of our affairs; and shall begin with asking the following question: Why is it that the enemy Obama regime has left the realm of abiding by the law? The answer is easy: The Obama regime is infested with criminals and anti-American crap. I have been tender in raising the cry against these persons, and used numberless arguments to show them as being the danger, but it will not do to sacrifice a world either to their folly or their baseness. The period has now arrived, in which either they or we must change our sentiments, or one or both must fall. What is an Obama? Good God! What is he? I should not be afraid to go with a hundred American Patriots against a thousand Obamas, were they to attempt to get into arms. Every Obama is a coward; for servile, slavish, self-interested fear is the foundation of Obamaism; and a man under such influence, though he is a cruel criminal, never can be brave. But, before the line of irrecoverable separation be drawn between the Obama side and American Patriots, let us reason the matter together. Our conduct of doing nothing is an invitation to the enemy Obama regime, yet not one in a thousand of you has heart enough to join them unless you are a republican in name only. The Obama regime is as much deceived by you as the American cause is injured by you. They expect WE the People will all take up arms, and flock to Washington, with rifles on our shoulders and pistols in our holsters. Our opinions are of no use to him, unless you

4

support him personally, for 'tis POLDS, and not American Patriots that he wants.

I once felt all that kind of anger, which a man ought to feel, against the mean principles that are held by the enemy Obama regime when they express: "Well! He gives us peace in our day." Not a man lives on the continent but fully believes that a conflict must some time or other finally take place, and a generous patriotic statement is, "If there must be trouble, let it be in my day, that my child may have peace;" and this single reflection is sufficient to awaken every patriot to duty. Not a place upon earth might be as happy as America. Her situation is separate from the entire wrangling world, and she has nothing to do but to protect herself from them. A man can distinguish himself between temper and principle, and I am as confident, as I am that God governs the world, that America will never be happy till she gets clear of Obama dominion. Destruction, without ceasing, will break out till that period arrives, and WE the People must in the end be conqueror; though the flame of Liberty sometimes ceases to shine, the fire of Liberty can never expire. Patriotic America does not want to use force; but wants a proper application of that force. Wisdom is not the purchase of a day, and it is no wonder that we should err at the first setting off. From an excess of tenderness, we were unwilling to formulate a resistance, and trusted our cause to the temporary defence of a pseudo-well-meaning charlatan politician. A too-many years' experience has now taught us better; yet our patriotic forces, while they were collecting, have been able to set bounds to the progress of the Obama enemy, and, thank God! WE the People are again assembling. I always considered American Patriots as the best troops in the world for a sudden exertion, and they must do for a long campaign, after which Obama and his regime will be ruined. If he succeeds, our cause is not ruined. He stakes all on his side against WE the People. The consequence will be that patriotic armies from both ends of the continent will march to assist their suffering fellow patriots. Obama and his thugs cannot go everywhere, it is impossible. I consider Obama as the greatest enemy the United States of America has ever had. He is bringing a class war into this country, He must be expelled. I wish with all the devotion of a Christian that the Obama regime be expelled from the continent and the Congress appropriate their possessions to the relief of those who have suffered by Obama's destructive doings. A single successful victory in November 2014 will settle the whole. America could carry on for two more years of Obama's destruction. Yet it is folly to argue against determined hardness; eloquence may strike the ear, and the language of sorrow draw forth the tear of compassion, but nothing can reach the heart that is steeled with procrastination. I turn with the warm ardor of a friend to those who have nobly stood, and are yet determined to stand the matter out: I call not upon a few, but upon all: not on this state or that state, but on every state: up and help us; lay your shoulders to the grindstone; better have too much force than too little, when so great an object is at stake – freedom from Obama and his destructive regime.

Let it be told to the future world that in the depth of destruction, when nothing but patriotic hope and virtue could survive, that the city and the country, alarmed at one common danger, came forth to meet and to repulse it. Say not that thousands are gone, turn out your tens of thousands; throw not the burden of the day upon Providence, but "show your faith by your works," that God may bless you. It matters not where you live, or what rank of life you hold, the evil or the blessing will reach you all. The far and the near, the home country and the back, the rich and the poor, will suffer or rejoice alike. The heart that feels not now is dead; the blood of the children will curse the coward who shrinks back at a time when a little might have saved the whole, and made them happy. I love the American Patriot who can smile in trouble, who can gather strength from distress, and grow brave by reflection. 'Tis the business of little minds to shrink; but he whose heart is firm, and whose conscience approves his conduct, will pursue his principles unto death. My own line of reasoning is to myself as straight and clear as a ray of light. Not all the treasures of the world, so far as I believe, could have induced me to support an offensive revolution against the enemy Obama regime for the sake of revolting. But if a thief breaks into my house, burns and destroys my property, and kills or threatens to kill me, or those that are in it, and to "bind me in all cases whatsoever" to his absolute will, am I to suffer it? What signifies it to me, whether he who does it is an illegal usurper or a common man; my countryman or not my countryman; whether it be done by an individual villain, or an army of them? If we reason to the root of things we shall find no difference; neither can any just cause be assigned why we should punish in the one case and pardon in the other. Let them call me a patriotic rebel and welcome, I feel no concern from it; but I should suffer the misery of devils, were I to make a whore of my soul by swearing allegiance to one whose character is that of a sottish, stupid, stubborn, worthless, brutish thug. I conceive likewise a horrid idea in receiving mercy from a being, that at the last day shall be shrieking to the rocks and mountains to cover him, and fleeing with terror from the orphan, the widow, and the slain of America.

There are cases which cannot be overdone by language, and this is one. There are persons, too, who see not the full extent of the evil which threatens them; they solace themselves with hopes that the enemy Obama, if he succeeds, will be merciful. It is the madness of folly to expect mercy from those who have refused to do justice; and even mercy, where conquest is the object, is only a trick of lying; the cunning of the fox is as murderous as the violence of the wolf, and we ought to guard equally against both. Obama's first object is, partly by threats and partly by promises, to terrify or seduce the people to deliver up their constitutional rights and receive mercy. This is what he calls making peace, "a peace which passeth all understanding" indeed! A peace which would be the immediate forerunner of a worse ruin than any we have yet thought of. Ye Patriots of America, do reason upon these things! Were the countryside to give up their arms, they would fall an easy prey to Obama's forces, who are all armed: this perhaps is what some of Obama's forces would not be sorry for. Were the cities to deliver up their arms, they would be exposed to the resentment of the countryside that would then have it in their power to chastise their defection at pleasure. And were any one state to give up its arms, that state must be garrisoned by all of Obama's forces to preserve it from the anger of the rest. Mutual fear is the principal link in the chain of mutual love, and woe be to that state that breaks the compact. Barack Hussein Obama is mercifully inviting you to barbarous destruction, and men must be either rogues or fools that will not see it. I dwell not upon the vapors of imagination; I bring reason to your ears and, in language as plain as A, B, C, hold up truth to your eyes.

I thank God that I fear not. I see no real cause for fear. I know our situation well, and can see the way out of it. While our forces were not collected the Obama regime did not risk a confrontation, but it is great credit to us, that, with a handful of patriots, WE the People have sustained OURSELVES throughout his usurped presence, fought off cries of being racist and suffered innumerable insults from all anti-Americans. The sign of fear is not seen in our camp. Our American Patriots at both ends of the continent are recruiting fast, and we shall be able to open the next campaign to regain America with thousands of freedom-loving supporters well versed in their political and constitutional rights. This is our situation, and who will, may know it. By perseverance and fortitude we have the prospect of a glorious issue; by cowardice and submission, the sad choice of a variety of evils: incarcerated citizens without due process of law – a ravaged country – depopulated cities without safety, and slavery without hope – our homes turned into barracks and bawdy-houses for POLDS, and a future race to provide for illegal immigrants. With our Founding Fathers, look on this picture and weep over it! And if there yet remains one thoughtless wretch who believes it not, let him suffer it unlamented. Fight for your country! Throw Obama and his thugs out! Away with them! The present time is ripe and worth an age, if rightly employed; but, if lost or neglected, all of the United States of America will partake of the evil; and there is no punishment that man does not deserve, be he who, or what, or where he will, that may be the means of sacrificing an opportunity so precious and useful.

These are the times that try American Patriots' souls. Indeed! WE the People value our souls and the soul of the United States of America as it developed out of the American Revolution. The principles established as law in the *Constitution for the United States of America* are the guarantees of our freedom. The policies of Barack Hussein Obama and his thug regime are anti-American to the core. WE the People shall never allow an enemy to steal and obliterate our unalienable rights!

===================★★★★★★★★★★★★★===================

Frederick William Dame
Patriotic, Steadfast, and True
January 15, 2014

Frederick William Dame

The American Crisis

People Who Rebel In Defense Of Reason

Rebel Against Tyranny

A Call To Take Action

Number Two

A universal audience is the prerogative of a writer. His concerns are with all mankind, and though he cannot command their obedience, he can assign them their duty. The impetus of this writing at this time in the American Crisis is directed at American Patriots. The Republic of Letters is more ancient than dictatorship, and of far higher character in the world than the Barack Hussein Obama regime; he who rebels against reason is a real rebel, but he who in defence of reason rebels against tyranny has a better title to leadership than Barack Hussein Obama.

A military man may hold out the sword of war, and call it the *ultima ratio regum*: the last reason of kings; we American Patriots in return can show Barack Hussein Obama the sword of justice, and call it "the best scourge of tyrants." The first of these two may threaten, or even frighten for a while, and cast a sickly languor over an insulted people, but reason will soon recover the debauch, and restore them again to tranquil fortitude. Barack Hussein Obama with his executive orders and signature, I find, has published proclamations; I have published American Crisis papers. As they stand, they are the antipodes of each other; both cannot rise at once, and one of them must descend; and so quick is the revolution of things, that Obama's performance, I see, has already fallen many degrees from its first place, and is now just visible on the edge of the political precipice.

It is surprising to what a pitch of infatuation, blind folly and obstinacy will carry mankind, and Obama's false promises and dictatorship proclamations are proof that it does not even quit them in their sleep.

Perhaps Barack Hussein Obama thought America, too, was taking a nap, and therefore chose, like Satan to Eve, to whisper his delusion softly, lest he should awaken WE the People. This country is too extensive to sleep all at once, and too watchful, even in its slumbers, not to startle at the unhallowed foot of a usurper. Barack Hussein Obama! You may issue your proclamations, and welcome, for we have learned to "reverence ourselves," and scorn the insulting ruffian that is you! America would gladly have shown you respect and it is a new aggravation to her feelings, that Barack Hussein Obama should be insulting, and raise his sword against those, who at their own desire raise themselves to liberty. But you and your thugs have not enough of nature left to be moral. Surely there must be something strangely degenerating in the love of the Obama regime that can so completely wear a man down to an ingrate, and make him proud to lick the dust that you, this evil person, have trod upon. A few more years, should Americans survive, will bestow on you and your thugs the title of "old criminals" and in some hour of future reflection you may probably find the fitness of Thomas Wolsey's despairing penitence: "had I served ... God as faithful as I have served [Satan], He would not thus have forsaken me in my old age."

The character in which you appear to us is truly ridiculous. Your friends, the Chicago thugs and the DemocRATS, announced your coming, with high descriptions of unlimited powers; but your proclamations have given them the lie, by showing you to be a commander-in-chief without authority and reason. Had your powers been ever so great they were nothing to us, further than we pleased; because we had the same right which other nations have, to do what we think is best. "The United States of America," will sound pompously in the world or in history; the character of a new General Washington will fill pages with as much lustre as that of the Founding Fathers: and the Congress have as much right to command the putative Obama regime and force them to desist from continued thuggery.

Citizens of America! Suppose how laughable such acts of dictatorship would appear coming from American Patriots, and then, in that merry mood, do but turn the tables upon yourselves, and you will see how Obama's proclamations are received by American Patriots. Barack Hussein Obama! Having thus placed you in a proper position in which you may have a full view of your folly, and learn to despise it, I hold up to you, for that purpose, the following policy from your own lunarian proclamation. "King Obama does command all such persons as are assembled together, under the name of federal or state congresses, committees, conventions or other associations, by whatever name or names known and distinguished, to continue all such treasonable actings and doings."

In his speeches Barack Hussein Obama always sinks himself below any positive character. That I may not seem to accuse him unjustly, I shall state a circumstance: by verbal invitations of his, communicated to Congress he signified his desire of conferring with some members of that body as private persons. It is beneath the dignity of the American Congress to pay any regard to such a suggestion that at best was but a genteel affront, and had too much of the commander-in-chief complexion of tampering with private persons; and which might probably have been the case, had the gentlemen who were deputed on the business possessed that kind of easy virtue which a proper patriotic politician is so truly distinguished by. Obama's request, however, was complied with, for dishonest men are naturally tenderer of their political fame than their civil fame. The interview ended as every sensible American Patriot thought it would; on his part, he had nothing to say, more than to request, in the room of demanding, the entire surrender of the Congress; and then, if that was complied with, to promise that the Congress persons should be re-elected to their positions. This was the upshot of the conference. Obama informed the conferees that he would work with them. We ask, what work? For as a golfer he has none. If he means the power of dictatorship, it is an oblique proof that he is determined to sacrifice all before him. Another evidence of his savage obstinacy! From his own account of the matter WE the People may justly draw these two conclusions: first, that Obama is a monster; and second, that there never was a politician being more foolish than himself. This plain language may perhaps sound uncouthly to an ear vitiated by refinements of political correctness, but words were made for use, and the fault lies in deserving them, or the abuse in applying them unfairly.

Soon after Obama returns from the golf course, and while Valerie Jarrett continues playing president, he throws a very illiberal and unmanly threat against the Congress; for it was certainly stepping out of the line of common civility, first to screen his national pride by soliciting an interview with them as private persons, and in the conclusion to endeavor to deceive the multitude by making an attack on the whole body of the Congress. Obama got them together under one name, and abused them under another. But the cause he supports, affords him so few instances of acting the gentleman, that out of pity to his situation the Congress pardoned the insult in their political correctness by taking no notice of it.

Obama says "that they, the Congress, disavowed every purpose for reconciliation not consonant with their extravagant and inadmissible claim of independence." Why, God bless me! What has Obama to do with Congress' independence? We ask no leave of Obama's to set it up; we ask no money of Obama's to support it; we can do better without his lies and propaganda than with them. The Obama regime may soon have enough to do to protect themselves without being burdened with us. We are very willing to be at peace and to work for our living; therefore, why do they want us, WE the People on the dole, when WE know they cannot spare it, and WE do not desire the country to run into debt? I am willing that Obama should see his folly in every point of view I can place it in, and for that reason descend sometimes to tell him what I wish him to see in earnest. But to be more serious with Obama, why does he say, "their independence"? To set you right, Barack Hussein Obama, we American Patriots tell you, that the independency is ours, not yours. The Congress were authorized by every state in the country to publish its source of authority as being WE the People to all the world, and in so doing are not to be considered as the inventors, but only as the heralds that proclaim it, or the office from which the sense of the people received a legal form; and it was as much as any or all their heads were worth, to have treated with Barack Hussein Obama on the subject of submission under any name whatever. But WE know the men in whom WE the People have trusted; can Obama say the same of his regime?

I come now more particularly to Obama's speeches on hope and change. Had Obama gained an entire conquest over all of America, and then put forth a statement, offering what Obama calls hope-and-change paradise of the private person, his conduct would have had some specious show of brainwashing to creep by surprise his policies and endeavor to terrify and seduce the inhabitants from their just allegiance to the rest by promises, which he neither meant nor is able to fulfill, is both cruel and unmanly: cruel in its effects; because, unless he can keep all the promises he has stated, how can he, in the words of his speeches, secure to his proselytes "the enjoyment of their lives?" What is to become either of his new adopted subjects, or our old patriotic friends in the many other places, where Obama proudly campaigned for a few days, and then fled with the precipitation of a pursued criminal and traitor? What, I say, is to become of those wretches? What is to become of those who went over to him from this city or that State? What more can we American Patriots say to them than "shift for yourselves?" Or what more can they hope for than to wander like vagabonds over the face of the America? Obama may now tell them to take their leave of the America of bygone days, and all that once was theirs. Recommend them, for consolation, to his dictatorship; there perhaps they may make a shift to live on the scraps of some dangling parasite, and choose companions among thousands like themselves. A traitor is the foulest fiend on earth.

In a political sense American Patriots ought to thank you, Barack Hussein Obama, for thus bequeathing hate to America; we shall soon, at this rate, be able to carry on a revolution and grow rich in patriotism by the ill policy of the Obama kingship, and expose traitors Americans were at first unwilling to suspect. But these men, you'll say, "are your most faithful subjects;" let that dishonor, then, be all their ill fortune, and let King Obama take them to his narcissistic self.

I am thoroughly disgusted with the Barack Hussein Obama regime; they live in ungrateful ease, and bend their whole minds to mischief. It seems as if God had given them over to a spirit of infidelity, and that they are open to conviction in no other line but that of punishment. It is time to have done with tarring, feathering, carting, and taking securities for their future good behavior; every sensible man must feel a conscious shame at seeing a poor fellow hawked for a show about the streets, when it is known he is only the tool of some principal villain, biased into his offence by the force of false reasoning, or bribed thereto, through sad necessity. We dishonor ourselves by attacking such trifling characters while greater ones are suffered to escape; 'tis our duty to find them out, and their proper punishment would be to exile them from the United States of America forever. The circle of them is not as great as some imagine; the influence of a few have tainted many who are not naturally corrupt. A continual circulation of lies among those who are not much in the way of hearing them contradicted, will in time pass for truth; and the crime lies not in the believer but the inventor. I am not for declaring war with every man that appears not so warm as myself: difference of constitution, temper, habit of speaking, and many other things, will go a great way in forming the outward character of a man, yet simple honesty may remain at bottom. Some men have naturally a military turn, and can brave hardships and the risk of life with a cheerful face; others have not; no slavery appears to them so great as the fatigue of arms, and no terror so powerful as that of personal danger. What can we say? We cannot alter nature, neither ought we to punish the son because the father begot him in a cowardly mood. However, I believe most men have more courage than they know of, and that a little at first is enough to begin with. I knew the time when I thought that the roar of ammunition would have frightened me almost to death; but I have since tried it, and find that I can stand it with as little discomposure, and, I believe, with a much easier conscience than you, Barack Hussein Obama, and your regime thugs. The same dread would return to me again were I in your situation, for my solemn belief of your cause is, that it is hellish and damnable, and, under that conviction, every thinking man's heart must fail him.

From a concern that a good cause should be dishonored by the least disunion among us, I said in my former Call To Take Action that there is a knot of men among us of such a venomous cast, that they will not admit even one's good wishes to act in their favor. Instead of rejoicing that heaven has, as it were, providentially preserved this country from total plunder and destruction, these men are continually harping on the great sin of our bearing arms, but the King of Washington, D. C. may lay waste the world in blood and terror, and they, poor fallen souls, have nothing to say.

In some future Call To Take Action I intend to distinguish between the different kind of persons who have been denominated DemocRATS; for this I am clear in that all are not so who have been called so, nor all men Republicans who were once thought so; and as I mean not to conceal the name of any true friend when there shall be occasion to mention him, neither will I that of an enemy, who ought to be known, let his rank, station or religion be what it may. Much pain has been taken by some to set your private character in an amiable light, but as it has chiefly been done by men and women who know nothing about you, and who are no ways remarkable for their attachment to WE the People, WE American

Patriots have no just authority for believing what they say. King Obama has imposed similar lies upon us by the same arts, but time, at length, has proven him a charlatan. Your avowed purpose here is to kill, conquer, plunder, brainwash, and enslave: and the ravages of your domestic thug army will have been marked with as much barbarism as if you had openly professed yourself the prince of ruffians; not even the appearance of humanity has been preserved on your ascendancy to power. No executive order that I could ever learn, has ever been issued to prevent or even forbid your thugs from insulting your opponents, wherever they came, and the only instance of justice, if it can be called such, which has distinguished you for impartiality, is, that you have treated and plundered all alike. There was a time when the Americans confided much in your supposed genius, and they rested themselves in your favor. How Americans may rest under your character I know not; but this I know, that you sleep and rise with the daily curses of thousands upon you, Barack Hussein Obama!

Imagine the following scenario: His evilness, the Commander-in-Chief in Washington, D. C. orders that all inhabitants who shall be found with arms shall be immediately taken and hung up!

A bad cause will ever be supported by bad means and bad men; and whoever will be at the pains of examining strictly into things, will find that one and the same spirit of oppression and impiety, more or less, governs through your whole DemocRAT Party: Not many days ago, I accidentally fell in company with a person noted for espousing your cause, and on my remarking to him, "that it appeared clear to me, by the late providential turn of affairs, that God Almighty was visibly on our side," he replied, "We care nothing for that you may have Him, and welcome; if we have but enough of the devil on our side, we shall do." However carelessly this might be spoken, matters not, 'tis still the insensible principle that directs all your conduct and will at last most assuredly deceive and ruin you.

If ever a nation was mad and foolish, blind to its own interest and bent on its own destruction, it is Obamanation. There are such things as national sins, and though the punishment of individuals may be reserved to another world, national punishment can only be inflicted in this world. Obamanation, as a nation, is, in my inmost belief, the greatest and most ungrateful offender against God on the face of the whole earth. Blessed with all the commerce America could wish for, and furnished, by a vast extension of dominion, with the means of civilizing both the eastern and western world, the Obama regime has made no other use of both than proudly to idolize Obama's own thunder, and rip up the bowels of whole countries for what he could get. A destroyer of freedom, Obama has made war his sport, and inflicted misery for prodigality's sake. The blood of Obama's involvement in Libya, Egypt, and Syria is not yet repaid, nor the wretchedness he has allowed to be permitted in Africa yet requited. Of late Obama has enlarged his list of national cruelties by not combating the Islamic butchery of Christians and the destruction of Christian churches throughout Syria and Africa. These are serious things, and whatever a foolish tyrant, a debauched regime, a trafficking bureaucracy, or a blinded people may think, the national account with heaven must some day or other be settled: all countries have sooner or later been called to their reckoning; the proudest empires have sunk when the balance was struck; and Barack Hussein Obama, like an individual penitent, must undergo his day of sorrow, and the sooner it happens to him the better. As I wish it over, I wish it to come, but withal wish that it may be as thorough as possible.

Perhaps Obama has no taste for serious things; but I ask him:

By what means, do you expect to conquer America? If you could not effect it in the first four years, when our patriotic forces were less than yours, or we had none, how are you to do it? In point of leadership you have been outwitted, and in point of fortitude outdone; your advantages turn out to your loss, and show American Patriots that it is in our power to ruin you. WE the People can always prevent a total defeat. You cannot be so insensible as not to see that WE have two to one the advantage of you, because WE conquer by patriotism, and you lose by it. I have no other idea of retaking the United States of America than by subduing the traitors who think they are patriots: have you done this, or can you do it?

Were you to obtain possession of this country, you would not know what to do with it more than to plunder it, which you are now doing every day. To hold it in the manner you hold your private life would be an additional dead weight upon your hands; and if a general conquest is your object, you had better be without the country than with it. When you have

16

defeated all American Patriots, America will fall into your hands of itself; but you lie to them in the manner of Satan. Your behavior is like robbing an orchard in the night before the fruit be ripe, and running away in the morning. Your experiment with America is sufficient to teach you that you have something more to do than barely to get into other people's houses; and your new converts, to whom you promised all manner of protection, and seduced into new guilt by pardoning them from their former virtues, must begin to have a very contemptible opinion both of your power and your policy. Your authority is now reduced to the small circle which your regime occupies, and your proclamations are nowhere else seen unless they are laughed at. The mighty subduers of the country have retreated into a nutshell, and the proud forgivers of our capitalist, free market sins are fled from those they came to pardon. In short, you have managed your experiment so very sophomorically, that the brainwashed only are conquerors, because none will dispute the air with them.

In all foreign campaigns which you, Barack Hussein Obama, have formerly been concerned you had only foreign armies to contend with; in this case you have both an American Patriot army and a country to combat with. If the Obama thugs get possession of this country, you will be obliged to shut yourselves up in it, and can make no other use of it, than to spend your shameful lives in its prisons for treason.

I wish to see the United States of America saved from the scoundrels, the spiritless, and the dehumanizers that are your regime. When I put all the circumstances together which ought to be taken, I laugh at your notion of conquering America and turning it into Obamanation. Because your heritage is a hut village in Kenya, where tribal kings might run over the whole in a few days, and where a single company of savages might put a multitude to the rout, you expected to find it the same here. It is plain that you brought from your heritage with you all the narrow notions you were bred up with, and imagined that a proclamation as a king was to do great things; but American Patriots always search for knowledge, and they will appear much wiser than when you arrived on the political scene.

WE the People may be surprised by events WE did not expect, and in that interval of recollection the Obama regime may gain some temporary advantage: but WE the People ripen again into reason, collect our strength, and while you are preparing for a triumph, WE the People will come upon you with a defeat. In order to secure our subjection, (for remember you can do it by no other means except by thuggery) your regime would be like a stream of water running to nothing. By the time you extended across America, you would be reduced to a string of drops not capable of hanging together; while we, by retreating from State to State, like a river turning back upon itself, would acquire strength in the same proportion as you lost it, and in the end be capable of overwhelming you. The country, in the meantime, would suffer, but it is a day of suffering, and we ought to expect it. What WE contend for is worthy the affliction WE may go through. If WE get but bread to eat, and any kind of raiment to put on, WE ought not only to be contented, but thankful. More than that WE ought not to look for, and less than that heaven has not yet suffered US to want. He that would sell his birthright to Satan is as worthless as he who sold it for money; and he that would part with it for a position if illegally gained power, or to claim to be a new king, ought forever to be a slave in buff. What are money, power, and evil to the inestimable blessings of "Liberty and Safety?" Or what are the inconveniences of a few months to the tributary bondage of ages? The meanest Patriot in America, blessed with these sentiments, is a happy man compared with an Obama thug; he can eat his morsel without repining, and when he has done, can sweeten it with a repast of wholesome air; he can take his child by the hand and bless it, without feeling the conscious shame of neglecting a parent's duty.

In publishing these remarks I have several objects in view.

On your part, Barack Hussein Obama, they are to expose the folly of your pretended authority as a commander-in-chief; the wickedness of your cause in general; and the impossibility of your conquering America at any rate. On the part of the American public, my intention is, to show them their true and solid interest; to encourage them to their own good, to remove the fears and falsities which the bad Obama regime has spread, and weak Obama fools have encouraged; and to excite in all Americans a love for union, and cheerfulness for duty.

I shall submit one more case to you, Barack Hussein Obama, respecting your conquest of this country, and then proceed to new observations.

Suppose our American Patriots in every part of this country were immediately to disperse, every man to his home, or where else he might be safe, and engage to reassemble again on a certain future day; it is clear that you would then have no adversary to contend with, yet you would be as much at a loss in that case as you are now; you would be afraid to send your thugs in parties anywhere, either to disarm or prevent us from assembling, lest they should not return; and while you kept them together, having no arms of ours to dispute with, you could not call it a conquest; you might furnish out a pompous page in the *Huffington Post* or the *New York Times*, but when we returned at the appointed time, you would have the same work to do that you had at first.

It has been the folly of the Obama regime to suppose itself more powerful than it really is, and by that means has arrogated to itself a rank in the world it is not entitled to: for more than these five years past the Obama regime has not been able to carry on a war of hope and change without threats that have become dope and chains. The level of intelligence of captive, lamestream leftists assisting the Obama regime have been about equal with the intelligence of the regime's thugs. Thus, the Obama regime cuts but a poor figure in its undertakings concerning the environment scandal, the IRS scandal, the Associated Press scandal, the Fast and Furious scandal, the Benghazi scandal, the closing-down-of-federal-parks-and-public-monuments scandal, the Snowden-NSA scandal, and the ObamaCare scandal, to name only eight of the over 100 scandals that have occurred under your non-leadership. They are symbols of thuggery at its best. Barack Hussein Obama was never famous by himself. His supporters are generally considered to be cowards, have more of the air of a dancing master, and by the examples of the supporters WE the People have seen, WE give the preference concerning uprightness and patriotism to ourselves. Obama's strength has lain in his extravagant brainwashing.

Michelle Obama's finances and credit are now low, because the taxpayers who foot her bills are saying they have had enough. As a person she belongs to the poorest in character; for were the whole family, and all that is in it, to be put up for sale like the estate of a bankrupt, it would not fetch as much as she owes; yet this thoughtless wretch must go on spending, and with the avowed design, too, of making us beasts of burden, to support her as a false queen in debauchery, and to pay her bills because she and Obama feel that Americans owe it to them. This ingratitude may suit them or the unchristian peevishness of a fallen character, but none else.

'Tis the unhappy temper of the Obama regime to be pleased with their undertaking, right or wrong, be it but successful; but they soon grow discontented with ill fortune, and it is an even chance that they are as clamorous for peace, as Michelle Obama is for the next taxpayer-funded vacation. In this natural view of things, you Barack Hussein Obama, your liked-to-have-had lordship stands in a very critical situation: your whole character is now staked upon your self-given laurels; they will wither, you will wither with them; they will not flourish, you cannot live long to look at them; and at any rate, the black account hereafter is not far off. What lately appear to us to be misfortunes are only blessings in disguise; and the seeming advantages on your side have turned out to our profit. Even losses of political position, as far as we can see, might be a principal gain to us: the more surface you spread over, the thinner you will be, and the easier wiped away; and our consolation under that apparent disaster would be, that the estates of the Obama thugs would become securities for the repairs. In short, there is no old ground we can fail upon, but some new foundation rises again to support us. "We have put, Barack Hussein Obama, our hands to arms, and cursed be he that looketh back."

You have done just enough to lay the foundation of your own ruin. You have become a principle evil prop in the DemocRAT Party; their fortunes rest on yours; by a single express you can fix their value with the public, and the degree to which their spirits shall rise or fall; they are in your hands as stock, and you have the secrets of the Chicago alleys with you. Thus situated and connected, you become the unintentional mechanical instrument of your own and their overthrow. The self-appointed king and his thug ministers put conquest out of doubt. To support them in the interim, it is necessary that you should make the most of everything. With a list of ethical victories – namely none – the DemocRAT Party cannot expect you will ask new sacrifices; and to confess your want of them would give the lie to your triumphs, and impeach the self-anointed king and his thug ministers of treasonable deception. If you make the necessary demands at home, your party sinks; if you make them not, you sink yourself; to ask for DemocRAT Party sacrifices now is too late, and to ask them before was too soon, and unless they arrive quickly will be of no use. In short, the part you have to act, cannot be acted; and I am fully persuaded that all you have to trust to is, to do the best you can with what thugs you have got. Though WE the People have greatly exceeded you in point of leadership and bravery of men, – even by just sitting in our armchairs – yet, as a people, we have not entered into the full soul of enterprise; for I, who know the people and the disposition of the people well, am confident, that it is easier for us to effect a revolution, than you a conquest; a few thousand men occupying Washington, D. C. with the declared design of deposing the self-appointed dictator king, bringing his thug ministers to trial, and setting up a provisional government in their stead, would assuredly carry our point, while you are groveling on the golf course, ignorant of the matter. As I send all my papers throughout the land, this, like the Call to Take Action, Number One, will find its way there; and though it may put some false patriots on their guard, it will inform the other real patriots, and the American nation in general, of our design to help them.

Thus far, Barack Hussein Obama, I have endeavored to give you a picture of present affairs: you may draw from it what conclusions you please. I wish as well to the true prosperity of the United States of America, but I consider independence from you and your thug regime as America's natural right and interest. This is my creed of politics. If I have anywhere expressed myself over-warmly, 'tis from a fixed, immovable hatred I have, and ever had, to cruel men and cruel measures. I have likewise an aversion to your character. What I write is pure nature, and my pen and my soul have ever gone together. My writings I have always given away, reserving only the expense of research, paper, and printing, and sometimes not even that. I never courted either fame or interest, and my manner of life, to those who know it, will justify what I say. My study is to be useful, and if you appreciate mankind as well as I do, you would, seeing you cannot conquer us, cast about and lend your hand towards accomplishing a return of America to WE the People. OUR independence with God's blessing WE will maintain against all the world; but as WE wish to avoid evil ourselves, WE wish not to inflict it on others. I am never over-inquisitive into the secrets of the thug cabinet, but I have some notion that, if you neglect the present opportunity, it will not be in OUR power to save you and your thug regime from being prosecuted for your treasonous actions against WE the People of the

United States of America. A lasting independent America is my wish, end and aim; and to accomplish that, I pray God the American Patriots may never be defeated, and I trust while they have good men and women, and are well prepared, and willing to be commanded, that they never will be defeated. WE the People who rebel in defense of reason rebel against tyranny.

★★★★★★★★★★★★★

Frederick William Dame
Patriotic, Steadfast, and True
January 22, 2014

Frederick William Dame

The American Crisis

Never Did Americans Lose So Much Freedom

In So Short A Time

A Call To Take Action

Number Three

★★★★★★★★★★★★

In the progress of politics, as in the common occurrences of life, we are not only apt to forget the ground we have travelled over, but frequently neglect to gather up experience as we go. We expend, if I may so say, the knowledge of every day on the circumstances that produce it, and journey on in search of new matter and new refinements: but as it is pleasant and sometimes useful to look back, even to the first periods of infancy, and trace the turns and windings through which we have passed, so we may likewise derive many advantages by halting a while in our political career, and take a review of the wondrous complicated labyrinth of little more than yesterday.

Once upon a time there was a place where the people had what had become very rare. The people knew what they had was rare and they were happy! Others said that the people were unhappy and that they had to live a life of hope and change. What was once rare no longer exists and the people are not happy! Truly may we say, that never did Americans lose so much freedom in so short a time! We have crowded the business of an age into the compass of a few months, and have been driven through such a rapid succession of things, that for the want of leisure to think, we unavoidably wasted knowledge as we came, and have left nearly as much behind us as we brought with us: but the road is yet rich with the fragments, and, before we finally lose sight of them, it will repay us for the trouble of stopping to pick them up.

Were a man or woman to be totally deprived of memory, they would be incapable of forming any just opinion; everything about him would seem a chaos: they would have even their own history to ask from everyone; and by not knowing how the world went in his absence, they would be at a loss to know how it ought to go on when they recovered, or rather, returned to it again. In like manner, though in a less degree, a too great inattention to past occurrences retards and bewilders our judgment in everything; while, on the contrary, by comparing what is past with what is present, we frequently hit on the true character of both, and become wise with very little trouble. It is a kind of counter-march, by which we get into the rear of time, and mark the movements and meaning of things as we make our return. Applied to the course of American history, this process assuredly underscores OUR culture, traditions, and patriotism.

There are certain circumstances which at the time of their happening, are like riddles, and as every riddle is to be followed by its answer, so those kinds of circumstances will be followed by their events, and those events, when analyzed with logic, lead always to the true solution. A considerable space of time may lapse between, and unless we continue our observations from the one to the other, the harmony of them will pass away unnoticed: but the misfortune is, that partly from the pressing necessity of some instant things, and partly from the impatience of our own tempers, we are frequently in such a hurry to make out the meaning of everything as fast as it happens, that we thereby never truly understand it; and not only start new difficulties to ourselves by so doing, but, as it were, embarrass Providence in her good designs.

I have been civil in stating this fault on a large scale; yet, as it now stands, it does appear to be leveled against a particular set of men; and to refine the fault a little further, it can surely be applied to the DemocRATS with a degree of striking propriety: those persons have been remarkable for drawing sudden conclusions from single facts. The least apparent mishap on the part of American Patriots, or the least seeming advantage on our part, will determine with the enemy Obama regime the fate of a whole political age. By this hasty judgment, the enemy, with the Obama regime scandals, has converted retreats into a defeat. The majority of people mistake Obama's errors for leadership; while every little advantage inadvertently given to WE the People, either to weaken our strength by dividing us, embarrass our councils by multiplying their objects, or to secure a greater post by the surrender of a less, has been instantly magnified into a false conquest. Thus, by

24

quartering ill policy upon ill principles, the Obama regime in its call for hope and change has frequently promoted the cause they designed to injure, and injured that which they superficially intended to promote with hope and change.

It is probable that retorts to earlier Calls To Take Action may arise before this number comes from the press. The enemy Obama regime thugs have not long lain idle, and have amused themselves with carrying on the war against America by dictatorial proclamations only. While they continue their delay, our strength increases, and were they to move to action now, it is a circumstantial proof that they have no reinforcement coming in this election year; wherefore, in either case, the comparative advantage will be ours. Like a wounded, disabled whale, they want only time and room to die in; and though in the agony of their exit, it may be unsafe to live within the flapping of their tail, yet every hour shortens their date, and lessens their power of mischief. If anything happens while this number is in the press, it will afford me a subject for the last pages of it. At present I am tired of waiting; and as neither the enemy Obama thug regime, nor the state of politics have yet produced anything that is not evil, for it has continued to be evil, I am thereby left in the field of general matter, undirected by any striking or particular object. This American Crisis paper, therefore, will be made up rather of variety than novelty, and consist more of things useful than things wonderful.

The success of the cause retaking America by WE the People, the union of the people, and the means of supporting and securing both, are points which cannot be too much attended to. He who doubts of the former is a desponding coward, and he who willfully disturbs the latter is a traitor. Their characters are easily fixed, and under these short descriptions I leave them for the present.

One of the greatest degrees of sentimental union which America will ever know is in denying the right of the Obama regime to bind the States and the citizens in all cases whatsoever, particularly regarding the dissolution of the *Bill of Rights*. The attempt to destroy the *Constitution for the United States of America* is in its form, an almighty one, and is the loftiest stretch of arbitrary power that ever one set of men and women claimed over another. This undertaking will be nothing more than putting the declared illegality into practice; and this failing, recourse will be had

25

to proclaiming martial law as a means to establish both the right and the practice, or to answer a worse purpose, which will be mentioned in the course of this number. Further, in order to repay themselves and to profit by their own injustice, the States will, by an emergency law, be declared to be in a condition of actual rebellion, and of consequence all property therein would then fall to the conquerors. The States, on their part, will have been, first, denied their rights; secondly, the use of their own laws will have been suspended; and these failing; thirdly, their property will be taken by force, as soon as the State is forcibly invaded. This is a future scenario. Even so, this is the same situation that caused the publication of the *Declaration of Independence* in 1776, wherein is composed the right of self-protection.

These, in a few words, are the different stages of the government-citizen quarrel; and the parts are so intimately and necessarily connected with each other as to admit of no separation. A person, to use a trite phrase, must be an American Patriot or an Obama regime lump. The American Patriots' feelings may be wounded; the American Patriots' charity, as a Christian, may be moved; yet, the American Patriots' political principles must go through all the cases on one side or the other. The American Patriot cannot be pro-America in this stage, and pro-Obama in that. If he says he is for the continued united independence of the separate States, he is to all intents and purposes against Obama, who wants everything under federal control, in all the rest; because he argues that the last comprehends the whole. The American Patriot may just as well say that Obama is right in declaring us rebels; right in pursuing us; and right in declaring the federal government has the right to bind the States and the citizens in all cases whatsoever. It signifies nothing what neutral ground, of Obama's own creating, he may skulk upon for shelter, for the quarrel in no stage of it hath afforded any such ground; and either WE the People or the Obama thugs are absolutely right or absolutely wrong through the whole.

The Obama regime, like a gamester nearly ruined, has now put all its scandals into one bet, and is playing a desperate game for the total. If the regime wins it, the regime wins from me my life; the regime wins America as the lost property of rebels; the right of imprisoning those that are left as reduced subjects; and the power of binding them as slaves to the Obama regime: and the single die which determines this unparalleled event is, whether we support our economic freedom and our political independence or whether the Obama regime overturns it. This is coming to the point at once. Here is the touchstone to try men by. He who is not a supporter of the independent States of America is, in the American Patriots' sense of the word, **an Obama thug**; and the instant that he endeavors to bring his thuggery into practice, he becomes **a Traitor**. The first can only be detected by a general test, and the law hath already provided for the latter.

It is unnatural and impolitic to admit men and women who would root up our economic freedom and political independence to have any share in our legislation, either as electors or representatives; because the support of our economic freedom and political independence rests, in a great measure, on the vigor and purity of our public bodies. Yet these are deteriorating. For example, the Obama regime would like nothing better than to have illegal aliens decide elections to be carried by men and women who professed themselves to be not America's subjects, or decide who is to sit in Congress, or to place the United States of America under the auspices of the United Nations.

But there are a certain species of Obama thugs with whom conscience or principle has nothing to do, and who are so from avarice only. Some of the fortunes in America result from the avarice of the leftists. They are interested in wealth only. Can anything be a greater inducement to a miserly person, than the hope of making his Mammon safe? And though the scheme be fraught with every character of folly, yet, so long as Obama and his like suppose, that by doing nothing materially criminal against America on one part, and by expressing his private disapprobation against individual independence from the chains of the Obama regime, as a palliative with the remark "Trust me!" On the other part, he stands in a safe line between both; while, I say, this ground be suffered to remain, craft and the spirit of avarice, will point it out, and people will not be wanting to follow this most contemptible of all characters.

These people, ashamed to own the sordid cause from whence their disaffection springs, add thereby meanness to meanness, by endeavoring to shelter themselves under the mask of hypocrisy; that is, they had rather be thought to be pro-American from some kind of principle, than anti-

American by having no principle at all. But till such time as they can show some real reason, natural, political, or conscientious, on which their objections to economic freedom and political independence from the chains of Obama are founded, we are not obliged to give them credit for being pro-Americans of the first stamp, but must set them down as anti-Americans of the last.

In the second number of *The American Crisis*, I endeavored to show the impossibility of the enemy's making any conquest of the United States of America, that nothing was wanting on our part but patience and perseverance, and that, with these virtues, our success, as far as human speculation could discern, seemed as certain as fate. But as there are many among us, who, influenced by others, have regularly gone back from the principles they once held, in proportion as we have gone forward; and as it is the unfortunate lot of many a good man and woman to live within the neighborhood of disaffected ones; I shall, therefore, for the sake of confirming the one and recovering the other, endeavor, in the space of a page or two, to go over some of the leading principles in support of economic freedom and political independence from Obama thuggery. It is a much pleasanter task to prevent vice than to punish it, and, however our tempers may be gratified by resentment, or our national expenses increased or eased, harmony and friendship with honesty, is, nevertheless, the happiest condition a country can be blessed with.

The principal arguments in support of economic freedom and political independence and with it necessary distance from the federal government may be comprehended under the four following headings and commentaries:

I.   The natural right of the individual to have economic freedom and political independence from the federal government.

The natural right of the individual to independence and economic freedom is a point which never yet was called in question. It will not even admit of a debate. To deny such a right, would be a kind of atheism against nature: and the best answer to such an objection would be, "The fool hath said in his heart there is no God."

II.   The interest in being economically free and politically independent from the federal government.

28

The interest of the individual in being economically free and politically independent is a point as clearly right as the former. Before the arrival of Barack Hussein Obama, Americans, by their own internal industry, had arrived at a pitch of greatness, trade and population, which was the interest of Obama to exploit, lest the United States of America should grow too powerful. Barack Hussein Obama has begun to view this country with the same uneasy malicious eye, with which a covetous guardian would view his ward, whose estate he had been enriching himself by for twenty years, and saw him just arriving at manhood.

America owes no more to Barack Hussein Obama, than the ward would to the guardian for being twenty-one years of age and saw him just arriving at manhood. That America had flourished at the time she was under the previous government, is true; and there is every natural reason to believe, that would she be uncontrolled by the present regime, she would be much greater worth than now. The case is simply this: American citizens have always been able to fend for themselves; the first settlers in the different Colonies were left to shift for themselves, unnoticed and unsupported by any socialist-communist form of government; but whereas formerly the tyranny and persecution of WE the People drove numbers to declare their first independence and as with time, by the favor of heaven on their industry and perseverance, they grew in importance, so, in a like degree, they became an object of Obama's socialist-communist thugs for destruction. It was impossible, in this state of development – the dumbing down of the American electorate has been going on for generations – that they could resist the power of any anti-American invader that should seek to bring them under his authority.

In this situation, Obama thinks it worth his while to claim America for socialism-communism, and the electorate received and acknowledged the claimer. It was, in reality, of no very great importance who was to be elected as long as hope and change was present, seeing, that from the force and ambition of the propaganda powers, the electorate decided to acknowledge The One. The clamor of Obama promising protection from the wealthy, likewise, was all a farce; because, in order to make that protection necessary, he had to first, by his own arguments and against all rationality and logic, create the wealthy as enemies. Hard Saul Alinsky terms indeed!

To know whether it be the interest of the individual to be economically free and politically independent, we need only ask this easy, simple question: Is it the interest of a man to be a boy all his life? The answer to one will be the answer to both.

America hath been one continued scene of legislative contention from the first congressional representatives to the last; and this was unavoidably founded in the natural opposition of interest between the old generations and the new. A usurper president elected by the dumbed-down and receiving his authority from them, ought never to have been considered in any other light than that of a spy, whose private business was information, and his public business a kind of civilized oppression. In the first of these characters he watches the tempers, sentiments, and disposition of the people, the demise of the economy, and the increase of private thug fortunes; and, in the latter, to suppress all such acts of the State assemblies, however beneficial to the people, which did not directly or indirectly throw some increase of power or profit into the hands of his regime.

America can now, never be called a free country, because her legislation depends on the will of a man an infinity of miles distant from the interests of WE the People, and who, by a single "no," can forbid or change what law he pleases, as he has done with the Affordable Care Act, known as ObamaCare. Thus he does not care!

It is impossible that any country can flourish, as it otherwise might do, whose commerce is engrossed, cramped and fettered by the laws and mandates of evil, and more than I can here enumerate, the country has suffered by being under the Obama regime. The principle source of wealth depends on a capitalistic market economy. With economic freedom we clear the whole at once – put an end to the business of unanswered petitions and fruitless remonstrances – exchange socialist-communist economics for free market capitalism – shake hands with the world – live at peace with the world – and trade to any market where we can buy and sell.

III.   The necessity of being economically free and politically independent from the federal government.

The necessity, likewise, of being economically free and politically independent, even before it was declared in 1776, became so evident and important, that the country ran the risk of being ruined every day that she delayed it. There is now reason to believe that Obama would endeavor to make a United Nations matter of American economic freedom and political independence, and, rather than lose the whole, would dismember America, and dispose of her several claims to the highest bidder, probably Arab-Muslim countries, seeing that this is where his sympathies and Islam allegiance lie. Such traffics were common in the old world. In Obama's world WE the People have no ambassador in any part of the world to counteract his acts of treasons, and by that means he has the range of every foreign government uncontradicted on our part. WE the People would even know nothing of such treaties till they are concluded, and foreign troops ready to occupy us. Had we been independent before, we had probably prevented her obtaining them. We have no credit abroad not only because of Obama's rebellious dependency on the United Nations, but also because of his ability to pat a friendly country like Israel on the back with a dagger in his hand. Under control of the United Nations our ships could claim no protection in foreign ports. WE the People would be United Nations subjects and at the same time fight against the power which we were once hoodwinked to acknowledge. It would be a dangerous development. If the grievances justified our taking up arms, they would justify our call for separation from the United Nations; if the grievances did not justify our separation; neither could they justify our taking up arms. All anti-American countries and coalitions would be interested in reducing us as rebels, and none – or the greatest part at least – would be interested in supporting us as independent States not under United Nations control. What did the present Secretary of State John Kerry once say? "I'm an internationalist. I'd like to see our troops dispersed through the world only at the directive of the United Nations."

At home our condition is still worse: our currency has no foundation, and the fall of it will ruin WE the People, but not Obama and his thugs, who would probably request and receive sanctity in some Islamic Jannah. We have no other basic law than a kind of Obama-ripped-apart United States *Constitution*; no other civil power than honest American Patriots; and no other protection than the temporary attachment of one patriot to another. If economic freedom and political independence from the Obama regime is delayed any longer, this country will be plunged into irrecoverable confusion: some violent for it, some against it, till, in the general cabal, those who are well to do will be ruined, and the poor destroyed to a level below poverty. It is to freedom and economic independence that every American Patriot owes the present safety which he lives in; for by that, and that only, WE the People at one time emerged from a state of dangerous suspense, and became a regular people.

The necessity, likewise, of being economically free and politically independent of the Obama regime, is based on the increasing importance of commerce, the weight, and ethics of legislation, and the justice-oriented condition of American politics. Daily, this has shown us the impossibility of continuing subordination to Obama's wishes; for, after the coolest reflections on the matter, this must be allowed, that Obama is too jealous of America to govern it justly; too ignorant of it to govern it well; and too far intellectually distant from it to govern it at all.

IV.   The moral advantages arising from economic freedom and political independence from the federal government

What weigh most with all men and women of serious reflection are, the moral advantages arising from economic freedom and political independence from the federal government: war and desolation were the trade of the old world; and America neither could nor can be under the government of the United Nations without becoming a sharer of its guilt, and a partner in all the dismal commerce of death. The ancient spirit of dueling – also an armed conflict – extended on a national scale, is a proper character for global wars. They have seldom any other motive than pride, or any other object than fame. The conquerors and the conquered are generally ruined alike, and the chief difference at last is, that the one marches home with his honors, and the other without them. 'Tis the natural temper of thugs to fight for a feather, if they suppose that feather to be an affront; and America, without the right of asking why, must abet in every quarrel, and abide by its fate. It is a shocking situation to live in that one country must be brought into all the wars of another, whether the measure be right or wrong, or whether that country will or not; yet this, in the fullest extent, was, is, and ever will be, the unavoidable consequence of the connection. The goal of Obama's evilness is to penetrate and permeate America's soul until like a cancer it will have destroyed America's being.

Dictatorships, for centuries past, have been nearly fifty years out of every hundred at war with some power or other. It certainly ought to be a conscientious as well as a political consideration with America, not to dip her hands in the bloody work of becoming a dictatorship and police state. Our situation affords us a retreat from their cabals, and the present happy union of the states bids fair for extirpating the future use of arms from one quarter of the world; for example, to propagandize an African or Syrian springtime to another; yet such have been the irreligious politics of the present leaders of the Obama thug regime, that, for the sake of they scarce know what, they would cut off every hope of such a blessing by tying this country to the United Nations, like Hector to the chariot wheel of Achilles, to be dragged through all the miseries of endless springtime wars.

The connection, viewed from this ground, is distressing to every patriot who has the feelings of humanity. By having the United Nations for our master, we will be placed on an accusation block as enemies to the greatest part of the world, and they to us will force us to comply with their resolutions: and the consequence will be inevitable. By being our own masters, independent of any foreign one, we can choose our friends, and the prospect of an endless peace among ourselves. Those who are advocates for the United Nations government over these still somewhat independent States, are obliged to limit both their arguments and their ideas to the period of a false United Nations peace only; the moment the United States of America become plunged in a policing somewhere in the world, every supposed convenience to us is vanished, and all we can hope for is not to be ruined. Can this be a desirable condition for a free and independent country to be in?

America, considered as a subject of the United Nations, would ever be the seat of war, and the bone of contention between aggressive powers.

On the whole, if the future expulsion of arms from any quarter of the world would be a desirable object to a peaceable man; if the freedom of trade to every part of it can engage the attention of a man of business; if the support or fall of millions of currency can affect our interests; if the entire possession of certain energy sources deserves the regard of possessing property; and if the right of making our own laws, uncontrolled by the United Nations-oriented Obama regime, spies or mandates, be worthy our care as freemen; – then all men are interested in the support of economic freedom and political independence; and may he that supports it not, be driven from the blessing, and live unpitied beneath the servile sufferings of scandalous subjection!

We have been amused with the tales of ancient wonders; we have read, and wept over the histories of other nations: applauded, censured, or pitied, as their cases affected us. The fortitude and patience of the sufferers – the justness of their cause – the weight of their oppressions and oppressors – the object to be saved or lost – with all the consequences of a defeat or a conquest – have, in the hour of sympathy, bewitched our hearts, and chained it to their fate: but where is the power that ever made WE, the independent, freedom-loving People subjects? Nowhere! It is in OURSELVES to say NO!

We may not, perhaps, be wise enough to make all the advantages we ought of our economic freedom and our political independence; but they are, nevertheless, marked and presented to us with every character of great and good, and worthy the hand of him who protects them. I look through the present trouble to a time of tranquility, when we shall have it in our power to set an example of peace to all the world. Were the Obama regime really impressed and influenced by the quiet principles the hypocrites profess to hold on the one hand, they would, however they might disapprove the means, be the first of all men to approve of American economic freedom and political independence, because, by separating ourselves from the cities of Sodom and Gomorrah, it affords an opportunity never given to man before of carrying their favourite principle of peace into general practice, by establishing governments that shall hereafter exist without warring on its citizens. O! ye fallen, cringing, thug- and Obama-ridden people! What more can we say of ye than that a criminal Obama thug is an evil character, and a political Obama thug a real hypocrite.

Having thus gone over some of the principal points in support of economic freedom and political independence, I must now request the reader to return back with me to the period when it first began to be a public doctrine, and to examine the progress it has made among the various classes of men. The area I mean to begin at, is the breaking out of hostilities on April 19th, 1775. Until this event happened, the country seemed to view the dispute over economic freedom and political independence as a kind of law-suit for a matter of right, litigating between the old country and the new; and she felt the same kind and degree of horror, as if she had seen an oppressive plaintiff, at the head of a band of ruffians, enter the court, while the cause was before it, and put the judge, the jury, the defendant and his counsel, to the sword. Perhaps a more heart-felt convulsion never reached a country with the same degree of power and rapidity before, and never may again. Pity for the sufferers, mixed with indignation at the violence, and heightened with apprehensions of undergoing the same fate, made the affair of Lexington and Concord the affair of the country. Every part of it felt the shock, and all vibrated together. A general promotion of sentiment took place: those who had drank deeply into WE the People patriotic principles, that is, the right and necessity not only of opposing, but wholly setting aside the power of the oppressor as soon as it became practically dangerous – for in theory it was always so – stepped into the first stage of political independence; while another class of patriots, equally sound in principle, but not so sanguine in enterprise, attached themselves the stronger to the cause, and fell close in with the rear of the former; their partition was a mere point.

In 2008 and again in 2012 numbers of the moderate men and women, whose chief fault, at that time, arose from entertaining a better opinion of Barack Hussein Obama than he deserved, have now been convinced of their mistake, have given him up, and publicly declared themselves good, new patriots. While the thugs, seeing it is no longer a laughing matter, either sink into silent obscurity, or content themselves with coming forth and abusing true American Patriots: not a single American Patriot appears to justify the actions of these days; it seems to appear to everyone with the same magnitude, to strike every one with the same force, and create in everyone the same abhorrence. From this period in 1776 and in the Obama years we may date the true growth of and the beginning of a new American independence.

If the many circumstances which happened at that memorable time be taken in one view, and compared with each other, they will justify a conclusion which seems not to have been attended to; I mean a present fixed design in King Obama and his thugs of driving America into arms, in order that they might be furnished with a pretence for seizing the whole country, as the immediate property of the socialists-communists. A noble plunder for hungry scum!

It ought to be remembered, that the first crisis of usurpation of WE the People was at this time unanswered on the part of the anti-American enemedia: the vetting of Barack Hussein Obama and his foul play in getting elected. This being a just state of the case, I then ask: Why were there no cries from the enemedia that a wrong had been achieved and there were no assemblies meeting to deliberate upon it? Degrading and infamous as their behavior was, there is nevertheless reason to believe that Obama and his adherents were afraid WE the People would arise at that moment, and lest WE should, took effectual care WE should not, by provoking us with calls of racism hostilities in the interim. They had not the least doubt at that time of conquering America at one blow; and what they expected to get by a conquest being infinitely greater than anything they could hope to get either by taxation or accommodation, they seemed determined to prevent even the possibility of hearing each other, lest Americans should disappoint their greedy hopes of the whole, by listening even to their own terms. On the one hand, they refused to hear accusations that Barack Hussein Obama is an illegal, unconstitutional person and unfit to occupy the Oval Office of the country, and on the other hand, the thugs and the enemedia took effectual care the country should not hear the accusations.

That the motions keeping Barack Hussein Obama's origins a secret and the orders for commencing propaganda hostilities were both concerted by the same thug persons or thug groups, is evident from the following behavior: Obama's idea of disarming American Patriots is a public propaganda, yet it requires him to be master of the country, in order to enable him to execute it. This was prior to the commencement of the second term of office, and consequently now in the second term it is time for the payback voiced by Valerie Jarrett, the illegal, shadow president. *"After we win this election, it's our turn. Payback time. Everyone not with us is against us and they better be ready because we don't forget. The ones who helped us will be rewarded, the ones who opposed us will get what they deserve. There is going to be hell to pay. Congress won't be a problem for us this time. No election to worry about after this is over and we have two judges ready to go."* Perhaps it may be asked, why is this payback being undertaken – particularly against the armed forces – and why is no opposition being formed? One reason is that there is hope of dividing WE the People. This is publicly tempting Americans to reject American military leaders on trumped up charges of wrong doing. This is an outright insult. Yet, performing a payback enables them in their wicked idea of politics, among other things, to purge the American military according to the personal wishes of Barack Hussein Obama and to blot out any mark of future disobedience and rebellion. Obama thug powers have undertaken means not to allow American Patriots to bear arms, possess ammunition, and etc. Out of incense of them against us, they attempt to on their own part some seeming reputable reason why. Yet there is no reputable reason. The guarantee of bearing arms and possessing ammunition, and etc, is guaranteed by the second amendment to the *Constitution for the United States of America.*

The true Obama regime hope and change is established on the concept of dividing, for by dividing, there is a tendency to weaken the States, and likewise to perplex the adherents of Americans to the *Constitution*. But the principal scheme, and that which has marked their character in every part of their conduct, was a design of precipitating a State into a condition which they might afterwards deem rebellion, and, under that pretence, put an end to all future complaints, petitions and remonstrances, by seizing the whole at once. The Obama regime has caused ravage in more than one part of the globe, till it can glut it no longer; their prodigality requires a new type of plunder, and through the destruction of the *Bill of Rights* the Obama thugs hope to transfer their rapine from a Chicago-Saul-Alinsky quarter throughout the rest of America. Every designed quarrel has its pretence; and the same barbarian avarice has accompanied the plant to all of America, which is ruining the country.

That men and women never turn rogues without turning fools is a maxim, sooner or later, universally true. Hostilities will commence. The distress the country feels at this unparalleled outrage gives a stability to that body which no other circumstance could have done. It has suppressed, too, all inferior debates, and bound them together by a necessitous affection, without giving them time to differ upon trifles. The suffering likewise has softened the whole body of the people into a degree of pliability, which has laid the principal foundation-stone of disunion, disorder, and non-government; and which, at any other time, might only have fretted and then faded away unnoticed and unimproved. But Providence, who best knows how to time her misfortunes as well as her immediate favors, has chosen this to be the time of the WE the People and WE the American Patriots, and who dare dispute it?

It does not seem the disposition of WE the People, at this crisis, to heap petition upon petition. They will remain unanswered. The prayers of congressional politicians appeal solely to what is called the prerogative of the Obama regime, while the matters in dispute are confessedly constitutional. But congressional offerings, flattering as they are, are still not as harmonious as the chinks of cash, and consequently not sufficiently grateful to the tyrant and his thug regime. From every circumstance it is evident, that it is the determination of the Obama regime to have nothing to do with America but to conquer her fully and absolutely. They are certain of success, and the field of battle is the only place of treaty. I am confident there are thousands and tens of thousands in America who wonder now that they should ever have thought otherwise; but the sins of those election days in 2008 and 2012 is the collective sin of civility; yet it operated against our present good in the same manner that a civil opinion of the devil would against our future peace.

Economic freedom and political independence is a doctrine scarce and rare; all our politics are founded on the expectation of making the matter true. Barack Hussein Obama's hope and change is conquest and confiscation. Good heavens! What volumes of thanks does America owe to Barack Hussein Obama? What infinite obligation to the tool that occupies, with paradoxical vacancy, the Oval Office? Nothing but the sharpest essence of villainy, compounded with the strongest distillation of folly, can produce a menstruum that will effect a separation. Economic freedom and political independence has been a settled system with America. This single circumstance is sufficient to acquit America before any jury of nations, of conducting a revolt against the Obama regime; a charge which is true and honorable. Either the amazing ignorance or the willful dishonesty of the Obama regime is effectually proved by it.

Any petition to the Obama regime to correct its political course will be rejected because they are too determined in their villainy even to act it artfully, and in their rage for conquest neglect the necessary subtleties for obtaining it. They have divided, distracted, and played a thousand tricks with us with their cunning and cruelty. This indignity of the Obama regime gives a new American spring to economic freedom and political independence. Those who know the savage obstinacy of the dictator Barack Hussein Obama, and the jobbing, gambling spirit of the thug ministers, predict the fate of the American Patriots, for the thugs being known, their measures are easily foreseen. As patriotic politicians we ought not so much to ground our hopes on the reasonableness of the thing we ask, as on the reasonableness of the persons of whom we ask it: Who would expect discretion from a fool, candor from a tyrant, or justice from a villain?

As every prospect of accommodation seems now to fail fast, Americans are beginning to think seriously on the matter; and their reason being thus stripped of the false hope and false change which had long encompassed the Obama regime politics, have not become approachable by fair debate: yet still the bulk of the people hesitate; they startle at the novelty of a new start toward the goal of economic freedom and political independence, one from Barack Hussein Obama without once considering that our getting into arms at first is a more extraordinary novelty, and that the Founding Fathers had gone through the work of economic freedom and political independence before us. They doubt likewise the ability of the country to support it, without reflecting that it requires the same force to obtain independence by arms as it does to keep independence. If the one is acquirable, the other is the same; because, to accomplish them, it is necessary that our strength should be too great for Obama to subdue; and it is too unreasonable to suppose, that with the power of being our own masters, we should submit to be servants.

The caution of American Patriots at this time is exceedingly misplaced; for if they were at one time in American history able to defend their property and maintain their rights by arms, they, consequently, are able to defend and support their independence and economic freedom and retake America; and in proportion as these men of 1776 saw the necessity and correctness of the measure, they honestly and openly declared and adopted it, and the part that the American Patriots have acted since has done them honor and fully established their characters. Error in opinion has this peculiar advantage with it, that the foremost point of the contrary ground may at any time be reached by the sudden exertion of a thought; and it frequently happens in sentimental differences, that some striking circumstance, or some forcible reason quickly conceived, will effect in an instant what neither argument nor example could produce in an age. That was the circumstance and reason in 1776 and it is now the present circumstance and reason: loss of economic freedom and political independence.

I find it impossible in the small compass I am limited to, to trace out the progress which economic freedom and political independence has made on the minds of the different classes of men, and the several reasons by which they were moved. With some, it was a passionate abhorrence against King Obama and his despots, as a set of savages and brutes; and such persons, governed by the agony of a wounded mind, are for trusting everything to hope and change and hell, and bidding defiance at once. With others, it is a growing conviction that the scheme of the political thugs is to create, ferment, and drive on a quarrel, for the sake of confiscated plunder. While a third class conceive it is the true interest of America, internally and externally, to be her own master, and give their support to economic freedom and to political independence, step by step, as they see her abilities to maintain it enlarge. With many, it is a compound of all these reasons; while those who are too callous to be reached by either, still remain dumbed-down anti-Americans.

The legal necessity of being economically free and politically independent, with several collateral reasons, is pointed out in an elegant masterly manner. This necessity can be read in the original *Declaration of Independence* of 1776. The same necessity is present today. The principal causes why new economic freedom and political independence have not been as universally supported as they ought, are fear and indolence, and the causes why they have been so far opposed, are, avarice, down-right villainy, and lust of personal power. There is not such a being in America as an Obama follower from conscience; some secret defect or other is interwoven in the character of all those, be they men or women, who can look with patience on the brutality, luxury, and debauchery of the Obama regime, and the violations of law they commit in America. Even a woman's virtue must sit very lightly on her who can

40

even hint a favorable sentiment in their behalf. Yet those women who do sympathize and support Barack Hussein Obama constitute a whole race of prostitute sympathizers; and the schemes for supporting the Obama cause are concerted and carried on by common hawkers of dejected feminists, assisted by those who keep them.

The connection between vice and meanness is a fit subject for satire, but when the satire is a fact, it cuts with the irresistible power of a diamond. If an American Patriot, in defence of his just rights, his property, and the chastity of his house, takes up a rifle or a pistol, he is arrested by the police; but the present dictator-king in Washington, D. C., threatens American citizens and kills them with drones. One week after Obama Narcissist received the Nobel Prize for Peace he sanctioned the drone killing in Yemen of 41 civilians, including at least 21 children and 12 women – five of who were pregnant; and with this singular act of peace Obama became lord high executioner. Barack Hussein Obama is reverenced and supported by repeated testimonies, while the friendly-like noodle who gives the drone orders continues a drudge service of his narcissistic being, is as proud as if he were being cuckolded by a creature called Michelle.

Our support and success depend on such a variety of men and circumstances that everyone who does but wish well, is of some use: there are men who have a strange aversion to arms, yet have hearts to risk every cent in the cause, or in support of those who have better talents for defending it. Nature, in the arrangement of mankind, has fitted some for every service in life: were all soldiers, all would starve and go naked, and were none soldiers, all would be slaves. As disaffection to new economic freedom and political independence is the badge of a DemocRAT, so affection to it is the mark of an American Patriot; and the different services of the American Patriots, down from those who nobly contribute everything, to those who have nothing to render but their wishes, tend all to the same center, though with different degrees of merit and ability. The larger we make the circle, the more we shall harmonize, and the stronger WE the People shall be. All WE want to shut out is disaffection and tyranny, and, that excluded, WE must accept from each other such duties as WE are best fitted to bestow. A narrow system of politics like socialism-communism without economic freedom and political independence is calculated only to sour the temper, and be at variance

41

with mankind. All we want to know in America is simply this: Who is for a new economic freedom and political independence, and who is not? Those who are for it, will support it, and the remainder will undoubtedly see the reasonableness of paying the charges; while those who oppose or seek to betray it, must expect the more rigid fate of the jail and the gibbet.

There is a bastard kind of generosity, which being extended to all men, is as fatal to society, on one hand, as the want of true generosity is on the other. A lax manner of administering justice, falsely termed moderation, has a tendency both to dispirit public virtue, and promote the growth of public evils. Had the enemedia and the false patriots taken cognizance of the true American Patriots and proceeded against such delinquents as were concerned in the society, they would have, probably, prevented the treasonable plans which have been concerted by Barack Hussein Obama then and since. When one villain is suffered to escape, it encourages another to proceed, either from a hope of escaping likewise, or an apprehension that we dare not punish. It has been a matter of general surprise that no notice was taken of the incendiary publications of Barack Hussein Obama's various executive orders, and in the signing of the martial law bill – which makes the indefinite detention of American citizens now legal; a law evidently intended to do away with all freedoms and independence. It encourages the ruling thug enemies to proceed on with their treasonous and evil police state.

I herewith present the reader with a memorial which is laid before the American People: Never did Americans lose so much freedom in so short a time as they have under the thug-in-chief Barack Hussein Obama! He hopes that his acts suffer to pass away unnoticed because they promote and encourage the enemy thugs to commit new acts of treason and hide the general danger of their cause.

Barack Hussein Obama and his thug regime are the disgrace to the United States of America.

★★★★★★★★★★★★★★

Frederick William Dame
Patriotic, Steadfast, and True
January 30, 2014

Frederick William Dame

The American Crisis

Our Part Is Finding The Traitors And Exhibiting

Them To Justice

A Call To Take Action

Number Four

At a recent meeting of a reputable number of American Patriots impressed with a proper sense of the justice of the cause which this country is engaged in, and animated with a generous fervor for supporting the same, it was resolved that the following be laid before the American People:

We profess liberality of sentiment to all men; with this distinction only, that those who do not deserve it would become wise and seek to deserve it. We hold the pure doctrines of universal liberty of conscience, and conceive it our duty to endeavor to secure that sacred right to others, as well as to defend it for ourselves; for we undertake not to judge of the religious rectitude of tenets, but leave the whole matter to Him who made us.

We persecute no man, neither will we abet in the persecution of any man for religion's sake – like Islam does; our common relation to others being that of fellow-citizens and fellow-subjects of one single community; and in this line of connection we hold out the right hand of fellowship to all men. But we should conceive ourselves to be unworthy members of the free and independent United States of America, were we unconcernedly to see or to suffer any treasonable wound, public or private, directly or indirectly, to be given against the peace and safety of the same. We inquire not into the rank of the offenders, nor into their religious persuasion; we have no business with either, our part is finding the traitors and exhibiting the traitors to justice.

The *Bill of Rights* guaranteeing basic freedoms to American citizens is no more! The National Defense Authorization Act (NDAA), a law signed on January 3, 2014 by the putative president Barack Hussein Obama, whom we do not suppose to be a natural born citizen of this country, has scarcely been discussed by the enslaved enemedia. Had the formulators of that law conceived it their duty to exhort American citizens to a patient submission under the trying visitations, and humbly to wait the event of heaven towards them, they had therein shown a Christian temper, and WE the People had been silent; but the anger and political virulence with which their instructions are given, and the abuse with which they stigmatize all ranks of men not thinking like themselves, leave no doubt in our minds from what spirit their law proceeded: and it is disgraceful to the pure cause of truth, that men can dally with words of the most sacred import, and play them off as mechanically as if politics consisted only in contrivance.

We know of no instance in which American Patriots are forbidden by the *Constitution for the United States of America* to bear arms, or to do anything which might strain their conscience; wherefore their position to withstand and refuse to submit to the arbitrary instructions and ordinances of the government appear to us a proper standpoint, and could only be reasonably calculated to gain favor with the like-minded Americans, when the Obama regime is seemingly on the brink of invading free and separate States, or, what is still worse, on the way to weakening the hands of our defence, that Obama's total control of American citizens might be made practicable and easy. Is it not feasible that this would be accomplished with the assistance of foreign forces?

We disclaim all tumult and disorder in the execution of the Obama regime proclamations and dictatorial decrees; and wish to be governed, not by evil but by reason. We are sensible that our cause has suffered by the two following errors: first, by ill-judged lenity to traitorous persons; and, secondly, by only a weak, superficial condemnation of them. For the future we disown both, and wish to be steady in our proceedings, and serious in our punishments of traitors and anti-American criminals.

Every State in America should, by the repeated voice of its inhabitants, direct and authorize the Congress to publish a formal and renewed *Declaration of Independence*, and separation from the oppressive Obama regime; and WE the People look on every man and woman as an enemy who does not in some line or other give his assistance towards supporting the same; at the same time WE the People consider the offence to be heightened to a degree of unpardonable guilt, when such persons, under the show of peace – like Muslims do – endeavor, either by writing, speaking, or otherwise, to subvert, overturn, or bring reproach upon the independence of this country as heralded by the *Declaration of Independence* and the *Constitution for the United States of America.*

When Barack Hussein Obama and his regime refuse to be obedient to the *Constitution for the United States of America* and federal and State ordinances that have so long guaranteed liberty, tranquility, and peace, then such action, if it is not treason, we know not what may properly be called by that name.

To American Patriots it is a matter of surprise and astonishment that politicians with the words "peace, peace, peace" continually on their lips, should be so fond of living under and supporting a dictatorial regime, and at the same time call it "happy", which is never better pleased than when it calls for class conflict and united regime thugs to cut the throats of the freemen of America, Black and White. We conceive it a disgrace to this country to harbor or wink at such palpable hypocrisy. But as we seek not to hurt the hair of any man's head when we can make ourselves safe without, we wish such persons to restore peace to themselves and to us, by removing themselves to some part of the other world of dictators, as by that means they may live unmolested by us and WE the People by them; for our fixed opinion is that those who do not deserve a place among us, like Barack Hussein Obama and his regime, ought not to have one.

We conclude with requesting the American People to take into consideration the unlawful acts of the Barack Hussein Obama regime and its scandals, and if it shall appear to them to be of a dangerous tendency, or of a treasonable nature, that they would commit the accused, together with such other persons as they can discover were concerned therein, into custody, until such time as some mode of trial shall ascertain the full degree of their guilt and punishment; in the doing of which, we wish their judges, whoever they may be, to disregard the person, his connections, interest, riches, poverty, or principles of religion, and to attend to the nature of his offence only: **TREASON**!

The most caviling sectarian cannot accuse the foregoing with containing the least ingredient of persecution. The free spirit on which the American cause is founded disdains to mix with such an impurity, and leaves it as rubbish fit only for narrow and suspicious minds to grovel in. Suspicion and persecution are weeds of the same dunghill, and flourish together.

Had the Obama thugs been stopped before their criminal politics became business, had their evilness been stifled, Americans might have lived through these present times in enviable ease, and no one would have molested them. The common phrase with these people is, *Our principles are hope and change! What difference does it now make? If you like your health plan you can keep your health plan. If you like your doctor, you can keep your doctor. That's a promise. Al-Qaida is on the run! We will bring terrorists to justice.* To which must be replied because their practices are the reverse; for never did the conduct of men and women oppose their own doctrine more notoriously than the present race of the Obama thugs. They have artfully changed themselves into a different sort of people from Americans than what true Americans thought them to be, and yet they have the address to persuade each other that they are not altered; like antiquated virgins, they see not the havoc deformity has made upon them, but pleasantly mistaking wrinkles for dimples, conceive themselves yet lovely and wonder at the stupid world for not admiring them.

Did no injury arise to the public by this apostasy of the Obama followers from themselves? The American Patriotic public would have nothing to do with it; but as both the design and consequences are pointed against a cause in which the whole community are interested, it is therefore no longer a subject confined to the cognizance of the participants only, but comes, as a matter of criminality before the authority either of the particular State in which it is acted, or of the country against which it operates. Every attempt now to support the authority of the Obama regime over America is treason against every State; therefore it is impossible that anyone can pardon or screen from punishment an offender against all.

46

But to proceed: while the infatuated progressives, obots, liberals, dumbed downers, and socialists-communist of the United States of America are talking of control and rule making, and the Lord knows what stuff and nonsense, their good King Obama and ministry thugs are glutting themselves with the revenge of reducing America to unconditional submission, and solacing each other with the certainty of conquering it in one final act of despotism.

We American Patriots will be obstinate, undutiful, and ungovernable from the very beginning. I am every day more and more convinced that WE the People never will be brought back to do Obama's will, and stand in subordinate relation to him. If WE the People will be reduced to unconditional, effectual submission, no concession on our part, no lenity, no endurance, will have any other effect but that of increasing our insolence.

The struggle is now a struggle for power; the die is cast and the only point which now remains to be determined is in what manner the re-taking of America can be most effectually prosecuted and speedily finished in order to procure that unconditional submission, which has been so ably stated by the noble *Declaration of Independence*, and I have no reason to doubt that the measures now pursuing will put an end to the Obama regime in the course of a single, up-coming election. Should it linger longer, we shall then have reason to expect that Barack Hussein Obama's power will interfere and take advantage of our domestic troubles and civil distractions.

My sentiments are pretty well known. I shall only observe now that lenient measures have had no other effect than to produce insult after insult; that the more we conceded, the higher Barack Hussein Obama rose in his demands, and the more insolent he has grown. It is for this reason that I am now for the most effective and decisive measures; and am of opinion that no alternative is left us, but to regain America forever and to compel Obama and his minions to acknowledge the source of legislative authority of this country – WE the People; and it is the principle of an unconditional submission on Obama's part I would be for maintaining.

Can words be more expressive than these? Surely WE the People will believe the American Patriots! The truth is, WE the People do believe American Patriots and know as fully as any anti-American knows, that King Obama and his regime never had the least design of an accommodation with America, but an absolute, unconditional conquest. The part which Barack Hussein Obama and his thugs were to act was by downright lying to endeavor to put the country off its guard, and to divide and sow discontent in the minds of such Americans as they might gain an influence over. In short, it was to keep up a distraction that the Obama forces might be able to conquer as quickly as possible. The bastard lamestream media and the Obama thugs were, by a different game, playing into each other's hands. The cry of the DemocRATS in Washington was, "No reconciliation, no accommodation," in order to maintain the greater hand; while those in America were crying LISTEN TO US, WE THE PEOPLE!

But this second and more evil Obama term is almost over and America has not been conquered by him. The whole work is yet to do, and the force much less to do it with. Their condition is both despicable and deplorable: out of cash – out of heart, and out of hope, and out of change! A country whose American Patriots are furnished with arms and ammunition as American Patriots now are, with millions of inhabitants, and many miles distant from the Washington, D. C. enemy that can approach her, is able to look and laugh them in the face.

Obama appears to have two objects in view, either to lie, or to lie more. By lying he secures time; by lying more he must face revolution. Barack Hussein Obama's true business is to conquer the United States of America, and in proportion as he finds himself unable to the task, he will employ his strength to distress men, women, and weak minds in order to accomplish through their fears what he cannot accomplish by his own force. 'Tis a circumstance that proves his weakness: it has feebleness and cowardice on the face of it, and holds him up in a contemptible light to all who can reason justly and firmly.

By several sources of information, it appears that the Obama domestic army, made up of the Federal Emergency Management Authority (FEMA), the Corporation for National and Community Service (CNCS), Organizing for America, and union thugs, in general, both leaders and followers, have given up the expectation of conquering America easily, or at all; their eyes now fixed upon the spoil. America is rich with stores, and as they think to get more by robbing, their movement towards this goal is discernible. We are now contending against an army of lumps of thugs, against a band of thieves, who had rather plunder than fight, and have no other hope of conquest than by cruelty.

They expect to get a mighty booty, and strike another general panic, by making a sudden movement and getting possession of major sectors of society; but unless they can control the banks, the armed forces, the total media, they may probably be stopped with the stolen goods upon them. Barack Hussein Obama has never yet succeeded wherever he has been opposed without his teleprompters and Valerie (Rasputin) Jarrett. A community organizer will run away when confronted without the outcome clearly having been decided in his favor beforehand.

The necessity of always fitting our internal patriotic forces to the circumstances of the times we live in is something so strikingly obvious that no sufficient objection can be made against it. The safety of all societies depends upon it; and where this point is not attended to, the consequences will either be a general languor or a tumult. The encouragement and protection of the good subjects of any country, and the suppression and punishment of bad ones, are the principal objects for which all authority is instituted, and the line in which it ought to operate.

We have in this country a strange variety of men and characters, and the circumstances of the times require that they should be publicly known; it is not the number of DemocRATS and Obamas that hurt us so much as the not finding out who they are. Men and women must now take one side or the other, and abide by the consequences: the Republicans In Name Only (RINOS), trusting to their short-sighted sagacity, have, most unluckily for them, made their declaration. They have involuntarily read themselves out of belonging to the country, and cannot hope to be restored to it again but by payment and penitence. Men whose political principles are founded on avarice are beyond the reach of reason.

The only cure the DemocRATS and the Obama thugs envision are to tax. Perhaps those who want to tax should be those who should be taxed more! A substantial good drawn from a real evil is of the same benefit to society as if drawn from a virtue; and where men have not public spirit to render themselves serviceable, it ought to be the study of government to draw the best use possible from their vices. When the governing passion of any man or woman, or set of men or women, is once known, the method of managing them is easy; for even misers, whom no public virtue can impress, would become generous, could a heavy tax be laid upon covetousness, and it is covetousness the DemocRATS and the Obama-like politicians want – the coveting of other people's hard-earned money.

The Obama regime have endeavored to insure their property with the anti-American enemies like George Soros, by forfeiting their reputation with us; from which may be justly inferred that their governing passion is avarice. Make them as much afraid of losing on one side as on the other and you stagger their bank accounts; make them more so, and you reclaim them; for their principle is to worship the power which they are most afraid of.

This method of considering men and things together, opens into a large field for speculation, and affords me an opportunity of offering some observations on the situation of our currency so as to make the support of it go hand in hand with the suppression of disaffection and the encouragement of public spirit. The aspect which first presents itself in inspecting the situation of the currency is the federal banking system – the institution called the Federal Reserve System – that should be disbanded, for it has not, even under expanded powers, met the two key objectives of monetary policy presented in a 1977 amendment to the Federal Reserve Act to which it was assigned: a) to promote the *maximum* sustainable output and employment, b) to promote price stability. It appears that manipulating moderate, long-term interest rates is only a method to accomplish the two goals above. At the same time, it must be said that under the socialist-communist system of Barack Hussein Obama, interest rates must be done away with because interest rates mean capitalism and for Obama capitalism is a dirty ten-letter word.

The second matter that deserves inspecting is a return to the gold/silver standard. The natural, positive aspects of a gold/silver standard outweigh the constructed, negative attributes concocted by fly-by-night economists, particularly Keynesian and neo-Keynesian economic theorists. The gold/silver standard can better guarantee long-term price stability; can provide fixed, international exchange rates for countries participating in the gold/silver standard system, which means that gold/silver used to pay for imports reduces the importing nation's money supply, which in turn causes deflation, and thus makes them more competitive; and a gold/silver standard does not allow for a kind of tax called financial repression – the method by which wealth from creditors is transferred to debtors. The gold/silver standard stops deficit spending and guarantees property rights. The gold/silver standard means that imports cannot be purchased with money that is not genuine. Because the United States of America is not on a gold/silver standard the Federal Reserve can inflate the money supply at will. The result is that more and more currency chases the same amount of goods and services, which causes an increase in their prices, which, in turn, causes the currency to be worth less, which in turn, causes debt to become a burden.

Related to the increase in prices is the fact that the power of labor unions is so great that it is also they who drive prices upwards because they strike for exorbitant wages that are totally unreasonable, particularly for non-specialized workers and employees who never expended any amount of private money to receive a highly qualified education. This is the main argument why the power of unions and the thug members must be broken and the extravagant demands be brought down to normalcy and logic.

The third aspect is that there is too much money in circulation that has little worth. Because the United States of America no longer has a gold/silver standard to back up the currency, the more paper money there is in circulation, the less will be the value of the paper money. The equation is: the less amount of amount of currency there is in the economy, the higher the value of the currency and vice-versa. Simply stated we have too much of it, and that there is a necessity of reducing the quantity, in order to increase the value. The only reason why there have been no widespread increases in the prices of goods and services is because the *new money* has been kept out of normal circulation. Instead, the stock market, investors, and banks are sitting on mountainous heaps of the *new money*. They are waiting to see how the economy under Barack Hussein Obama and ObamaCare will develop. Whenever this *new money* is spent and loaned, it will circulate throughout the economy and cause huge price increases because even more money will be chasing

51

after the same quantity of goods and services. The fact that the United States dollar is backed up by the Federal Reserve System is meaningless and under Barack Hussein Obama the value of a dollar is 18 trillion meaninglessnesses.

Men are daily growing poor by the very means that they take to get rich; for in the same proportion that the prices of all goods on hand are raised, the value of all money laid by is reduced because gold or silver no longer backs up the value of the currency. An across the surface simple case will make this clear. Let a man have 100 separate dollars in cash in his pocket and as many goods on hand as will today sell for 20 dollars; but not content with the present market price, he raises the price by 20 dollars to 40 dollars and by so doing obliges others to raise their price to 40 dollars. In this case it is evident that his 100 dollars laid by in his pocket is reduced in value; whereas, if he had cut his price to 10 dollars and the other sellers on the market had cut their prices in half, the 100 separate dollars laid by in his pocket could now buy what previously would have required 200 dollars; because it would then purchase as many goods again, or assist in supporting his family as long again as before. Strange as it may seem, he is the poorer for raising his goods, to what he would have been had he lowered them; because the 40 dollars which his goods sold for, is, by the general raise of the market rendered of no more value than the 10 dollars would be had the market fallen in the same proportion; and, consequently, the whole difference of gain or loss is on the difference in value of the 100 dollars laid by, viz. from 50 to 200.

This rage for raising prices is for several reasons much the fault of the DemocRATS leveling of economics, and when such economics are instituted they blame the capitalists for its defects. Capitalism is blamed for results it did not cause. The DemocRATS become by far the most noisy and discontented. The greatest part of the DemocRATS, particularly those employed in some public service, are buyers only and not sellers, and as this evil has its origin in trade, it cannot be charged on those who are out of it.

But the grievance has now become too general to be remedied by partial methods, and the only effectual cure is to reduce the quantity of money: with half the quantity we should be richer than we are now, because the value of it would be doubled, and consequently our attachment to it increased; for it is not the number of dollars that a man or woman has, but how far they will go that makes them either rich or poor.

These two points being admitted, viz. that the quantity of money is too great, and that the prices of goods can only be effectually reduced by reducing the quantity of the money, the next point to be considered is the method how to reduce it.

The circumstances of the times, as before observed, require that the public characters of all men should now be fully understood, and the only general method of ascertaining it is by an oath or affirmation, renouncing all allegiance to the King of Washington, D. C., and to support the total independence of the United States of America, as declared by Congress. Be it nonetheless an over simplification, let, at the same time, a tax of ten, fifteen, or twenty percent per annum, to be collected quarterly, be levied on all property. These alternatives, by being perfectly voluntary, will take in all sorts of people. Here is the test; here is the tax. He who takes the former, conscientiously proves his affection to the cause, and binds himself to pay his quota by the best services in his power, and is thereby justly exempt from the latter; and those who choose the latter, pay their quota in money, to be excused from the former, or rather, it is the price paid to us for their supposed, though mistaken, insurance with the economists.

But this is only a part of the advantage which would arise by knowing the different characters of men. The DemocRATS stake everything on the issue of their fool-proof economics, all the while sapping and undermining America's strength; and, of consequence, the property of Americans is the more exposed thereby; and whatever injury their estates may sustain by the movements of the DemocRATS, must either be borne by themselves, who have done everything which has yet been done, or by those who have not only done nothing, but have, by their disaffection, invited the enemy on to continue false economic policies.

In the present crisis we ought to know, square by square and house by house, who are in real allegiance with the independent United States of America, and who are not. Let but the line be made clear and distinct, and all men will then know what they are to trust to. It would not only be good policy but strict justice to reverse the situation, to raise financial support out of the estates and property of the rich Obama votaries, to be paid to the federal treasury to bind the property of all such persons to make good the damages which they created and which the United States of America might sustain in the undistinguishable mode of conducting a repossession of the United States of America.

In every former publication of mine down to the last American Crisis, I have generally gone on the charitable supposition, that the DemocRATS were rather a mistaken group than a criminal people, and have applied argument after argument, with all the candor and temper which I was capable of, in order to set every part of the case clearly and fairly before them, and if possible to reclaim them from ruin to reason. I have done my duty by them and have now done with that doctrine, taking it for granted, that those who yet hold their disaffection are either a set of avaricious miscreants, who would sacrifice the continent to save themselves, or a banditti of hungry traitors, who are hoping for a division of the spoil. To which may be added a list of social parasite dependants, who, rather than go without a portion of power, would be content to share it with the Devil. Of such men there is no hope, and their obedience will only be according to the danger set before them and the power that is exercised over them.

A time will shortly arrive in which, by ascertaining the characters of persons now, we shall be guarded against their mischiefs then; for in proportion as the enemy despair of conquest, they will be trying the arts of seduction and the force of fear by all the mischiefs which they can inflict. But in our struggle, WE the People may be certain of these two things, viz. that cruelty in an enemy, and motions made with more than usual parade, are always signs of weakness. He who can conquer finds his mind too free and pleasant to be brutish; and he who intends to conquer never makes too much show of his strength.

We now know the enemy we have to do with. While drunk with the certainty of victory, they disdain to be civil; and in proportion as disappointment makes them sober, and their apprehensions of a conflict alarm them, they will become cringing and artful; honest they cannot be. But our answer to them, in either condition they may be in, is short and full – "As free and independent States we are willing to make peace with you tomorrow on our terms only, but we neither can hear nor reply in any other character."

If Barack Hussein Obama cannot conquer us, it proves that he is neither able to govern nor protect us, and our particular situation now is such that any connection with him would be unwisely exchanging a position of dominance for a position of subservience. Therefore, the only road to peace, honor, and commerce is independence from the Obama regime.

Find the traitors and exhibit them to justice!

Written this 238th year of the *Declaration of Independence*, which God preserve.

Frederick William Dame
Patriotic, Steadfast, and True
February 11, 2014

Frederick William Dame

The American Crisis

We Fight Not To Enslave But To Set Our Country Free

A Call To Take Action

Number Five

Those who expect to reap the blessings of freedom must, like men, undergo the fatigues of supporting it. Thus we are continuing the fight to set our country free. The events of these Barack Hussein Obama years are those kinds of alarms which are just sufficient to rouse us to duty, without being of consequence enough to depress our fortitude. It is not a field of a few acres of ground, but a cause that we are defending, and whether we defeat the Obama enemy in one battle, or by degrees, the consequences will be the same: FREEDOM!

Look back at the events of the past years and more! There you will find that the enemy's successes by lies and forgeries always contributed to reduce them. What they have gained in ground, they paid so dearly for in numbers of followers that their political bashings of WE the People have in the end amounted to defeats. WE the People have always been masters at the last push, and always shall be while WE do our duty. Barack Hussein Obama has been many times on the cozy propaganda couches and in the chairs of the enemedia, and from thence he has never been driven back with loss and disgrace by the enemedia. Why must we allow this to continue? Obama's political condition and ours are very different. In reality he has everybody to fight. WE the People have only his one regime to cope with and which wastes away at every engagement. WE the People can not only reinforce, but can redouble our numbers; he is cut off from all patriotic reality, and must sooner or later inevitably fall into our hands, for fight WE American Patriots will. It would be amenable to defeat Obama and his regime non-violently. Yet, American Patriots will not shrink from active revolution, if necessary, to achieve the goals of OUR *Declaration of Independence* and the guarantees of OUR *Constitution*.

Shall a band of regime robbers, who are this day less in strength than they were last year, conquer America, or subdue even a single State? The thing cannot be, unless we sit down and suffer them to do it. Notwithstanding WE American Patriots should lose the ground, WE would by ever confronting the enemy argumentation, propaganda, and thuggery put them in a condition to be afterwards totally defeated.

Could our whole body of American Patriots attack Obama and his regime at one time, and continuously without political correctness interruptions, the consequences would be more profitable for the whole country because the enemedia would have to take notice of it. Our having different parts of the country under control would pit us against the enemedia still under control of Obama's financial support and thug controllers; and the uncertainty which approach the enemy would attempt to take, naturally affords us an opportunity of gathering our patriot forces together for various media forrays with their main political bodies at their studios and offices; for it must strike every thinking man with conviction, that it requires a much greater force to oppose an enemy in several places, than is sufficient to defeat him in any one place.

Men who are sincere in defending their freedom will always feel concern at every circumstance which develops to take action against them; it is the natural and honest consequence of all affectionate attachments, and the want of it is a vice. But the dejection lasts only for a moment; they soon rise out of it with additional vigor; the glow of hope, courage, and fortitude, will, in a little time, supply the place of every inferior passion, and kindle the whole patriotic heart into heroism.

There is a mystery in the countenance of some causes, which we have not always present judgment enough to explain. It is distressing to see an enemy regime advancing as a mob to take over this country, but throughout America is the only place in which we can beat them, for it is the source from which we have always had fortitude to eventually defeat our enemies, whenever they made the attempt to conquer us. Obamaism is a killer disease and the nearer any disease approaches to a crisis, the nearer it is to a cure. Danger and deliverance make their advances together, and it is only the last push, in which one or the other takes the lead. There are many men who will do their duty when it is not wanted; but a genuine public patriotic spirit always appears most when there is most occasion for it. Thank God! Our patriots, though fatigued by many years of congressional inaction and wishy-washy political correctness, are yet entire. The attacks made against us in the past were under many disadvantages, naturally arising from the uncertainty of knowing which type of illegal actions and propaganda the socialist-communist enemy would take; and, from that circumstance, the whole of our patriotic force could not be brought up together in time enough to engage all at once. Our patriotic strength is yet reserved; and it is evident that Obama does not think himself a gainer by the scandals of his non-leadership, otherwise he would not have acted as a king-dictator, as a sulking narcissist before the Congress in the 2014 State of the Union farce.

Men and women of America's cities and countryside, it is in your power, by a spirited improvement of the present circumstance, to turn it to a real advantage. Barack Hussein Obama! You are now weaker than before, and every propaganda shot of truth from WE the People will contribute to reduce you. You are more immediately interested in yourself than in any other part of the country. Your all is at stake; it is not so with the general cause; you are devoted, because you are the enemy, to plunder and destruction. It is the encouragement which you, the plunderer-in-chief have promised his plundering regime. Thus circumstanced, you may think you are saving yourselves by a considering a pseudo-justifiable resistance, but you can have no hope in any other conduct. I never yet knew one weakness our brave American Patriots, or any part of WE the People, women or men, out of heart, and I have seen them in circumstances a thousand times more trying than the present. It is only those that are not in action, that feel languor and heaviness, and the best way to rub that off is to turn out, and make sure the work of our future election and propaganda encounters, and if need be, our active, even violent revolutionary encounters with the Obama side come to fruition.

Our American Patriots must undoubtedly feel fatigue, and want a reinforcement of rest though not of valor. Our own interest and happiness call upon us to give every American support in our power, and make the burden of the day, on which the safety of this nation depends, as light as possible. Remember, that we have patriotic forces throughout the United States of America, and if the enemy be but checked till all American Patriots can mobilize, this country will be saved, and the enemy finally routed. WE the People have too much at stake to hesitate. WE the People ought not to think an hour upon the matter, but to spring to action at once. Other States like Texas, Florida, Georgia, North Carolina, Virginia, Missouri, Wisconsin, Alabama, South Carolina, Louisiana, Oklahoma, Mississippi, and Kansas have confronted Obama on his destructive politics, particularly the Affordable Care Act, and have so far driven off the future invaders. More states are fighting Obama and his thugs. Now our time and turn is come, and perhaps the finishing stroke is reserved for us. When we look back on the dangers we have been saved from, and reflect on the success we have been blessed with, it would be sinful either to be idle or to despair.

I close this paper with a short address to Barack Hussein Obama. You are only lingering out the period that shall bring with it your defeat. You have yet scarce begun upon the encounter with us. It will come before you will ever know! The further you push the forray, the faster will your troubles thicken. What you now enjoy is only a respite from ruin; an invitation to destruction; something that will lead on to our deliverance at your expense. We know the cause which we are engaged in, and though a passionate fondness for it may make us grieve at every injury which threatens it, yet, when the moment of concern is over, the determination to duty returns. WE the People are not moved by the gloomy smile of a worthless, self-appointed dictator-king serviced by a body servant. WE the People are moved by the ardent glow of generous patriotism. Contrary to Your DemocRATS and socialist-communist thugs, WE the People fight not to enslave, but to set OUR country free, and to make room upon the earth for honest men to live in. In such a case WE the People are sure that WE are right; and WE leave to you the despairing reflection of being the tool of a miserable tyrant: yourself!

Frederick William Dame
Patriotic, Steadfast, and True
February 12, 2014

59

Frederick William Dame

The American Crisis

Barack Hussein Obama Becomes

A Proverb Of Contempt

A Call To Take Action

Number Six

Barack Hussein Obama! To argue with a man who has renounced the use and authority of reason, and whose philosophy consists in holding The United States of America in contempt, is like administering medicine to the dead, or endeavoring to convert an atheist by scripture. Enjoy your insensibility of feeling and reflecting. It is the prerogative of animals. And no man will envy you these honors in which a savage only can be your rival and a bear your master. You have added absolutely nothing of value to the United States of America. Indeed, you possess no human honor. You are contemptible.

You think that this country will reward your disservices of the past years with an elegant monument on Mount Rushmore. You feel it is consistent that America should bestow some mark of distinction upon you, that you certainly deserve her notice, and a conspicuous place in the catalogue of extraordinary persons. Yet it would be more apt to pass you from the world in state, and consign you to magnificent oblivion among the tombs, without telling the future beholder why. Judas is as much known as John, yet history ascribes their fame to very different actions.

You have undoubtedly merited a monument; but of what kind, or with what inscription, where placed or how embellished, is a question that would puzzle all the heralds of the Vatican in the profoundest mood of historical deliberation. We are at no loss to ascertain your real character, but somewhat perplexed as to how you desire to perpetuate its identity, and preserve it uninjured from the transformations of time or mistake. A statuary may give a false expression to your bust, or decorate it with some equivocal emblems by which you may happen to steal into reputation and impose upon the hereafter traditional world. Ill nature or ridicule may conspire, or a variety of accidents combine to lessen, enlarge, or change your infamy; and no doubt but he who has taken so much pains to be singular in his conduct would choose to be just as singular in his exit, his monument, and his epitaph.

The usual honors of the dead, to be sure, are not sufficiently sublime to escort a character like you to the great slang bin of psychologically disturbed mental dust and non-conscience ashes; for however men may differ in their ideas of grandeur or of government here, the grave is nevertheless a perfect place for you. Death is not the monarch of the dead, but of the dying. The moment one obtains a conquest he loses a subject, and like the foolish ideology you serve, will, in the end, class war yourself out of all his dominions.

As a proper preliminary towards the arrangement of your funeral honors, we readily admit of your new rank of self-appointed dictatorship-kingship. The title is perfectly in character and is your own more by merit than creation. There are politicians of various orders, from the politicians fighting the windmill to the politicians with their open hand under the table. The former is your patron for exploits, and the latter will assist you in settling your accounts. No honorary title could be more happily applied! The ingenuity is sublime! Your quean Michelle has discovered more genius in fitting you therewith, than in generating the most finished figure for a button, or check writing on the properties of a button mould.

O my goodness! How shall we dispose of you? The invention of a statuary is exhausted, and there are no suggestions of providing you with a monument, except as a seated Satan. America is anxious to bestow her funeral favors upon you, and wishes to do it in a manner that shall distinguish you from all the deceased heroes of her history. Although the Egyptian method of embalming is now known to the present age, and hieroglyphical pageantry has been deciphered, such aspects cannot be used for you because unlike the Egyptians, your being is below scum. Some other method, therefore, must be thought of to immortalize the black night fighter of the windmill and lord of the under-the-table-open handshake. Of course, to your narcissism, you are not oppressed with very delicate ideas. You surely have ambitions of being wrapped up and handed about in myrrh, aloes, and cassia. Less expensive odors will suffice ... such as those of a cesspool; and it fortunately happens that the simple genius of America has discovered the art of preserving bodies, and embellishing them too, with much greater frugality than the ancients. In balmage of humble tar you will be as secure as a Pharaoh, and in a hieroglyphic of feathers rival in finery all the mummies of Egypt.

As you have already made your exit from the moral world, and by numberless acts both of passionate and deliberate injustice engraved a "here lieth" on your deceased honor, it must be mere affectation in you to pretend concern at the humors or opinions of mankind respecting you. What remains of you may expire at any time. The sooner the better. For he who survives his reputation lives out of despite of himself, like a man listening to his own reproach.

Thus entombed and ornamented, I leave you to the inspection of the curious and return to the history of your yet surviving actions. The questionable character of your being has undergone some extraordinary examinations since your arrival in America. It is now fixed and known; and we have nothing to hope from your candor or to fear from your capacity. Indolence and inability have too large a share in your composition ever to suffer you to be anything more than the hero of little villainies and unfinished adventures and exploitations. That, which to some persons appeared moderation in you at first, was not produced by any real virtue of your own, but by a contrast of passions, dividing and holding you in perpetual irresolution. One vice will frequently expel another without the least merit in the man; as powers in contrary directions reduce each other to rest.

It became you to have supported a dignified solemnity of character; to have shown a superior liberality of soul; to have won respect by an obstinate perseverance in maintaining order, and to have exhibited on all occasions such an unchangeable graciousness of conduct, that while we beheld in you the resolution of an enemy, we might admire in you the sincerity of a clown. You came to America under the high sounding titles of foreign student and Harvard Law Review editor; not only to suppress what you call inferiors, by teleprompter oratory of racism, but to shame them out of countenance by the excellence of your example, which, you have been the patron of low and vulgar frauds, the encourager of media cruelties; and have imported a cargo of vices blacker than those which you pretend to suppress.

Mankind is not universally agreed in their determination of right and wrong; but there are certain actions which the consent of all nations and individuals has branded with the unchangeable name of meanness. In the list of human vices we find some of such a refined behavior that they cannot be carried into practice without seducing some virtue to their assistance; but meanness has neither alliance nor apology. It is generated in the dust and sweepings of other vices, and is of such a hateful figure that all the rest conspire to disown it. Barack Hussein Obama, the commissioner of hate, has at last vouchsafed to give it rank and pedigree. He has placed himself in the Oval Office at the council board, and dubbed it Companion of the Order of Evil.

A particular example of meanness which I allude to in this description is forgery. You have abetted and patronized the forging and the uttering of counterfeit birth certificates. In the same newspapers in which your own proclamation under your authority was published, offering, or pretending to offer, protection to these States, there were repeated advertisements of counterfeit certifications of live birth, and persons who have come officially from you, and under your sanction, have been taken up in attempting to vouch for them.

A conduct so basely mean in a public character is without precedent or pretence. All nations on earth, whether friends or enemies, ought to unite in despising you. You are conducting an incendiary war upon American society, which nothing can excuse or palliate – an improvement upon beggarly villainy – and shows an inbred wretchedness of heart made up between the venomous malignity of a serpent and the spiteful imbecility of an inferior reptile.

The laws of this civilized country do condemn you to the gibbet without regard to your usurped rank or titles, because it is an action foreign to the usage and custom of America; and should you fall into the hands of American Patriots, which pray God you may, it will not be a doubtful matter that we will consider you as a military prisoner and as a prisoner for felony.

Besides, it is exceedingly unwise and impolitic in you, or any other person in your regime, to promote or even encourage, or wink at the crime of forgery in any case whatever. Because, as the riches of a country, as a nation, are chiefly in true values and legal birthrights, and the far greater part of trade among individuals is carried on by the same medium of commercial truth, that is, by honest behavior with one another, they, therefore, of all people in the world, ought to endeavor to keep forgery and dishonesty out of sight, and, if possible, not to revive the idea of them. It is dangerous to make men familiar with a crime which they may afterwards practice to much greater advantage against those who first taught them. Several politicians in the past have made their exit at the gallows for forgery on their agents; for we all know, who know anything of history, that there is not a less necessitous body of men, taking them generally, than what the charlatans are. They contrive to make a show at the expense of the tailors, and appear clean at the charge of the washer-women.

America has at this time relatively not a little national debt, but nearly eighteen trillion dollars of it. Under your non-leadership America now has the greatest quantity of paper currency debt in all of its totaled history of financial debt and the least quantity of gold and silver of any nation; the real specie serves only as change in large sums, which are always for the payment of interest on the national debt. Thus circumstanced, the American nation is put to its wit's end, and obliged to be severe almost to criminality to prevent the practice and growth of forgery debt. Scarcely a session passes on Wall Street but witnesses this truth, yet you, regardless of the policy which America out of necessity is obliged to adopt, have made your whole regime intimate with the crime. As politicians of your make at the conclusion of an election are too apt to carry into practice the vices and illegal sanctions, it will probably happen, that you and your regime will hereafter abound in more forgeries, to which art the practitioners were first initiated under your authority. You have the honor of adding a new vice to the Oval Office catalogue; and the reason, perhaps, why the invention was reserved for you, is because no occupier of the Oval Office before you was mean enough even to think of it.

That a man whose soul is absorbed in the low traffic of vulgar vice is incapable of moving in any superior region is clearly shown in you by the event of every political campaign and your speeches. Your exploits have

64

been without patriotic plan, patriotic object or patriotic decision. Can it be possible that you and your regime suppose that the possession of America will be any ways equal to the expense or expectation of the evil which supports you? What advantages are derived from any achievements of yours? It is perfectly indifferent what place you are in, so long as the business of exploitation is performed and the charge of maintaining you remains the same.

If the principal events of your politics be ever attended to by historians, the balance will appear against you at the close of each. It is pleasant to look back on dangers past, and equally as pleasant to meditate on present ones when the way out begins to appear. That period has now arrived, and the long doubtful Obama term of office is changing to the sweeter prospects of victory and joy. By what miracle the country was preserved in these seasons of danger is a subject of admiration!

The principal plan of American Patriots now is to wear away the time with as little political loss as possible, and to raise WE the People for the autumn election. You, Barack Hussein Obama, do not have a superior force that is known under any expectation for their being patriotic quality. You are wasted, your numbers reduced, and your vanity amused by your thinking that you are superior. It is intended by fate to put the prize of defeat into your hands with much dishonor to yourself.

The utmost hope of America in the year 2014 reaches no higher than that she might not then be conquered by socialism-communism. Even the most cowardly DemocRAT allows that could America withstand the shock of your regime, her independence would be past a doubt. WE the People have then greatly the advantage over you. You are not formidable. Your knowledge of politics is supposed to be that of a genius. You have neither experience nor feelings for American Patriotism. You and the DemocRATS have nothing to do but to be defeated in November 2014, and your chance lay in the first vigorous onset of American Patriotism.

American Patriots are not young and unskilled. America is obliged to trust her defence to time and practice; and has, by mere dint of perseverance, maintained her cause, and brought the enemy Obama regime to a condition in which she is now capable of meeting Obama and his criminal thugs on any grounds.

Every advantage obtained by American Patriots is by fair and hard fighting. The defeat of DemocRATS disguised as socialists-communists – or is that what they really are in their non-souls? – will be complete. The eventual victory of WE the People will be an instance of their heroic perseverance very seldom to be met with. And the victory over the evil Barack Hussein Obama by American Patriots will ever give them a place in the first rank in the history of great actions.

In the future when I look back on the gloomy days of the Obama regime and see America suspended by a thread, I will feel a triumph of joy at the recollection of America's delivery, and a reverence for the patriotic men and women who snatched her from destruction. To doubt now would be a species of infidelity, and to forget the instruments which saved us then would be ingratitude. The close of such an election victory leaves us with the spirit of conquerors. We will begin to feel and be important and pleasantly await the future without you, your like, and the DemocRATS.

However confident you might have been on your first arrival in Washington, D. C., the result of your years there have given you some idea of the difficulty, if not impossibility of conquest. The face of matters in the first years gave you no encouragement to pursue a discretionary exploitation of America; for though success, in that case would have given you a double portion of fame, yet the experiment was too hazardous. You have failed and the whole blame is upon you, which means that you are condemned at once to execution.

The splendid laurels of the United States of America have flourished in the past and they will flourish again in future. America has surprised the world, and laid the foundation of her glory.

WE the People know the real value of those advantages. WE the People also know that WE have experienced all the tracings and colorings of horror, despair, and misery under your non-leadership.

I admire the distribution of patriotic laurels around the country. It is the earnest of continued union. Some States have had their day of sufferings and of fame. Other States have exerted themselves in proportion to the enemy Obama regime they have encountered or been insulted by. Some States have been called upon and have done their duty nobly. All have been witnesses to the almost expiring flame of human freedom. It has been the close struggle of life and death, the line of invisible division; and on which the unabated fortitude of WE the People prevail, and save the spark that will blaze with unrivalled lustre.

Let me ask you, Barack Hussein Obama, what great exploits have you performed? Through all the variety of changes and opportunities which your terms of office have produced, There are no actions of yours, excluding your felonies, that are styled masterly. You have moved in and out, backward and forward, round and round, scandal upon scandal as if valor consisted in a political jig. The history and figure of your movements would be truly ridiculous could they be justly delineated. They resemble the labors of your dogs Bo and Sunny pursuing their own tails; the end is still at the same distance, and all the turnings round must be done over again.

WE the People know what WE are about, what WE have to do, and how to do it.

Your actions have been marked by no capital stroke of policy or heroism. Your principal scheme is too visible to succeed. It is, therefore, necessary to trepan you into a situation in which you can only be on the defensive, without the power of the enemedia affording you assistance.

Having got you into this situation, the genius of American Patriotism will be on the rise, her power approaching to superiority. The obscurity of the morning is your best friend, for a fog is always favorable to a hunted enemy. Slow and sure is sound work. No sooner will that shout of joy ring throughout the land than you would hide yourself behind your woman and children, and sleep away defeat in expensive inactivity. Your thug goons can never be conquerors. Your situation admits only of defeat. The reason why you will lose must be either prudence of American Patriots or cowardice on your part; the former supposes your inability and the latter needs no explanation. I draw no conclusions but such as are naturally deduced from known and visible facts, and such as will always have a being while the facts which produce them remain unaltered.

It is my sincere opinion that matters are in much worse condition with you than what is generally known. Your recent speech on the State of the Union is like a soliloquy on ill luck. It shows you not coming to reason,

67

for sense of pain is the first symptom of recovery in profound stupefaction. Your condition is deplorable. You deliver the insults to American citizens, and it is deplorable that you know exactly what insults you read from the teleprompter. You resent America and Americans. You are thankful for the most trivial evasions to the most humble remonstrances. The time was when you could not deign an answer to a normal question from WE the People, and the time now is when you dare not give an answer with logic to anything or anyone. May our farewell to you and your regime be not only in all America but in the entire world.

Never did a nation invite destruction upon itself with the eagerness and the ignorance with which the United States of America did in 2008 and 2012. Bent upon the ruin of a successful and unoffending country, you have drawn the sword that has wounded to the heart, and in the agony of your resentment have applied a poison for a cure. Your conduct towards America is a compound of rage and lunacy; you aim at the government of it, yet preserve neither dignity nor character in your methods to obtain it. Were government a mere manufacture or article of commerce, immaterial by whom it should be made or sold, we might as well disperse it to anyone who is not a natural born citizen. But, when we consider it as the fountain from whence the general manners and morality of a country take their rise, that the persons entrusted with the execution thereof are by their serious example an authority to support these principles, how abominably absurd is the idea of being hereafter governed by a set of men and women who have been guilty of forgery, perjury, treachery, theft, and every species of villainy which the lowest wretches on earth could practice or invent! What greater public curse can befall any country than to be under such authority, and what greater blessing than to be delivered therefrom. The soul of any man of sentiment would rise in brave rebellion against you, and you and your like from the earth. You and your regime have proven the truth stated by the Founding Father George Washington: "Arbitrary power is most easily established on the ruins of liberty abused to licentiousness."

The malignant and venomous tempered Barack Hussein Obama has amused his savage fancy in symbolically ravaging the whole of America and Barack Hussein Obama has endeavored to justify it and declared his wish to systematically destroy the houses of all well-to-do persons in the country, except Barack Hussein Obama's wealthy, dumb, robotic

68

followers. Such a confession from one who was once entrusted with the powers of civil government, is a reproach to the character. But it is the wish and the declaration of a man whom anguish and disappointment have driven to despair, and who is daily decaying into the grave with immoral rottenness.

There is not in the compass of language a sufficiency of words to express the baseness of you and your regime, your ministries and minions. They have refined upon villainy till it wants a name. To the fiercer vices of former ages they have added the dregs and scummings of the most finished rascality, and are so completely sunk in serpentine deceit, that there is not left among them one generous creature.

From such men and women and such masters may the gracious hand of Heaven preserve America! And though the sufferings she now endures are heavy and severe, they are like straws in the wind compared to the weight of evils she would feel under the continued government of your dictator kingship and your criminal thugs.

There is something in meanness which excites a species of resentment that never subsides, and something in cruelty which stirs up the heart to the highest agony of human hatred. Barack Hussein Obama has filled up both these characters till no addition can be made, and has not reputation left with us to obtain credit for the slightest promise. The will of God is upon us and the deed is registered for eternity. When you shall be a spot scarcely visible in the world, America shall flourish the favorite of heaven and the friend of mankind.

For the domestic happiness of the United States of America and the peace of the world, I wish you had not a foot of land but what is circumscribed within your circle of Kenyan huts. Extent of dominion has been your ruin, and instead of civilizing others you have brutalized yourself and those who come in contact with you. Your mere presence is a cancer in the atmosphere. You are the only power who could practice the prodigal barbarity of your being.

When we take a survey of mankind we cannot help cursing the wretch, who, to the unavoidable misfortunes of nature, shall willfully add to the calamities of socialist-communist politics. One would think there were evils enough in the world without studying to increase them, and that life

69

is sufficiently short without shaking the sand that measures it. The histories of Lenin, Stalin, Hitler, Mao, the evil Kims – and now Barack Hussein Obama – are the histories of human psychopathic devils. A good man cannot think of their actions without abhorrence, nor of their deaths without rejoicing. To see the bounties of heaven destroyed, the beautiful face of nature laid waste, and the choicest works of creation and art tumbled into ruin would fetch a curse from the soul of piety itself. But in this country the aggravation is heightened by a new combination of affecting circumstances. America is still young, and, compared with other countries, is virtuous. None but a Herod of uncommon malice would have made domestic war upon infancy and innocence: and none but a people of the most finished fortitude, dared under those circumstances, have resisted the tyranny. To you, Barack Hussein Obama, WE the People are indebted for nothing. The country is the gift of heaven, and God alone is our Lord and Sovereign.

The time will come when you, in a melancholy hour, shall reckon up your miseries by your murders in America. Life with you wears a clouded aspect. The vision of pleasurable delusion is wearing away and changing to the barren wild of age and sorrow. The poor reflection of having served your evilness will yield you no consolation in your parting moments. Your thugs will crumble to the same undistinguished ashes with yourself, and have sins enough of their own to answer for. It is not the farcical benedictions of a bishop, nor the cringing hypocrisy of a court of chaplains, nor the formality of an act of Congress that can change guilt into innocence, or make the punishment one pang the less. You may, perhaps, be unwilling to be serious, but this destruction of the goods of the United States of America, this havoc of socialism-communism forced upon WE the People, and this sowing of American identity with mischief must be accounted for by you who made and executes it. To us they are only present sufferings, but to you they are your downfall.

If there is a sin superior to every other, it is that of willful and offensive disrespect of guaranteed freedoms. Most other sins are circumscribed within narrow limits, that is, the power of one man cannot give them a very general extension, and many kinds of sins have only a mental existence from which no infection arises; but he who is the author of a country's destruction lets loose the whole contagion of Hell and opens a

70

vein that bleeds a nation to death. We leave it to you and your regime thugs to boast of these honors; we feel no thirst for such savage glory; a nobler flame, a purer spirit animates America. She has taken up the sword of virtuous defence. She has bravely put herself between Tyranny and Freedom, between a curse and a blessing, determined to expel the one and protect the other.

It is the object only of defeating you that makes it honorable. And if there was ever a just revolution since the world began, it is this in which American Patriots are now engaged. American Patriots do not invade the Kenyan land of yours. American Patriots do not burn your villages, massacre their inhabitants like Islamic terrorists do. America wants nothing from you, and is indebted for nothing to you: and thus circumstanced, her defence is honorable and her prosperity is certain.

Yet it is not on the justice only, but likewise on the importance of this cause that I ground my seeming enthusiastical confidence of our success. The vast extension of America makes her of too much value in the scale of Providence to be cast like a pearl before swine at the feet of a usurper. There has been such a chain of extraordinary events in the development of this country at first, in the peopling and planting it afterwards, in the rearing and nursing it to its present state, and in the protection of it against the present evil dictatorship. That no man can doubt. Providence has some nobler end to accomplish than the gratification of the petty Barack Hussein Obama and Valerie Jarrett, or the ignorant and insignificant Michelle Obama.

As the blood of the martyrs has been the seed of the Christian Church, so the political persecutions done by your regime will and have already enriched American Patriotism with industry, experience, union, and importance. Always under the DemocRATS, America was a mere chaos of States, individually exposed to the ravages of that political party. At one time America had nothing that she could call her own. Her felicity depended upon accident. The convulsions of history might have thrown her from one conqueror to another, till she had been the slave of all, and ruined by everyone; for until she had spirit enough to become her own master, there was no knowing to which master she should belong. That period, thank God, is past, and she is no longer the dependent and disunited Colonies, but the independent and United States of America, knowing no master but heaven and herself. You may call this "delusion," "rebellion," or what name you please. To us it is perfectly indifferent. The issue will determine the character, and time will give it a name as lasting as its own.

You have now tried the fate of the country and can fully declare that nothing is to be got on your part, but blows and broken bones, and nothing but waste of trade and credit, and an increase of poverty and taxes. You are now only where you were when you started: not a step more forward towards the conquest of the country; because, as I have already stated, an Obama regime in Washington, D. C. can never be a conquering regime. The full amount of your losses since the beginning of your terms exceeds any conservative estimate, beside trillions of debt, for which you have nothing in exchange. Our expenses, though great, are circulated within ourselves. Yours is a direct sinking of money, and that from both ends at once. First, illegally supporting union thugs, and secondly, in paying them afterwards, because the money in neither case can return to the government. WE the People are already in possession of the prize, you only in pursuit of it. To US it is a real treasure; to you it would be only an empty triumph. OUR expenses will repay themselves with tenfold interest, while yours entail upon you everlasting poverty.

Take a review of the ground which you have gone over and let it teach you policy, if it cannot honesty. You stand but on a very tottering foundation. A change of the government in November may probably bring your measures into question and your head to the block. Without successes, you will have some difficulty in escaping, and yours being all a war against America, will afford you less pretensions, and WE the People more grounds for impeachment.

Go home, wherever that is, and endeavor to save the remains of your own ruined country that is threatened by the madness of Islamic terrorists. A few moments well applied may yet preserve it from political destruction. I am not one of those who wish to see a country in flames, because I am persuaded that such an event will not shorten the terror. The rupture at present is confined between you, your regime and WE the People. American Patriots find that you cannot conquer America, but have the wish to conquer you and your like. You are fighting for what you can never obtain, and WE are defending what WE never mean to part with. A few words, therefore, settle the bargain. Mind your own business and WE will mind ours. Govern your body servants, and WE will govern OURSELVES. You may then lie where you please unmolested by US – but not in the United States of America. WE the People will lie where WE please unmolested by you. If it were possible that you could carry on the destruction of America for twenty years you must still come to this point at last, or worse, and the sooner you think of it the better it will be for you.

My situation enables me to know the repeated insults which you have placed on America and the wretched shifts that you are driven to. I will never forget them! Your reduced strength and exhausted coffers have given a powerful superiority to WE the People. You are not a match for American Patriots. But if neither councils can prevail on you to think, nor sufferings awaken you to reason, you must even go on, 'till Barack Hussein Obama becomes a proverb of contempt, and everyone dubs you as the Commander-in-Chief of Fools.

Barack Hussein Obama! You are not my friend! You are not my countryman!! You are my enemy and I am yours!!!

Frederick William Dame
Patriotic, Steadfast, and True
February 19, 2014

Frederick William Dame

The American Crisis

The Obama Regime Is Corrupt And Americans

Are Sinking Into Despotism And Slavery

A Call To Take Action

Number Seven

★★★★★★★★★★★★★

WE the People are sinking into despotism and slavery under a corrupt government! In the United States of America today there is no difference between DemocRATS and a government that is ruled by the tyrant Barack Hussein Obama and his thugs. You are all the same!

I have been meeting with American Patriots. No person voluntarily exchanges good company for bad. However, I am forced to return to the subject at hand in this American Crisis: Barack Hussein Obama. It is nearly six years since the tyranny of Barack Hussein Obama received its first constitutional attempt to be repulsed by a few American Patriot lawyers, only to be rebuffed at every opportunity to allow justice to be done with the judicial system argument that the plaintiffs have no standing. Using the no standing argument as a valid reason to allow Barack Hussein Obama to continue his treason against the United States of America and WE the People is tantamount to the judicial system of the United States of America saying in Shakespearian manner: *Obama is vile stuff and we hold vile stuff so dear!* These past years are a period in American history that has given birth to an evil government because the dumb voters elected a charlatan imposter as the folly of the world.

I cannot help being sometimes surprised at the complimentary references which I have seen and heard made to ancient histories and transactions. The wisdom, civil governments, and sense of honor of ancient Greece and Rome are frequently held up as objects of excellence and imitation. Americans have lived to very little purpose, if, at this period of the world, they must go two or three thousand years back for lessons and examples.

74

We do great injustice to ourselves by placing them in such a superior line. We have no just authority for it, neither can we tell why it is that we should suppose ourselves inferior, unless we admit that under the present dictatorship rule of Barack Hussein Obama we have become inferior.

Could the mist of antiquity be cleared away and men and things be viewed as they really were, it is more than probable that antiquity would consider us as being inferior. Throughout the past two hundred and forty-four years America has surmounted a greater variety and combination of difficulties than, I believe, ever fell to the share of any one people in the same space of time, and has replenished the world with more useful knowledge and sounder maxims of civil government than were ever produced in any age before. Had it not been for America, there would have been no such thing as freedom left throughout the whole universe. But ... under Barack Hussein Obama WE the People have lost many of our freedoms in a long chain of wrong reasoning from wrong principles, and it is from this situation now that America must learn the resolution to redress herself, and the wisdom how to accomplish it.

The Grecians and Romans were strongly possessed of the spirit of liberty but not the principle, for at the time that they were determined not to be slaves themselves, they employed their power to enslave the rest of mankind. But this distinguished era is blotted by not one misanthropical vice. In short, if the principle on which the cause is founded, the universal blessings that are to arise from it, the difficulties that accompanied it, the wisdom with which it has been debated, the fortitude by which it has been supported, the strength of the power which American Patriots had to oppose in 1776, and the condition in which American Patriots undertook it then, be all taken in one view, we may justly style the patriotic action as the most virtuous and illustrious revolution that ever graced the history of mankind. WE the People have now arrived at a condition in which it is necessary to undertake a new revolution against the oppressive Barack Hussein Obama thug regime.

A good opinion of ourselves is exceedingly necessary in private life, but absolutely necessary in public life, and of the utmost importance in supporting national character. I have no notion of yielding the palm of the United States to any group of charlatans or despots that were ever born. WE the People have patriotically equaled the bravest in times of danger, and excelled the wisest in construction of civil governments.

From this agreeable eminence let us take a review of present affairs. The spirit of corruption is so inseparably interwoven with Obama's politics that his puppet ministries suppose all mankind are governed by the same motives. They have no idea of a people submitting even to temporary inconvenience from an attachment to rights and privileges. Their plans of business are calculated by the hour and for the hour, and are uniform in nothing but the corruption which gives them birth. They never had, neither have they at this time, any regular plan for the governing of America by good, patriotic policies. They know not how to go about it, neither have they power to effect it if they did know. The thing is not within the compass of human practicability, for America is too extensive to be fully conquered by a dictator. America can be defended by actively defeating or making legal prisoners of those who threaten or attack her. And this is the only system of defence that can be effectual in such a large country.

There is something in a domestic war carried on by subversive activities which makes it differ in circumstances from any other mode of war, because he who conducts it cannot tell whether the ground he gains be for him, or against him, when he first obtains it. In the elections of 2008 and 2012, Barack Hussein Obama was successful with an air of victory declared through the enemedia before the elections were over, the consequence of which was their seeing Obama as a savior not only of America, but of the world. But America needs no savior and the world needs more than one. In November 2014 and again in two years American Patriots will turn Barak Hussein Obama's first triumphs into a trap in which the will be totally routed. WE the People will attend to the circumstances and events of a domestic war carried on by subversion and Barack Hussein Obama will find that he will be defeated in the end.

I confess myself one of those who believe the defeat of Barack Hussein Obama to be attended with more advantages than present injuries. The case stands thus: The Obama enemy imagines life under his rule to be of more importance to us than it really is; for we all know that it has long ceased to be special: not positive developments for living Americans have transpired since the Obama regime usurped powers in 2008 and again in 2012. Yet, the enemy believes the conquest of it to be practicable, and to that belief has added the absurd idea that the soul of all America is centered in them! ... and WE the People would be conquered and forced into their socialist-communist straightjacket. It naturally follows that WE the People must break up the plans that Americans had so foolishly gone upon. WE the People must force the Obama regime thugs out of office and if they cannot be impeached, we must make sure that they will never again raise their ugly heads in American political life.

WE the People never had so evil an enemy to fight against, nor so fair an opportunity of final success as now. The death wound is already given. The day is ours if we follow it up. The enemy, by his situation, is within our reach, and by his reduced strength is within our power. The Obama regime thugs may rage as they please, but our part is to conquer and defeat them into political oblivion: Progressives, Obots, Liberals, Dumbed downers, Socialists (POLDS)! Let them wrangle and pout, but let it not draw our attention from the one thing needful. Here, in this spot is our own business to be accomplished, our felicity secured. What we have now to do is as clear as light, and the way to do it is as straight as a line. It needs no commentary, yet, in order to be perfectly understood I will put a case that cannot admit of a mistake.

WE the People should certainly think ourselves the greatest heroes in the world; and should, as soon as possible, indeed immediately, collect together all the patriotic force of the country and lay siege to the usurped White House, for it requires a much greater force to besiege an enemy in the District of Communists than to defeat them in the field. The case now is just the same as if it had been produced by the means I have here supposed. Innumerable victims have been laid waste by the Obama regime. Guns and munitions stores in our possession, which are guaranteed by the Second Amendment to the Constitution, are being stolen by the regime because of their apprehensions of a defeat if they continue their politics of domestic war on Americans, or their conscious inability of keeping the home field safe. I see no advantage which can arise to America by hunting the enemy from State to State. It is a triumph without a prize, and wholly unworthy the attention of a people determined to conquer. Neither can any State promise itself security

77

while the enemy remains in a condition to transport themselves from one part of the country to another.

The Obama regime cannot conquer where WE the People oppose them. Any undertakings by them are mean and cowardly, and reduce Barack Hussein Obama to a common pilferer. He will be despised if he appears in public. If he hides, he may be shut up and starved out, and the country, if he advances into it will become his Waterloo. He has his choice of evils and WE the People of opportunities. If he moves early, it is not only a sign but a proof that he expects no victory, and his delay will prove that he either waits for the arrival of a plan to go upon, or force to execute it, or both; in which case our strength will increase more than his; therefore, in any case we cannot be wrong if we do but proceed to revolt against him. We can begin by holding patriotic, anti-Obama meetings on weekends, picketing town and state government offices, signing petitions, writing letters to the media contacting senators and representatives, giving speeches, etc. Post your anti-Obama positions and calls for impeachment on all social networks. Write your Congress men and women and tell them that they can begin impeachment at any time, regardless of the fact that the Senate may not have a Republican majority to convict Barack Hussein Obama and his thugs for treason and felonies. Remind the sit-on-its-posterior, docile Congress that the words of the Roman emperor Tiberius apply to them as a collective body of inaction belonging to self-seekers possessed of moral cowardice: "Those men (and women) are fit to be slaves."

The particular condition of the DemocRAT Party deserves the attention of all the States. Their strength must not be estimated by the number of inhabitants. Here are men of all heritages, characters, professions, and interests. Here are the firmest American Patriots, surviving, like sparks in the ocean, unquenched and uncooled in the midst of discouragement and disaffection. Here are men and women losing their all with cheerfulness, and collecting fire and fortitude from the flames of their own estates. Here are others skulking in secret, many making a market of the times, and numbers who with new patriotic hopes are changing to become American Patriots with the circumstances of every day. It is by a mere dint of fortitude and perseverance that the American Patriots of some States that have such patriots have been able to maintain so good a countenance, and do even what they have done.

We want help, and the sooner it can arrive the more effectual it will be. The individual States, be they which they may, will always feel an additional burden upon their backs with Obama's policies, and be hard set to support its own civil power with sufficient authority; and this difficulty will rise or fall, in proportion as the other states throw in their assistance to the WE the People and our patriotic common cause: the retaking of America, our country!

The enemy will most probably make many manoeuvres in the course of the future election campaigns to amuse and draw off the attention of the several States from the one thing needful: an immediate change of government! We may expect to hear of alarms and pretended political expeditions to this place and that place, to the southward, the eastward, the westward, and the northward, all intended to prevent WE the People from forming into one awesome body. The less the Obama enemy's strength is, the more subtleties of this kind will they make use of. Their existence depends upon it, because the force of America, when collected, is sufficient to swallow up their present thug goons. It is, therefore, our business to make short work of it by bending our whole attention to this one principal point, for the instant that the main political body of the DemocRATS is defeated, all the inferior alarms throughout the country, like so many shadows, will follow their and Obama's downfall.

The only way to finish a domestic war with the least possible bloodshed, or perhaps without any, is to collect an American Patriot force against the power of which the enemy shall have no chance. By not doing this, we prolong the domestic war, and double both the calamities and expenses of it. What a rich and happy country would America be, were she, by a vigorous exertion, to execute Barack Hussein Obama to a reduction to nothingness as she has reduced all of her enemies! Her currency would rise to millions beyond its present value. Every man would be rich, and every man would have it in his power to be happy. And why not do these things? What is there to hinder us? America is her own mistress and can do what she pleases.

If we had not at this time a man in the field, we could, nevertheless, raise an American Patriot force in a few weeks sufficient to overwhelm all the obot goons which dictator Obama at present thinks he commands. Vigor and determination will do anything and everything. We began the war in

1776 with this kind of spirit. Why not end it with the same spirit in 2014 and again in 2016? Here, fellow Americans is the enemy. Here are WE the People and the American Patriots! The interest, the happiness of all America, is centered in this ruined spot, the District of Communist Poverty. Let's change it into the District of Conservative Principles. Come and help us in 2014 and 2016. Here are laurels, come and share them! Here are evil Obama regime thugs, come and help us to expel them! Here are true Americans that will make you welcome, and enemies that dread your coming!

The worst of all policies is that of doing things by halves. Penny-wise and dollar-foolish have been the ruin of thousands. Pennies no longer count and dollars are valueless under Barack Hussein Obama. The present spring, summer and fall, if rightly improved, will free us from our troubles, and save us the expense of millions. We have now only one enemy to cope with. No opportunity can be fairer; no prospect more promising.

That in which every man is interested is every man's duty to support. Any burden which falls equally on all men, and from which every man is to receive an equal benefit, is consistent with the most perfect ideas of liberty. I would wish to revive something of that virtuous ambition which first called Americans into the field in 1776. Then every American was eager to do his part, and perhaps the principal reason why we have in any degree fallen therefrom, is because we did not set a right value by it at first, but left it to blaze out of itself, instead of educating, regulating, and preserving it by just proportions of memorials and service. Patriotism is an ever-occurring process and must always be properly honored and passed on from generation to generation. This has not happened in the United States of America. What is left in education nowadays is the evil progressive process called Common Core, which has no core and is so commonly communicated that two plus two no longer equals four. America! Your citizens are being made dumb by POLDS and their like!

We must undertake this important revolution step-by-step and there are some basic rules to follow:

1. Band together under the call for freedom of the Founding Fathers. *Don't Tread on me! Rally round the Liberty Tree! Let Freedom ring throughout the land!*

2. Let the names of Obama supporters be registered and their pictures be placed on a Wanted List so that all American Patriots can see who their enemies are.

3. Let the sums of money collected by the Obama regime be confiscated so that they may be used for the financial support of the new American Revolution.

4. Do not be politically correct, particularly with the enemedia. The enemedia are just as guilty as Barack Hussein Obama is in conducting the greatest scam the history of the world has ever experienced. Political correctness is a form of lying. Be honest, particularly with the enemedia. Call them out if they attempt to mock you, put words in your mouth, change the topic, etc. Tell them that if they do not support American Patriots and WE the People, they are traitors and no better than the Obama regime to which they have enslaved themselves into becoming non-entities.

As it will always happen that in the space of ground on which a hundred men shall live, there will be always a number of persons who, by age and infirmity are incapable of doing personal service, regard these people as equal American Patriots.

There never was a scheme against which objections might not be raised. But this alone is not a sufficient reason for rejection. The only line to judge truly upon is to draw out and admit all the objections which can fairly be made, and place against them all the contrary qualities, conveniences and advantages; then by striking a balance you come at the true character of any scheme, principle or position.

The advantages of the new American Revolution here proposed are ease, expedition, and cheapness; yet the men so raised get a much larger bounty than is anywhere at present given; because all the expenses, extravagance, and consequent idleness of recruiting are saved or prevented. The country incurs neither new debt nor interest thereon; the whole matter being all settled at once and entirely done with by WE the

People with what we have. Active support for WE the People and American Patriots can be accomplished without a tax, without either the charge or trouble of collecting one. True support comes from a moral conscience and a just heart. The American Patriots are ready for the field with the greatest possible expedition, because it becomes the duty of the inhabitants themselves, in every part of the country, to find their proportion of patriotic men and women.

WE the People will never forget that a corrupt government behavior causes a nation to lose its freedoms and sink into despotism and slavery.

Frederick William Dame
Patriotic, Steadfast, and True
February 21, 2

Frederick William Dame

The American Crisis

Every Logically Thinking Citizen Despises

Barack Hussein Obama

A Call To Take Action

Number Eight

Characters like Barack Hussein Obama are found in all democratic republics and are despised by their patriotic citizens. Barack Hussein Obama! Your kind of character has no dignity!! You are the epitome of nothingness!!!

There is a dignity in the warm passions of an American Patriot that is never to be found in the cold malice of Barack Hussein Obama. In the former there is the heat in the heart that permeates the body and soul. In the latter there is poison. The instant an American Patriot has it in his power to punish, he feels a disposition to forgive. But the canine venom of Barack Hussein Obama knows no relief but revenge. This general distinction will, I believe, apply in all cases and suits as well WE the People vs. the Obama thug regime.

Barack Hussein Obama! As I presume your last proclamations before Congress and your teleprompter speeches before the American public will undergo the strictures of other patriotic pens, I shall confine my remarks to only a few germane points that show your evilness. All that you have said might have been comprised in half the compass. What you say and feel is so important to you. However, it is really tedious and unmeaning, and only a repetition of many of your former follies, with here and there an offensive aggravation. Your cargo of lies will have no market. It is unfashionable to look at them – nay … even speculation is at an end. They have become your drug and are in no way calculated for the climate of rational thinking American Patriots.

In the course of your blabbering you argue that the policies as well as the benevolence of your regime have thus far checked the extremes of class conflict, yet you support and instigate class conflict as often as you can, particularly when they tend to distress a people still considered as our fellow citizens, and to desolate a country shortly at your instigation to become again a source of mutual hate. What you mean by the benevolence of your regime is to me inconceivable. To put a plain question: Do you consider yourselves humans or devils? For until this point is settled, no determinate sense can be put upon the benevolence. You have already equaled and in many cases excelled, the savages of other dictatorships in the world; and if you have a cruelty in store you must have imported it, unmixed with every human material, from the original warehouse of Hell.

WE the People are indebted to the interposition of Providence for the short chain that limits your ravages and her blessings on our endeavors. WE the People detest the so-called Obama regime's benevolence. Remember you do not, at this time, command a foot of land in the United States of America. WE the People circumscribe your power; wherever you are physically located, regardless of the geography of the golf course. To avoid a defeat, or prevent a desertion of your goon thugs, you have taken up your quarters in golf holes and caves on ski slopes of inaccessible security. You even resort to seek protection from something resembling the wild bellowing of a moose cow calling your opponents *Knuckleheads*. In order to conceal what everyone can perceive, you always endeavor to impose your propaganda upon us as an act of mercy. If you think to succeed by such shadowy devices, you and your obots are but infants in the political world; you have the A, B, C, of stratagem yet to learn and are wholly ignorant of the people you have to contend with. Like clowns in a state of intoxication you and your thugs forget that the rest of the world has eyes, and that the same stupidity which conceals you and your thugs from yourselves exposes you to the deserved satire and contempt of the world.

The politics of Barack Hussein Obama's socialism-communism professes the unnatural design not only of estranging Americans from Americans, but of mortgaging America and her resources to our enemies, such as your refusal to build the Keystone pipeline, which is only an extension and straightening of existing pipelines. You would rather have Americans

84

pay a dhimmi-jizya tax to Saudi Arabia and other Arab oil producing countries in the form of oil purchases at too expensive a price!

I consider your lying declarations like a madman biting in the hour of death. What you say ever contains likewise a fraudulent meanness; for, in order to justify barbarous conclusions, you advance false positions. The *Declaration of Independence* and the Constitution *for the United States of America* are open, noble, and generous. They are true policy, founded on sound philosophy, and neither a surrender nor mortgage, as you have scandalously insinuated and called for their revamping in your weird political direction. I have seen every proposal and speak from positive knowledge. In Barack Hussein Obama, Americans have never found an affectionate friend and faithful ally. In Barack Hussein Obama, Americans have found nothing but tyranny, cruelty, and infidelity. But the happiness is that the mischief you, Barack Hussein Obama, threaten is not in your power to execute; and if it were, the punishment would return upon you in a ten-fold degree. The humanity of America has hitherto restrained her from acts of retaliation. The affection she retains for many individuals has, to the present day, warded off her resentment and operated as a screen to the whole. But even these considerations must cease when national objects interfere and oppose them. Repeated aggravations will provoke a retort, and policy justifies the measure. WE the People mean now to take you seriously upon your own ground and principle, and as you do, so shall you be done by.

You ought to know that you and the DemocRAT Party are far more exposed to incendiary desolation than WE the People in OUR present state can possibly be. Americans occupy a country whose riches are in the *Declaration of Independence*, the *Constitution for the United States of America*, and patriotism. The wealth of DemocRATS lies chiefly in giving handouts of other people's money to the depositories of unions, fleets of dumbed-down followers, and society's parasites. There is not a DemocRAT's politically held office but may be laid in ashes by a single patriotic counter candidate. Your own may probably contribute to the proof: in short, there is no evil which cannot be returned when you come to incendiary political mischief. Such election losses that the DemocRATS will sustain when executed in the 2014 election season is infinitely greater than any loss you can inflict. Barack Hussein Obama and the DemocRATS neither are, nor can be secure from this sort of

85

election destruction, and, as political pundits justly observe, a loss at the November elections will bankrupt the DemocRATS and the Obama regime.

In the past is has been the custom of Republicans and DemocRATS to make honest accusations on each other. The honest accusation herewith is in reality a truth: just as there are Republicans In Name Only, there are DemocRATS who are nothing but RATS only.

Think not that our distance secures you, Barack Hussein Obama, or our invention fails us. WE the People can much easier accomplish such a point in our revolution against you than any dog gulping down its chuck. WE the People do not talk the same language. WE the People do not dress in the same $10,000 habit. WE the People do not appear with the same bullying manners as you. WE the People can pass from one part of America to another unsuspected; many of us are more acquainted with the country than you are, and should you apolitically provoke us, you will most assuredly lament the effects of it. Mischiefs of this kind require no intelligence to execute them. They require only hate and a love of evil. The meanness is obvious and the opportunities unguardable. I hold up a warning to your senses, if you have any left, and likewise to the very unhappy people who think their affairs are committed to you. I call not with the rancor of an enemy, but with the earnestness of a friend on the deluded people of Obamaland lest between your blunders and theirs, they sink beneath the evils that you have contrived for us all.

"He who lives in a glass house," says a Spanish proverb "should never begin throwing stones." This is exactly your case and you must be the most ignorant of mankind, or suppose us so, not to see on which side the balance of accounts will fall. There are many other modes of retaliation, which, for several reasons I choose not to mention. But be assured of this, that the instant you put your threats into execution, a counter-blow will follow it. You openly profess yourselves savages and it is high time WE the People should treat you as such, and if nothing but distress can recover you to reason, to punish will become an office of charity. Indeed, it is more than probable that your own folly will provoke a much more ruinous act. Say not when mischief is done that you had not warning and remember that WE the People do not begin it, but mean to repay it. This much for your savage and impolitic threats when you speak!

86

Regardless of what you say, surely the union of absurdity with madness was never marked in more distinguishable lines than those that come out of you foul mouth when you speak off your teleprompter. You may do well enough for you, who dare not inquire into the humble capacities of American Patriots; but WE the People, who estimate persons and things by their real worth, cannot suffer OUR judgments to be so imposed upon; and unless it is your wish to see yourself exposed, it ought to be your endeavor to keep yourself out of sight, preferably in a padded room enclosed by iron bars. The less you have to say about yourself the better. WE the People have done with you, and that ought to be answer enough. You have often been told so. Strange that the answer must be so often repeated. You go a-begging as a dictator-king and spoiled brat, or with some unsaleable commodity you were tired of; and though everybody tells you no, no, still you keep hawking you health care for the American people about whom you do not care. As WE the People have no inclination to welcome you and your product, WE the People bid nothing for it. However, there is one constitutional commodity that will have you in time.

The impertinent folly of your narcissistic self deserves no other notice than to be laughed at and thrown aside, for the principle on which you are founded is detestable. Americans are invited to submit to a man who has attempted by every cruelty to destroy them, and to join him in making socialism-communism the *joi d'vivre* in America? Your positions are the steer stools par excellence.

Can Bedlam in concert with Lucifer form a more mad and devilish request? Were it possible a people could sink into such apostasy they would deserve to be swept from the earth like the inhabitants of Sodom and Gomorrah. The proposition is a universal affront to the rank which man holds in the creation, and an indignity to Him who placed him there. It supposes that Americans are made up without a spark of honor, and under no obligation to God or man.

What sort of men or Christians must you suppose the Americans to be, who, after seeing their most humble lives insultingly rejected; the most grievous laws passed to distress them in every quarter; an undeclared domestic war let loose upon them, and everyone invited to the slaughter; who, after seeing their kinsmen murdered, their fellow citizens starving to death because they have no income, and their houses and property being reclaimed; who, after the most serious appeals to heaven, the most solemn abjuration by oath of all government connected with you, and the most heart-felt pledges and protestations of faith to each other; and who, after soliciting the friendship, and entering into alliances with other sections of the country, should at last break through all these obligations, civil and divine, by complying with your horrid and infernal proposal? Ought WE the People ever after to be considered as a part of the human race? Or ought WE the People not rather to be blotted from the society of mankind and become a spectacle of misery to the world? But there is something in corruption, which, like a jaundiced eye, transfers the color of itself to the object it looks upon, and sees everything stained and impure; for unless you were capable of such conduct yourselves, you would never have supposed such a curse of socialism-communism. The offer fixes your infamy. It exhibits you as a creature without faith; with which oaths and treaties are considered as trifles, and the breaking of them as the breaking of a bubble. Regard to decency or to rank might have taught you better; or pride inspired you, though virtue could not. There is not left a step in the degradation of character to which you can now descend; you have put your foot below the ground floor, indeed, below the domiciles of worms, and the key of the dungeon is turned upon you.

That the invitation to become socialist-communist may want nothing of being a complete monster, you have thought proper to finish it with an assertion which has no foundation, either in fact or philosophy. The only true assertion is: socialism-communism is evil! Therefore, WE the People style OURSELVES as the enemy of the Obama regime, and by way of propagandizing the establishment of estranging political ideas the Obama regime is styled the enemy of WE the People. Indeed, the Obama regime IS the enemy of WE the People. The Obama regime IS totally non-philosophical! The Obama regime IS barbarism! They are of the same species and when applied to beings of the same species, let their station in the creation be what it may. WE the People have a perfect idea of a natural enemy when the devil comes into the play, because the enmity is perpetual, unalterable, and unabateable. It admits neither of peace, truce, or treaty; consequently the warfare is eternal, and therefore it is natural. WE the People are humans confronting evil and know that

88

on moral and ethical grounds WE the People must be in opposition to the Obama evil that is a curse on the American society.

OUR quarrels are not accidental and they are not equivocally created. WE the People cannot become friends of the Obama regime based upon any concept of hope and change that is evil in its core. The Creator has constituted the Obama regime's socialism-communism as the enemy of mankind. He has not made socialism-communism any one order of beings. That comes from Satan. Even though WE the People may quarrel, WE the People will still hold together. If any two opposing opinions are so, then the offence of one opposing opinion frequently originates with the accuser. Yet, the Obama regime does not maintain it has an opinion only. It claims it has the doctrine that is the answer to America's troubles. Problems cannot be solved with evil solutions.

Separated from the reality of WE the People, the Obama regime has contracted an unsocial habit of manners, and imagines in others the jealousy it creates in its own sphere. Never long satisfied with peace, the Obama regime supposes the discontent universal, and buoyed up with its own importance, conceives itself the only object pointed at.

WE the People and the Obama regime are not natural enemies. There does not exist in Nature such a principle. WE the People receive our essence from the Laws of Nature. The Obama regime receives its existence from the antithesis to Nature: Satanic Hell!

The expression natural enemy has been often used, and always with a fraudulent design; for when the idea of a natural enemy is conceived, it prevents all other inquiries, and the real cause of the quarrel is hidden in the universality of the conceit. Men start at the notion of a natural enemy and ask no other question. The cry obtains credit like the alarm of a mad dog and is one of those kinds of tricks which, by operating on the common passions, secure their interest through their folly.

But WE the People are not to be thus imposed upon. WE the People live in a large world and have extended our ideas beyond the limits and prejudices of racist baiters. WE the People hold out the right hand of friendship to all the universe and WE the People conceive that there is a sociality in the manners of democratic republic countries that is much better disposed to peace and negotiation than that of negotiation with the evil Obama regime. Until the latter becomes more civilized – which will never happen because the Obama regime is uncivilized to the core – it cannot expect to live long at peace with any American Patriot. The Obama regime's common language is vulgar. It is offensive. It is permeated with the rudiments of insult. The Obama regime is Hell; the mighty arm of Satan that shakes the earth to its center and its poles; the scourge of good! Barack Hussein Obama is the terror of the world! Barack Hussein Obama governs with a nod and pours down vengeance as if he were some kind of god. His language neither makes a nation great or little; but it shows a savageness of manners and has a tendency to keep national animosity alive. The entertainments of his speeches are calculated to the same end, and almost every public exhibition of an Obama regime propagandist is tinctured with insult. Barack Hussein Obama is always in dread of the *Constitution*; terrified at the apprehension of the *Bill of Rights*; suspicious of being outwitted by WE the People; and privately cringing though he is publicly offending. Let him, therefore, return to Hell and he will find the idea of a natural enemy to be only a phantom of his own imagination.

Little did I think at this period of the domestic war to see a proclamation which could promise Barack Hussein Obama no one useful purpose whatever, and tend only to expose him. One would think that you were just awakened from a four years' dream, and knew nothing of what had passed in the interval. Is this a time to be offering laws by your phone and pen? Is it worth your while, after every force has failed you, to retreat under the shelter of a phone and pen? Or can you think that WE the People are to be begged or threatened into submission by a signature on a piece of paper or a phone call? But as the taxpayer supported, self-appointed dictator-king that you are, you conceive yourself bound to do something, and the genius of ill-fortune told you that you must pen or phone.

For my own part, I do not threaten to put phone to the ear or to put pen to paper in order to execute lies. I put pen to paper in order to tell the truth. One truth is that of all the words in the English language that are negative in their meaning, not one of them can be used to describe Barack Hussein Obama because that character is in a hole deeply below those negative meanings. Convinced of our superiority by the issue of every election campaign conducted legally, I am inclined to hope that that which all the

90

rest of the world now see would become visible to you, and therefore felt unwilling to ruffle your temper by fretting you with repetitions and discoveries. There have been intervals of hesitation in your conduct, apparently because you were high on some drug, or because you were infatuated with yourself, or because you were preoccupied the weird, unnatural love of a body servant, from which it seemed a pity to disturb you, and a charity to leave you to yourself. You have often stopped, as if you intended to think, but your thoughts have ever been too early, or too late, and always evil.

There was a time when Congress and the Courts disdained to answer, or even hear a petition from WE the People concerning your ineligibility. That time is past and they are petitioning our acceptance. WE the People now stand on higher ground and offer documented information supporting Barack Hussein Obama's impeachment, and the time will come when they, perhaps in vain, will take it from us. The latter case is as probable as the former ever was. Congress and the Courts cannot refuse to acknowledge our independence with greater obstinacy than they before refused to hear cases of Barack Hussein Obama's constitutional eligibility. There is something in obstinacy which differs from every other passion; whenever it fails it never recovers, but either breaks like iron, or crumbles sulkily away like a fractured arch. Most other passions have their periods of fatigue and rest; their suffering and their cure; but obstinacy has no resource, and the first wound is mortal. Congress and the Courts have already begun to give it up, and they will, from the natural construction of the vice Barack Hussein Obama has committed, find themselves both obliged and inclined to do so.

Barack Hussein Obama! If you look back you see nothing but loss and disgrace. If you look forward the same scene continues, and the close is an impenetrable gloom. You may plan and execute little mischiefs, but are they worth the expense they cost you, or will such partial evils have any effect on the general cause? Your propaganda expeditions will be felt at a distance like an attack upon a hen-roost, and expose you in the world with a sort of childish frenzy. Is it worthwhile to keep thugs and goons and dumb persons to protect you in writing proclamations? Possessing yourselves of yourselves is not conquest, but convenience, and in which you will one day or other be trepanned. American Patriots' morals and ethics – which you never had – will mean that your next political action will lock you into your bread-and-water cell.

It would puzzle all the politicians in the universe to conceive what you stay for, or why you should have stayed so long. You are prosecuting a domestic war in which you confess you have neither object nor hope, and that conquest, could it be effected, would not repay the charges: in the meanwhile the rest of your affairs are running to ruin and a revolution is kindling against you. In such a situation there is neither doubt nor difficulty; the first rudiments of reason will determine the choice, for if peace can be procured with more advantages than even a conquest can be obtained, he must be an idiot indeed that hesitates. Do not hesitate any longer. Resign from your usurped position and go into some self-imposed exile paid for by your friendly pay-to-play palls in Islamic cartels.

But you, Barack Hussein Obama, are probably buoyed up by a set of wretched mortals, who, having deceived themselves, are cringing with the duplicity of a spaniel for a little temporary bread. Those men and women will tell you just what you please. It is their interest to amuse in order to lengthen out their protection. They plan to keep you amongst them for that very purpose; and in proportion as you disregard their advice, and grow callous to their complaints, they will stretch into improbability and season their flattery the higher. Characters like these are to be found in every country, and every country will despise them. Barack Hussein Obama, you are one such character.

Frederick William Dame
Patriotic, Steadfast, and True
February 26, 2014

Frederick William Dame

The American Crisis

WE the People Will Not Let This Crisis Go To Waste!

A Call To Take Action

Number Nine

You POLDS! ... You Progressives, Obots, Liberals, Dumbed-downers, Socialists-Communists! Hear ye! Hear ye! Hear ye! Normal people use their ears to listen carefully and to place in their brains located between their ears important information that will assist them in becoming American Patriots. WE the People do this every day! You POLDS should also! Doing such will help you to change your attitude. Use *The American Crisis* to cure your anti-American illness!

There are stages in the business of serious life in which to amuse is cruel, but to deceive is to destroy; and it is of little consequence in the conclusion whether people deceive themselves, or submit by a kind of mutual consent to the impositions of each other. That the United States of America has long been under the influence of delusion, no ... mistake, needs no other proof than the unexpected and wretched situation that she is now involved in. So powerful has been the influence that no provision was ever made or thought of against the misfortune, because the possibility of its happening was never conceived, except by the Founding Fathers when they wrote the *Constitution for the United States of America*, specifically Article II, Section 1, Paragraph 5. However, they did not foresee that the brain-dead American voter, the DemocRAT Party, the United States Congress, and the Supreme Court of the United States of America would not care in 2008/2009 and again in 2012/2013. Indeed, will they ever care?

The general and successful resistance of American Patriots will result in the conquest of Barack Hussein Obama and his regime. It will usher in a new age in the truth of upholding the *Constitution* treated by WE the People as the dream of a political opposition with a patriotic goal. The

Barack Hussein Obama regime and its thugs are beheld as dangerous objects unworthy of attention, yet with the necessity of serious thought. The bare intimation of them affords the nighttime talk shows a triumph of laughter. But those are short triumphs! Everything which has been predicted against the Obama regime has happened, and all that it promised has failed. A long series of politics so remarkably distinguished by a succession of misfortunes, without one alleviating turn, must certainly have something in it systematically wrong. It is sufficient to awaken the most credulous into suspicion and the most obstinate into thought. Either the means in the Obama regime's power are insufficient or the measures ill planned. Either the execution has been bad or the thing attempted impracticable; or, to speak more emphatically, either you, Barack Hussein Obama, are not able, or heaven is not willing. For why is it that you have not conquered us? Who, or what has prevented you? You have had every opportunity that you could desire, and succeeded to your utmost wish in every preparatory means. Your fleets of DemocRAT Party Idiots and armies of Dumb Pelosis are all over America. No uncommon fortune has intervened. The patriotic opposition, either in or out of Washington, D. C., has disconcerted the Obama regime's measures; retarded and diminished your force. They have foretold the Obama regime's fate. Every regime scheme was carried with as high a hand as if the whole nation had been unanimous. Everything the regime thugs wanted was asked for, and everything asked for was granted by a wishy-washy Congress.

Barack Hussein Obama! A greater force than your thugs was not within the compass of your abilities to send, and at the time you sent them you were the most favorable person in America. For proof one only needed to ask you! You were then at rest with the whole world beside. You had the range of every enemedia ... uncontradicted and deceived. You excited Americans with tales of hope and change. Under that disguise you collected numerous brainwashed followers and came almost unexpectedly upon the nation as its next leader. Your accolades of promise were much greater than America looked for or needed, and that which American Patriots had to oppose it with was not believed because it was badly communicated and poorly presented by the enemedia. The hope and change dope was embodied only for a short time and expired within a few months after your illegal arrival in the Oval Office. You had a regime to form; measures to concert; and thugs to train, and every necessary article to import or to create in the form of dictatorial laws. Your socialist-communist scheme had exhausted the realm of imagination, and deceit intercepted our political calls for redress.

WE the People were unknown to you, unconnected with your political world of evil destruction, and strangers to the disposition of socialism-communism. Could you possibly have wished for a more favorable conjunction of circumstances? Yet all these have happened and passed away, and, as it were, WE the People now laugh at you. Indeed, you have become a laughing stock full of glitches. There are likewise events of such an original nativity as can never happen again, unless a new evil world should arise from Hell, from whence you came.

If anything can be a lesson to presumption, surely the circumstances of your domestic war will have their effect. Because Barack Hussein Obama will be defeated by American Patriotic Power, his pride will draw no consolation from the importance of his conquerors, the American Patriots. In the present case Barack Hussein Obama is excelled by those that he affected to despise, and his own opinions retorting upon himself become an aggravation of his disgrace. Misfortune and experience are lost upon mankind when they produce neither reflection nor reformation.

Evils, like poisons, have their uses and there are diseases which no other remedy can reach. It has been the crime and folly of Barack Hussein Obama to suppose himself invincible and without acknowledging or perceiving that the fullness of his strength has been drawn away by the country he is now at domestic war with.

The arm of the Barack Hussein Obama regime has been spoken of as The Arm of The One, and he has lived his whole life as if he thought the whole world was created for his diversion. His politics, instead of civilizing, have tended to brutalize mankind. Under the vain, unmeaning title of *Defender of the Islamic Faith*, he has made war like a terrorist against the religions of humanity in making absolutely no condemnations of Muslim terrorism against Christianity, or Hinduism, or Buddhism. His cruelties against the people living on the unsecured borders with Mexico will never be forgotten, and it is somewhat remarkable that the drug produce of that country, transported to America, should be allowed to destroy Americans. The chain of evil is continued, though with a mysterious kind of uniformity both in the crime and the non-punishment. The latter runs parallel with the former, and time and fate will give it a perfect illustration of blame and conviction of you, Barack Hussein Obama.

When information is withheld, ignorance becomes a reasonable excuse. One would charitably hope that the Obama regime does not encourage cruelty from choice but from mistake. But the evidence indicates the opposite. Their recluse situation, surrounded by their own perfectness, preserves them from the calamities of a domestic war and keeps them in the dark as to the conduct of their own DemocRATS.

The Obama thugs see not, therefore they feel not. They tell the tale that is told them and believe it, and accustomed to no other news than their own, they receive it, stripped of its horrors and prepared for the palate of the nation through the channels of the enemedia. They are made to believe that their propaganda and policies differ from those of other socialist-communist countries and have nothing of rudeness or barbarity in them. They suppose their propaganda and politics what they wish them to be. They feel a disgrace in thinking otherwise, and naturally encourage the belief from a partiality to themselves. There was a time when many Americans voted for Obama. They felt the same prejudices that he told them to feel and reasoned from the same errors that he convinced them were truths. But experience, sad and painful experience, has taught them better. If voting today, they would not give their ballot to Obama and the DemocRATS. Having seen and experienced reality, they are now being illegally audited by the Internal Revenue Service.

What the conduct will be after WE the People get rid of the Obama regime, I know not; but what the conduct of the present is, I well know. It is low, cruel, indolent, and profligate; and have the people of America no other cause for the impeachment of the Obama regime than what Obama and his policies have occasioned, that alone is cause sufficient.

The field of politics in Washington, D. C. is far more extensive than that of any news created by the enemedia. Men have a right to reason for themselves, and though they cannot contradict the intelligence in the patriotic media, they may frame upon it what sentiments they please. The misfortune is that a general ignorance has prevailed over the whole

96

nation respecting America under the Obama regime. The majorities and the minorities have both been wrong. Since 2008 the former have always been so and the latter have always been so.

Politics, to be executively right, must have a unity of means and time, and a defect in either overthrows the whole. The senators and representatives and court justices rejected the legal arguments of those petitioning the government and the Supreme Court for redress while they were practicable. They are now beginning to join in these petitions and are becoming aware of the investigations into the legal authenticity of Barack Hussein Obama at a time when the practicability of the Obama regime is sinking as if in quicksand. The danger still looms for the Obama regime. From wrong measures they got into wrong time, and have now completed the circle of absurdity by closing it upon themselves.

Americans who were in Washington, D. C. a few months before the breaking out of Obama hostilities against America in 2009 and 2013 found the disposition of the people such that they might have been led by a thread and governed by a reed. Their suspicion was quick and penetrating, but their attachment to Barack Hussein Obama was obstinate, and it was at that time a kind of treason to speak against it. They may have disliked the Obama regime, but they esteemed Obama's misinformation propaganda as supplied by the enemedia. Their idea of grievance operated without resentment, and their single object was reconciliation. I always believed the Obama regime to be capable of measures so rash and wicked as the commencing of domestic hostilities. I even imagined the DemocRATS in the nation would encourage it. I viewed the dispute as a kind of lawsuit in which I supposed the parties in the wishy-washy Congress would keep their necks out of the rope's loop and would find a way either to decide or settle disputes.

I have always had thoughts of calling for Congressional impeachment of all DemocRATS and RINOs who deserve impeachment – all of them! Moreover, I shall fight Barack Hussein Obama regarding all themes – with a weapon unknown to him – intellect coupled with American Patriotism without teleprompters and speech writers.

The world could not have persuaded me that I should be either a soldier or an author. I became both and many more. Thomas Jefferson inspired me to become in my own way a renaissance man. The talents for soldier and author were somewhat buried in me, and might ever have continued so, had not the necessity of the times with the illegal election of Barack Hussein Obama to the Oval Office dragged and driven them into action with the inestimable support of American patriotic colleagues. I had formed my plan of life, and conceiving myself happy, wished everybody else so. But when the country into which I entered life as a natural born citizen was set on fire about my ears, it was time to stir. It was time for every American patriotic man and woman to stir. Those who had been long settled had something to defend; those who had just come of age had something to pursue; and the call and the concern was equal and universal. In a country where all men and women were once concerned with their non-socialism-communism lives, the difference of a few years with government involvement taking action can make their confirmed status as free citizens independent of government become non-existent.

The breaking out of domestic revolt opens a new suspicion in the politics of America, which, though very rare, have since been proved to be very right. What I allude to is a secret and fixed determination in the Obama regime to sell out America to the United Nations as a conquered country under the inevitable control of the ludicrous Islamic countries who are a majority in that ludicrous body. This must be taken as the object. The whole line of conduct is uniform and consistent in its parts. This conduct pursued by the Obama regime is rash in its origin and ruinous in its consequences. Coupled with other policies like ObamaCare there is no proportion between the object and the charge. Nothing but the whole soil and property of the United States of America can be placed as a possible equivalent against the trillions which the Obama regime has expended. No taxes raised in America can possibly repay their expenditures.

If an American spends one dollar for every second, 24 hours a day, 7 days a week, 365 days a year, it would take that American 31,688 years to spend one trillion dollars. It would take the American Patriot 11.5 days to pay back one million dollars at the spending rate of one dollar per second; 32 years to pay back one billion dollars at a spending rate of one dollar per second, and 31,688 years to pay back one trillion dollars at a spending rate of one dollar per second. The national debt, not including

98

interest on the borrowed money is almost eighteen trillion dollars and growing. It will take 538,696 years and more for one person with a one-dollar-per-second spending rate to pay back the almost eighteen trillion dollars of debt without interest payments.

It is a moot question to ask: How much money have the Obamas and their thugs received in kickbacks during the past years? The Obamas and Valerie-slum-lord-psychopath Jarrett did not make sure that their friends received government contracts for nothing! There is only one solace: at the end of paying back one billion dollars, in the 32-year period, the Obamas and their thugs should be dead or near to death, and with the guidance of Providence, the United States of America will still exist, hopefully as the Founding Fathers conceived it.

Reconciliation never appears to have been the wish or the object of the Obama regime. They looked on conquest as certain and infallible, and, under that persuasion, sought to drive WE the People into what they might style a general rebellion, and then, crushing WE the People with force that dictators always use, reap the rich harvest of a general confiscation, and silence WE the People forever; whereas it is they that should be silenced forever. The profligacy of the Obama regime requires that a new gold mine should be opened and that gold mine could be no other than America, conquered, forfeited, and sold off. The Obamas and their regime have nowhere to go. Every channel of patriotic money has been drained; and their extravagance, with the thirst of a drunkard, is gaping for supplies. WE the People taxpayers will gladly pay for their keeping in iron bar cells until the devil comes to take them!

If the Obama regime denies the selling out of America to have been their plan, it becomes them to explain what was their plan. For either they have abused us in coveting property they never labored for, or they have abused us in expending an amazing sum with an incompetent spender. Taxation can never be worth the charge of obtaining it by fines; and any kind of formal obedience which WE the People could have made would have weighed with the lightness of a laugh against such a load of expense. It is, therefore, most probable that the Obama regime will at last justify their policy as they always do, by their dishonesty, and openly declare that their original design was the conquest of WE the People: and, in this case, it well becomes WE the People to consider how far the nation might be benefited by the success of American Patriots in the elections in 2014 and 2016.

In a general view there are few conquests that repay the charge of making them, and mankind are pretty well convinced that it can never be worth their while to go to revolution for profit's sake. If WE the People are made domestic war upon, OUR country plundered, or OUR existence at stake, it is OUR duty to defend and preserve OURSELVES, but in every other light, and from every other cause, is domestic war inglorious and detestable.

Barack Hussein Obama! When conquests are made of foreign countries, it is supposed that the commerce and dominion of the country which made them are extended. But this could neither be the object nor the consequence of the present domestic war. You enjoyed the whole of American capitalism before. There could be no possible addition by a conquest, but on the contrary, it must diminish as the inhabitants would be forced to reduce their wealth by becoming socialists-communists. You have the same dominion over the country which DemocRATS used to have, and you have no complaint to make against America for breach of any part of a fictitious contract between you or America, or contending against any established commercial, political, or geographical custom. The country and commerce were both your provider when you began to conquer in 2008/2009, essentially in the same manner and form as had been available to the DemocRATS throughout a hundred-plus years before.

Nations have sometimes been induced to make conquests for the sake of reducing the power of their enemies, or bringing an enemy country to a balance with their own. But this could be no part of your plan. No authority is claimed here, neither is any such authority suspected by you, or acknowledged or imagined by WE the People. What then, in the name of heaven, could you go to domestic war for? Or what chance could you possibly have in the event, but either to hold the same country which you held before and that you have placed in a much worse condition, or to lose, with an amazing expense, what you might have retained without a penny of charges?

Domestic war can never be the interest of a free nation. Yet a domestic war against WE the People is more than a quarreling comparable to people in business. But to make a domestic war with those who pay the greater majority of taxes, which you and Michelle expend as if it were pennies, is like setting two bull-dogs upon a customer at the shop door. The least degree of common sense shows the madness of the bull dogs, and it will apply with the same force of conviction. Piratical Islamic countries of Africa having neither commerce nor commodities of their own to lose, may make war upon all the world, and lucratively find their account in it; but it is quite otherwise with the Obama regime: for, besides the stoppage of the free market in time of the domestic war, WE the People expose more of our own property to be lost than WE the People have the chance of receiving our property from an evil government.

Barack Hussein Obama! Some hacks in Congress, practically all of them from the DemocRAT Party and slaves to the Obama regime, have mentioned the greatness of your Affordable Care Act as an apology for the greatness of being able to use free time to write poetry or partake in social chattings. The social parasites are living off the producers. This is miserable politics indeed, because it ought to have been given as a reason for your not engaging in socialism-communism at first.

The southern border of the United States America commands the Republic of Mexico trade almost as ineffectually as a non-existing border to permit free trade. But what is the trade? – open markets for drugs for POLDS' consumption in exchange for free firearms from the Obama regime Justice Department and the gunrunner-in-chief, Eric Holder.

In whatever light the domestic war with America is considered upon commercial drug principles, it is evidently the interest of the people of the United States of America and the Republic of Mexico not to support it; and why it has been supported so long against the clearest demonstrations of truth and national advantage, is, to me, and must be to all the reasonable world, a matter of astonishment; or is it a matter of crime with some aspects of payback for those at the top?

Perhaps it may be said that because I am American I write this from interest. To this I reply that my principle interest is American Patriotism and American Freedom from socialism-communism. My attachment is to a never existing socialism-communism and ever to an American Patriotism and Freedom. What I advance is right, no matter where it transpires or whom it touches. WE the People have received the proclamations of your DemocRATS in the enemedia. Yet, I have no doubt that my pen will not be given mass media attention. To oblige and be obliged is fair. But fairness means nothing to you, Barack Hussein Obama.

I shall mention one more circumstance in which I think the people of the United States of America have been equally mistaken. There is such an idea existing in the world as that of national honor, and this, falsely understood, is oftentimes the cause of war. In a Christian and philosophical sense, mankind seem to have stood still at individual civilization and to have retained as nations all the original rudeness of nature. Peace by treaty is only a cessation of violence for a reformation of sentiment. It is a substitute for a principle that is wanting and ever will be wanting till the idea of national honor be rightly understood. As individuals we profess ourselves Christians. As a nation America is a Christian nation. Regardless of your shooting the bull from your teleprompters, your statements regarding your lie that America is not a Christian nation are immoral! Your statements are indecent! Your language is improper! You are exposing your character and you do not cut a good figure! With your character non-qualities, you will never cut a good figure! In private, WE the People feel sorry for your odor, for utterance by someone of your rank cannot change your smell. It is below the stench of a skunk that has aimed at one of *dem RATS*. Your statements are a dishonor to the United States of America. Dishonor exudes out of the depths of a corrupt individual who thrives at living in a political cesspool! It is, I think, exceedingly easy to define what ought to be understood by national honor; for that which is the best character for an individual is the best character for a nation; and wherever the latter exceeds or falls beneath the former, there is a departure from the line of true greatness.

I have thrown out this observation with a design of applying it to the Obama regime. Their ideas of national honor seem devoid of that benevolence of heart, that universal expansion of philanthropy, and that triumph over the rage of vulgar prejudice, without which man is inferior to himself and a companion of common animals. To know who they shall regard or dislike, they ask what country they are of, if they are Muslim, or of the Muslim Brotherhood, and what amount of wealth they enjoy. Their idea of national honor seems to consist in national insult, and that to be a great people, is to be neither a Christian, nor a philosopher, nor a gentleman, but to threaten with the rudeness of a bear and to devour with the ferocity of a lion. This perhaps may sound harsh and uncouth, but it is too true, and the more is the pity.

I mention this only as the Obama regime's general character. But towards America the Obama regime has observed no character at all; and destroyed America by its conduct of what it assumed in its fake sense of perfection. The hope-and-change-in-chief set out with the title The One. The associations of ideas which naturally accompany this expression are filled with everything that is fond, tender, and forbearing. They have an energy peculiar to themselves, and overlooking the accidental attachment of common affections, apply with infinite softness to the first feelings of the heart. It is a political term which everyone can feel the force of, and every child can judge of. It needs no painting of mine to set it off, not even nature can do it justice. But has any part of your conduct to America corresponded with the title Hope And Change Set Up By The One? If in your general perception of national character you are unpolished and severe, in this you are inconsistent and unnatural, and you must have exceeding false notions of national honor to suppose that the world can admire a want of humanity, or that national honor depends on the violence of resentment, the inflexibility of temper, or the vengeance of execution.

I would willingly convince you, and that with as much temper as the times will suffer me to do, that as you opposed your own interest by quarrelling with WE the People, so likewise your conception of honor, rightly conceived and understood, as narcissism, is no ways called upon to enter into a domestic war with WE the People. Had you studied true greatness of heart, the first and fairest ornament of mankind, you would have acted directly contrary to all that you have done, and the world would have ascribed it to a generous cause, besides which you had (with the assistance of the enemedia) secured a powerful name – The One – by your hope-and-change speeches. Little did brain-dead Americans understand that your real meaning was dopes in chains! You were not

103

known and not dreaded; and it would have been wise in you to have suffered WE the People to have slept undisturbed under that idea. It was to you a force existing without expense. It produced to you all the advantages of real power; and you were stronger through the universality of that charm than any future fleets and armies could ever probably make you. Your greatness was so secured and interwoven with your The One narcissism that you ought never to have awakened WE the People, and had nothing to do but to look in a mirror. Had you and your regime thugs been true politicians you would have seen all this and continued to draw from the magic of a name, and brainwashed the force and authority of a nation.

Unwise as you were in breaking the charm, you were still more unwise in the manner of doing it. Samson only told the secret, but you have performed the operation. You have shaven your own head and wantonly thrown away the locks. America was the hair from which the charm was drawn that infatuated the world. You ought to have quarreled with no power; but with America upon no account. You had nothing to fear from any condescension you might make. You might have humored America, even if there had been no justice in your claims, without any risk to your reputation; for America, fascinated by your self-acclaimed fame, would have ascribed it to your benevolence, and America, intoxicated by your majesty's rankness, would have slumbered in her fetters and followed the pied piper into oblivion.

But this method of studying the progress of the passions in order to ascertain the probable conduct of mankind is a philosophy in politics which those who preside at any Obama regime meeting of thugs have no conception of. They, like you, Barack Hussein Obama, know no other influence than corruption and reckon all their probabilities from precedent. A new case is to them a new world, and while they are seeking for a parallel they get lost. The talents of any one of your thugs, particularly Valerie-the-slumlord-thug Jarrett can be estimated at best no higher than those of a sophist. Any one of your thugs may understand the subtleties but not the elegance of nature; and by continually viewing mankind through the cold medium of hate, never thinks of penetrating into the warmer region of the mind. As your adversary, it is happiness to have in them no philosophy and no sentiment, for they sleep the better for it. Punishment becomes your support, for while you will eventually suffer the lash for your sins, you keep yourself up by twirling about with a body servant. In politics you are a good steer stooler and in everything else nothing at all.

There is one circumstance which comes so much within George Soros' province as a financier that I am surprised it should escape him, which is, the different abilities of the DemocRATS in taking advantage of the George Soros monies but in not supporting the party's expenses. Strange as it may seem, DemocRATS are not a match for George Soros in this particular. By a curious kind of revolution in accounts, the people of rural America, where the DemocRAT Party platforms are planks on manure piles, are told to mistake America's poverty for America's riches; that is, they reckon the national debt as a part of the national wealth. What poor nation could amass such a national debt? Only rich America can do this and The One will pay for it. They make the same kind of error which a man would do, who after mortgaging his estate, should add the money borrowed to the full value of the estate in order to count up his worth, and in this case he would conceive that he got rich by running into debt. Just thus it is with your economics. According to the *Treasury's Debt to the Penny Calculator*, the national debt when Barack Hussein Obama putatively occupied the Oval Office on January 20, 2009 was 6.307 trillion dollars. The gross federal debt was about $10.627 trillion dollars. To the nation collectively it was so much poverty. There are as effectual limits to public debts as to private ones, for when once the money borrowed is so great as to require the whole yearly revenue to discharge the interest thereon, there is an end to further borrowing. In the same manner as when the interest of a man's debts amounts to the yearly income of his estate, there is an end to his credit. This is nearly the case with the Obama regime's economics. The projected interest on the debt for the year 2014 is $146,552,822,954.87. The projected revenue for 2014 is 5.7 trillion dollars. To the brain dead that means that the United States of America has approximately 5.5 trillion surplus. The brain-dead-in-chief thinks this also. Yes. ... in-debt America is wealthy! Moreover, Chief Brain Dead says that America can pay her debts easily. Just print more money!

The very reverse of this was the case with America in 1776. At that time Americans began the War for Independence without any debt upon America, and in order to carry it on, America neither raised money by

105

taxes, nor borrowed it upon interest, but created it out of patriotism and the work ethic; and America's situation at that time was so much the reverse of yours. When we shall have sunk the sum which has been created under your non-leadership, we shall then be out of debt, be just as rich as when we began, and all the while we are doing it shall feel no difference, because the value will rise as the quantity of the currency decreases.

There is not a country in the world so capable of not wanting to bear the expense of a socialist-communist state as America; not only because she was not in debt when she began, but because the country is still young and capable of infinite improvement, and has an almost boundless tract of new ideas in store; whereas socialism-communism has got a stench of age and growth, and has never occupied land or property successfully. The one is like a young heir coming to a large improvable estate; the other like an old man whose chances are over, and his estate mortgaged for half its worth.

In the second Call To Take Action of *The American Crisis* I endeavored to set forth the impracticability of conquering America. I stated every case that I conceived could possibly happen, and ventured to predict its consequences. As my conclusions were drawn not artfully, but naturally, they have all proved to be true. I am upon the spot; know the politics of America, her strength and resources, and by a train of services, the best in my power to render, was honored with the friendship of the remaining American Patriots who are my colleagues, those like-minded, those in the United States Armed Services, and the people for whom I stand. I consider the cause a just one. I know and feel it a just one, and under that confidence never make my own profit or loss the ultimate object. My endeavor is to have the matter well understood on both sides, and I conceive myself tendering a general service by setting forth to the one the impossibility of being conquered, and to the other the impossibility of conquering.

Most of the arguments made use of by your propaganda supporting the cause of socialism-communism are the very arguments that ought to have been used against supporting it; and the plans, by which you thought to conquer, are the very plans in which you are sure to be defeated. You have taken everything up at the wrong end. Your ignorance is astonishing, and were you in my situation you would see it. Some Americans may, perhaps, have your confidence, but I am persuaded that they would make very indifferent members of socialism-communism. I know what you are and what America is, and from the compound of knowledge, am better enabled to judge of the issue than what the King Obama or any one of his regime thugs are able to judge.

In this number I have endeavored to show the ill policy and disadvantages of the domestic war against WE the People. I believe many of my remarks are new. Those which are not so, I have studied to improve and herewith place in a manner that may be clear and striking. Your failure is, I am persuaded, as certain as fate. America is above your reach. She is more than your equal in the world and her independence neither rests upon your consent, nor can it be prevented by your evil. In short, all of you spend your substance in vain and impoverish yourselves without a hope. That is good change!

But suppose you and your regime thugs have conquered America. What advantages, collectively or individually, as merchants, manufacturers, scientists, or conquerors, could you have looked for? This is an object you seem never to have attended to. Listening for the sound of victory, and led away by the frenzy of evil, you neglect to reckon either the cost or the consequences. You must all pay; you must all bear a share, and it is both your right and your duty to weigh seriously the matter. If America is conquered by socialism-communism she will have to be parceled out in grants to the favorites at the Obama regime court for the simple reason that your tax revenues will be lessened because America will be in no condition to pay. WE the People are rich by contrivance of OUR own, which will cease as soon as you became total masters. OUR paper money is now of almost no use, and silver and gold we have none. In the last socialist-communist takeover in this world no freedom was achieved. As the taxes of socialism-communism pay for the charge of making them, has not the same been the case in every attempt at socialism-communism?

To the Congress I wish to address myself in a more particular manner. They appear to have supposed themselves partners on the golf course so that they could receive an expectation of a right to the booty; but in this it is most probable they would, as legislators, have been disappointed. The case of the pathetic Obama regime is quite a new one, and many unforeseen difficulties have arisen thereon. The Congress claimed a legislative right over America and the toleration of the Obama regime's pressure originated from that pretence. But if America is ever conquered through the means of a docile Congress, the claims of the legislature will be suffocated in the conquest. WE the People are out of the authority of Congress. But neither Barack Hussein Obama nor Congress is out of OUR authority. Congress has all this while been supporting measures not meant to assure the establishment of their authority in the issues of which they have been triumphed over by the Obama regime.

Had Congress remained the separate branch of government it is supposed to be, a new and interesting situation between the Congress and the Obama regime would have developed. You would have said that you conquered for yourself, and that to conquer for Congress was an unknown case. The Congress might have replied that WE the People are a country in rebellion. WE the People would say that you cannot conquer US! You cannot reduce US! WE the People are foreign to a socialist-communist state because we have a *Declaration of Independence* and a *Constitution for the United States of America* that say WE the People are the source of political power! You and Congress cannot insist that America is the sole property of The One! Congress is supposed to be the legal delegates of the people. This brings us to a set of very interesting and rational questions.

1st, What is the original fountain of power and honor in this country?

2nd, Whether the prerogative does not belong to the people?

3rd, Whether there is any such thing as the *Constitution*?

4th, Of what use is the Obama regime to the people?

5th, Whether he who invented the Obama regime is not an enemy to mankind?

6th, Whether it is not a shame for a woman to spend millions a year as would a quean and do no good for it, and whether the money might not be better applied?

7th, Whether such a person should exist at all?

8th, Whether a republic, constituted like that of America, is not the most happy and consistent form of government in the world?

9th, Whether the present usurped, docile Congress can completely be retaken in 2014 and 2016?

10th, Should not the Obama regime be indicted for, convicted of, and executed for treason?

In short, the contention about the dividend might have distracted the nation; for nothing is more common than to agree in the conquest and quarrel for the prize; therefore it is, perhaps, a happy circumstance that the successes of WE the People have prevented the dispute.

To the great bulwark of the nation, the legal citizens, I likewise present my address. It is their interest to see America as an independent and not a conquered socialist-conquered country. If conquered, she is ruined; and if ruined, poor. Consequently, the profits will be a trifle and her credit will remain non-existent at best. If independent, she flourishes, and from her flourishing profits arise. It matters to you who governs America. It matters nothing only to socialist-communist parasites that never do anything for America! A free market economy is at stake! Some articles will consequently be obtained from other places, and it is right that they should; but the demand for others will increase by the greater influx of legal inhabitants which a state of independence and peace will occasion, and in the event all immigration is regulated to zero, legal citizens may be enriched.

The commerce of America is perfectly free, and ever will be so. She will consign away no part of it to any nation, or to any international organization like the United Nations; neither to socialism-communism. She has not to her friends, and certainly will not to her enemies; though it is probable that your narrow-minded politicians, particularly DemocRATS and RINOs, thinking to please you thereby, may at some time or other, unnecessarily make such a proposal. Trade and democratic republicanism flourishes best when it is free, and it is weak policy to attempt to fetter it. America's treaties are made on the most liberal and

109

generous principles. American Patriots have proved themselves to be philosophers, politicians, and heroes.

The Obama regime has studied the ruin of this country during the past years from which it is not within the abilities of POLDS to rescue her. Attempts by the DemocRATS, Congress, or even Killary Klinton to recover America are as ridiculous as the Obama plans which involved America's demise.

Reading *The American Crisis* will give you POLDS more common sense than you ever before had. It is a long lane that has no turning. Any political period of misconduct and misfortune is certainly long enough for any one nation to suffer under; and upon a supposition that domestic war has no official declaration; I beg to place a line of conduct before you that will easily lead you out of all your troubles. It has been hinted before and cannot be too much attended to.

Regime thugs! Suppose America had remained unknown to Barack Hussein Obama. What, I ask, in that case, would have been your conduct towards America? For that will point out what it ought to be now. The problems and their solutions are equal, and the right line of the one is the parallel of the other. The question takes in every circumstance that can possibly arise. It reduces politics to a simple thought and is moreover a mode of investigation in which, while you are studying your interest, the simplicity of the case will cheat you into good temper. You have nothing to do but to suppose that you have found America and she appears found to your hand, and while in the joy of your heart you stand still to admire her, the path of politics rises straight before you.

Were I disposed to paint a contrast, I could easily set off what you have done in the present case, against what you would have done in that case, and by justly opposing them, conclude a picture that would make even thugs blush. But, as when any of the prouder passions are hurt, it is much better philosophy to let a man slip into a good temper than to attack him in a bad one, for that reason, therefore, I only state the case, and leave you to reflect upon it.

To go a little back into politics, it will be found that the true interest of WE the People lay in proposing and promoting the continuous independence of America immediately and continuously; for the expense which America had then incurred by having Barack Hussein Obama a major product in the previous term ought to have shown Americans the policy and necessity of changing the leadership of the country as the best probable method of preventing future non-covered expenses, and the only method by which she could hold the economy without the charge of sovereignty. Besides which, the title WE the People that America possessed from the beginning of her history, as a parent country to all legal citizens, led to, and pointed out the propriety, wisdom, and advantage of a republic. Just as in private life, children grow into men and women, and by setting up for themselves, extend and secure the interest of the whole family, so in the settlement of States large enough to admit of maturity, the same policy must be pursued, and the same consequences would then follow. Nothing hurts the affections both of parents and children so much as living too closely connected as well as keeping up the distinction too long. Domineering will not do over those, who, by a progress in life, have become equal in rank to their parents, that is when they have families of their own; and though they may conceive themselves the subjects of their advice, will not suppose them the objects of their government. By drawing this parallel I admit the simplicity of the relationship of the federal government with the state governments. It is time for the state governments to exercise their constitutional independence and tell the federal government under the Obama regime that they no longer desire to live in a government family based on the concepts of dictatorship and socialism-communism.

Barack Hussein Obama! When you saw the state of strength and opulence, and that by her own industry, which America in its history has arrived at, you ought to have advised her to continue to exercise democratic republicanism. You ought to have proposed an alliance of continued support with her for democratic republicanism, not for socialist-communist dope and chains. In so doing you and all Americans would have drawn more real economic advantage and freedom than from any weak and wrangling socialist-communist government that you could exercise over America. In short, had you studied only the domestic politics of a family, you would have learned how to govern. Instead of this easy and natural line, you flew out into everything that was wild and outrageous, till, by following the passion and stupidity of the ship's captain, you wrecked the vessel within sight of the shore. Family and children have no meaning to you unless they are controlled by the government.

Having shown what you ought to have done, I now proceed to show why it was not done. The caterpillar circle of the Obama regime court had an interest to pursue socialism-communism, distinct from, and opposed to WE the People; indeed, opposed to the interest of the nation. The loss of DemocRAT-held state governorships, DemocRAT-held Senate seats, and DemocRAT-held House of Representative seats, all with their appendages, is a shocking sound in the ear of a hungry dictator. Your present dictatorship-kingship and regime thugs will be the ruin of you; and you had better risk a revolution and call yourself defeated, than be thus led on from madness to despair and from despair to ruin. WE the People have set you the example and you may follow it and be free, or you may fight us in the coming revolt, be taken prisoner, tried, found guilty, and executed.

I now come to the last part: a domestic war with WE the People. This is what no man in his senses will advise you and all good men would wish to prevent. Whether WE the People will declare war against you is not for me in this place to mention, or to hint, even if I knew it; but it must be madness in you to do it first. The matter is come now to a full crisis; yet, peace is easy if willingly set about. Whatever you may think, Barack Hussein Obama, WE the People have behaved handsomely to you. WE the People would have been unjust to OURSELVES to have acted otherwise than we did. WE the People give you genteel notice that there is nothing in OUR conduct reserved or indelicate, and while WE the People announce OUR determination to support the *Declaration of Independence* and the *Constitution for the United States of America*, we leave you, Barack Hussein Obama, to give the first offence. American Patriots, on their part have exhibited a character of firmness to the world.

In 1776, unprepared and unarmed, without form or government, WE American Patriots singly opposed a kingdom that domineered over half the globe. The greatness of the deed demands respect – but you are unable to spell that wonderful word … probably because it is foreign to your behavior – and though you may feel resentment, you are compelled both to wonder and admire.

Here I rest my arguments and finish my address. Such as it is, it is a gift, and you are welcome for your unsaid and unthought-of Thank You! It was always my design to dedicate a crisis to you, Barack Hussein Obama, when the time should come that would properly make it a Crisis; and when, likewise, I should catch myself in a temper to write it, and suppose you in a condition to read it. That time has now arrived and with it the opportunity for conveyance. I wish you all the failure possible, even the failures with your private life and your body servants. May *The American Crisis* not wither about your ears, but that you write:

WE THE PEOPLE WILL NOT LET THIS CRISIS GO TO WASTE!

between your ears. Your intellectualism as shown by your non-leadership proves that surely there is more than enough space in your scelerous cavern.

★★★★★★★★★★★★★

Frederick William Dame
Patriotic, Steadfast, and True
March 9, 2014

Frederick William Dame

The American Crisis

The Golf-Course Politics Of Nothingness

A Call To Take Action

Number Ten

★★★★★★★★★★★★★

As recently as January 2014, Barack Hussein Obama says trust in him to his followers and subjects, the legal citizens and the illegal aliens in the United States of America, and then plays a round of golf.

As a God-fearing Christian, I trust in God, in the Divine Providence and in the justice of the American Patriots' cause. I am firmly resolved to prosecute the fight against Barack Hussein Obama with vigor and to make every exertion in order to compel the enemy Obama regime to the terms of defeat and failure. To this declaration the United States of America are witness. If the Barack Hussein Obama regime wants a fight, they will have it and shall have more than enough of it.

Barack Hussein Obama! The evil years have nearly elapsed since your commencement of hostilities against WE the People, and every campaign, by a gradual decay, has lessened your ability to conquer WE the People, without you producing a serious thought on the condition you are in or your fate. Like a prodigal lingering in a habitual consumption, you, Barack Hussein Obama, feel the relics of life and mistake them for recovery. New schemes, like new medicines, have administered fresh hopes and prolonged the disease instead of curing it. Even a change of military generals, like a change of physicians, serves only to keep the POLDS' flattery of you, their charlatan, alive, and furnish new pretences for new extravagances.

"Can Obama fail?" political pundits have taken pride in themselves when they have asked at the undertaking of every one of your enterprises; and that "whatever Obama wills is fate," has been given with the solemnity of prophetic confidence; and though the question has been constantly

114

replied to by disappointment, and the predictions falsified by the enemedia, yet still your insults continue, and Barack Hussein Obama's catalogue of national evils increases therewith. Eager to persuade the world of your power, you have considered the destruction of a once-proud world power as the ultimate sign of greatness, and conceived that the glory of the Obama regime lies in the number of foreign policy failures, the domestically unemployed, and the miseries which Barack Hussein Obama and his regime thugs inflict on the United States of America.

The results of the destruction of American-friendly allied governments such as that in Egypt under Hosni Mubarak in 2011, the hatred you have towards the government of Israel, and the eradication of a minion government under Muammar al-Gaddafi in Libya in 2011, have spread with wanton cruelty in the Middle East, along the coast of North Africa and into Africa proper. All the while you, with an uncontrolled desire to expend money that is neither yours nor that of your quean, remote from the scene of suffering, have nothing to lose and as little to dread. Information – if you ever attend your daily morning briefings – reaches you like a tale of antiquity in which the distance of time defaces the conception and changes the severest sorrows into conversable amusement – an attitude that allows you to play golf, have taxpayer-financed holidays, and soul concerts without a tear of guilt for those souls who are suffering under your dictatorship.

This present paper is addressed perhaps in vain, to you, the self-appointed King of Obamaland and your regime That advice should be taken wherever example has failed, or precept be regarded where warning is ridiculed, is like a picture of hope resting on despair: but when time shall stamp with universal currency the facts the Obama regime have long encountered with a laugh, and the irresistible evidence of accumulated losses, like the handwriting on the wall, shall add terror to distress, you will then, in a conflict of suffering, possibly learn to sympathize with others by feeling for yourselves. You, Barack Hussein Obama, deserve no pity!

The triumphant appearance of the combined Pelosis and Reids at your side when you babble at the mouth, and the expeditions of John Kerry, as of late to Ukraine located on the Black Sea, will, by placing in your mind the condition of an endangered country, read to you a stronger lecture on the calamities of your foreign policy of nothingness and bring to your mind a truer picture of promiscuous distress than the most finished rhetoric can describe or the keenest imagination conceive.

Hitherto you have experienced the expenses but nothing of the miseries encountered by WE the People. Your disappointments have been accompanied with no immediate suffering, and your losses come to you only by intelligence. Like fire at a distance you hear not even the cry; you feel not the danger, you see not the confusion. To you everything has been foreign – even the taxes to support your regime's policies. You know not what it is to be alarmed at midnight with an armed enemy in the streets. You are a stranger to the distressing scene of a family in flight, and to the thousand restless cares and tender sorrows that incessantly arise, more so when they are in a refugee camp. To see women and children wandering in the severity of winter in Syria, with the broken remains of a well furnished house, and seeking shelter in every cranny and makeshift tent, are matters that you have no conception of. You know not what it is to stand by and see your household furniture chopped for fuel and your beds and goods ripped to pieces to make packages of plunder.

The misery of others, like a tempestuous night, is added to the pleasures of your own security, your golf games, and the self-contenting ceremonies that you engage in with your body servants. You even enjoy the storm by contemplating the difference of conditions of using drones that carry sorrow into the breasts of thousands. They serve but to heighten in you a species of tranquil pride. Yes, you … kill innocent people and American military personnel with your ridiculous rules of engagement. Yet these are but the fainter sufferings of your inept foreign policy, when compared with carnage and slaughter of the Muslim Brotherhood that you unequivocally support, or a Syrian or African town in flames at the torch of Muslims … potential terrorists all, and the miseries of a beheaded Christian family of Muslim honor killing, all in the name of your peaceful Allah. You say Islam is peaceful! Respect it! For heaven's sake you cannot even spell *respect* correctly, to say nothing of your foolishness in understanding it.

116

The people of America, by anticipating distress, have fortified their minds against every species you are able to inflict. They have resolved to protect their homes, not to resign them to destruction, not to seek new settlements, and not to submit to your regime. Thus familiarized to misfortune before it arrives, WE the People will bear OUR portion with the less regret. The justness of OUR cause is a continual source of consolation, and the hope of final victory, which will never leave WE the People, serves to lighten the load and sweeten the cup of patriotism from which WE the People drink.

But more troubles shall become you and your foreign policy failures will be transferred upon you and not on John Kerry, for he is too much of a diplomatic imbecile. You will have neither expensive VIP golf courses to fly to, your body servants to comfort you, nor any hope to rest upon. Distress of you and your regime will not be sharpened by self-reflection. You and your regime will have brought it on yourselves. Although you have endeavored to avoid it, you will have descended even below the mark of a moral human. The national honor or the advantages of independence are matters which, at the commencement of the Obama regime's aggressiveness against WE the People, were never studied. It has only been at the last moment that you ever thought of national honor and concluded that it does not apply to socialism-communism, to say nothing of Islam's world dominating *Umma*. Thus circumstanced, you naturally and conscientiously feel a dependence upon providence, but it is the anti-providence of Satan. You have a clear pretension to it, and call for it because you fail. Your infidelity to morals and ethics has triumphed over you.

Your condition is the reverse of WE the People. Everything you suffer you have sought: nay, you have created mischiefs on purpose to inherit your inflicted sufferings. You could not have secured your title Mr. Zero by a firmer deed. The world awakens with no pity for your complaints. You felt none for others; you deserve none for yourselves. Nature does not interest herself in cases like yours, but, on the contrary, turns from them with dislike, and abandons them to punishment. You may now present memorials to whomever you please, but as far as America is the object, true American Patriots will not listen. The policy of the Obama regime and the propensity there in every mind to curb America's ambition, and bring cruelty to judgment, are unitedly your policy; and

117

where nature and interest reinforce with each other, the compact is too intimate to be dissolved.

Make but the case of others your own, and your own theirs, and you will then have a clear idea of the whole. Had any president – even James Earl Carter – acted towards Americans as you have done, he would have had to have branded them with every epithet of abhorrence; and had you stepped in to succor a struggling people, all the world would have echoed with your own applauses. But entangled in the passion of dispute you see America not as you ought, and form opinions thereon which suit with no interest but your own. You wonder that America does not rise in union with you to impose on herself socialism-communism and reduce herself to unconditional submission. You are amazed that the powers of the individual State governments do not assist you in conquering a country which is afterwards to be turned against itself; and that no one is interested in contributing to keep you in an America that already enjoys the free market for myriad products of the world.

You seem surprised that George Soros does not pour in his billions as succors to maintain you as a mistress of your body servants. Barack Hussein Obama! Stop twirling at midnight! America's economy is suffering! American foreign policy is suffering to the precipice of it being non-existent. No country will see America being successful while she is under your fetters.

Such excesses of passionate folly, and unjust as well as unwise resentment, have driven you on like the Pharaoh of ancient Egypt, to unpitied miseries, and while the importance of the quarrel shall perpetuate your disgrace, the flag of American freedom will carry it round the world. The natural feelings of every rational being will be against you, and wherever the story shall be told, you will have neither excuse nor consolation left. With an unsparing hand and an insatiable mind, you have desolated freedom-loving America to gain dominion and to lose it; and all the while, in a frenzy of avarice and ambition, the east and the west are doomed to bondage. You have rapidly earned destruction as the wages of a nation.

At the thoughts of a domestic war at home, every man and woman amongst your regime ought to tremble. The prospect is most dreadful in

118

America; more so than Russia under Vladimir Putin. You know who he is, don't you? He's your adversary who makes you look like a wimping pussy.

The DemocRAT Party has always been against the measures of the republican form of government and are, in general, composed of haters who add no strength whatsoever to the United States of America. There does not exist a being so devoid of sense and sentiment as to covet anything said by them or by you and therefore no patriotic man or woman in America can be with you and them in principle. Several might from a cowardice of mind, prefer you and them to the hardships and dangers of opposing you and them; but the same disposition that gives them such a choice, unfits them to act either for or against American Patriots with equal shares of resolution.

The principle which produced you – hope and change – now divides the nation. American patriotic animosities are in the highest state of fermentation. Both sides, by calls of the enemedia, are in arms. No human foresight can discern and no conclusion can be formed concerning what turns your golf-course-politics might take. Vladimir Putin you say is not now in a fit disposition to make sense out of your actions. Therefore, you fly to Florida for a weekend of golf taking with you your scrub thug Valerie Jarrett, whom Putin in one action would throw into a Chicago gutter where she belongs. You have no success to hope for abroad and nothing but expenses arising at home. Your everything is staked upon a midnight twirl, and the longer it gyrates the worse off you are.

There are situations that a nation may be in, which when abstracted from every other consideration, may be politically right or wrong. But with the wrongs of your policies you are not doing what is right for America and what is right for America you are not doing at all. Such was the situation of America at the commencement of your hostilities in 2008/2009 and again in 2012/2013. It is still the same.

That America is beyond the reach of foreign conquest is a fact which experience has shown and time confirmed, and this admitted, what, I ask, is now the object of contention? If there be any honor in pursuing self-destruction with inflexible passion – if your imposed national suicide be

119

the perfection of national glory, you may, with all the pride of criminal happiness, expire from America's borders unenvied and unrivalled. When the tumult of domestic war shall cease, and the tempest of present passions be succeeded by calm reflection, or when those, who, surviving the Obama regime's fury, shall inherit a legacy of debts and misfortunes, when the yearly revenue will scarcely be able to discharge the interest accumulated in one year, and no possible remedy be left for the others, ideas far different from the present will arise, and embitter the remembrance of former follies.

A mind disarmed of its rage feels no pleasure in contemplating a frantic quarrel. Sickness of thought, the sure consequence of conduct like yours, leaves no ability for enjoyment, no relish for resentment; and though, like a man in a fit, you feel not the injury of the struggle, nor distinguish between strength and disease, the weakness will nevertheless be proportioned to the violence you create, and the sense of pain will decrease with the recovery of America when you are gone.

To what persons or to whose system of politics you owe your present state of wretchedness is a really a matter of total indifference to the majority of Americans. They have contributed, however unwillingly, to set you above themselves because the enemedia have told them to do so, and you, in the tranquility of conquest, resign the inquiry. The case now is not so properly who began the fight for the implementation of socialism-communism, as who continues to combat it. That there are men and women in all countries to whom economic confusion and distress is a mine of wealth, is a fact never to be doubted. Characters like these naturally breed in the putrefaction of distempered times, and after fattening on the disease; they perish with it, or, impregnated with the stench, retreat into obscurity. This is your fate!

But there are several erroneous notions to which you likewise owe a share of your misfortunes, and which, if continued, will only increase your trouble and your losses. One opinion is that the patriotic men and women of America would relish conservative, moral measures under a different administration, which they would not from the present regime. Several possible survivors of your regime are steering the same course. Such distinctions in the infancy of the argument have some degree of foundation, but they now serve no other purpose than to avoid prison terms as co-conspirators in treason. The limits of this dispute will not be changed or altered by trivial circumstances.

The obots of the Obama regime sacrifice their time in disputing on a question with which they have nothing to do, namely, whether America shall continue to be independent or become a socialist-communist system under dictatorship. WE the People will decide that question and the answer will be continued freedom and nothing else. The only question that can come under the Obama regime determination is: When will they disappear? – The sooner the better! They confound a logical question with a political one, and undertake to supply by a vote what they will lose by a battle. Say America shall not be independent of socialism-communism, and it will signify as much as if they voted against a decree of fate, or say that she shall continue independence from socialism-communism, and she will be more independent than before. Such a dumb question of being socialist- communist serves only to show the folly of the Obama regime and the weakness of its disputants.

From a long habit of calling America your own, you suppose her governed by the same prejudices and conceits which govern yourselves. You have set up a particular denomination of pseudo-religion ideology, namely Obamaism, a cultic religion to the exclusion of all others. You, with an unsociable narrowness of mind, have cherished enmity against American Patriots.

You suppose America's alliance must be friendship with the Muslim Brotherhood and Islamic terrorists. But copying notions of the world from the Founding Fathers, America feels herself free, and the prejudices removed, she thinks and acts upon a different system. It frequently happens that in proportion as we are taught to dislike persons and countries, not knowing why, we feel an ardor of esteem upon the removal of the mistake: it seems as if something was to be made amends for, and we eagerly give in to every office of friendship, to atone for the injury of the error; but never under Islam and its terror.

Perhaps, there is something in the extent of countries, which, among the generality of people, insensibly communicates extension of the mind. The soul of a usurper, in its native state, seems bounded by the foggy confines of treason's edge, and all beyond affords to him matters only for

121

profit or curiosity, not for forgiveness. His usurpation is to him his world, and fixed to that, his everything centers in it; while those who are the legal inhabitants of America, by casting their eye over a larger field, take in likewise a larger intellectual circuit, and thus approaching nearer to an acquaintance with the universe, their atmosphere of thought is extended, and their intelligence fills a wider space.

In short, our American minds seem to be measured by countries when we are men, as they are by places when we are children, and until something happens to disentangle us from the prejudice, we serve under it without perceiving it. In addition to this, it may be remarked, that men who are not dumbed down by progressives, the principles of which are universally known, or admitted, and applied without distinction to the common demise, obtain thereby a larger share of philanthropy than those who remain dumb, social parasites, and unimproved. Anti-socialism-communism, anti-Muslim Brotherhood, and anti-progressivism carry the mind from the country to the creation and give it a fitness suited to the extent. It is honorable that a country's leader is also its natural born citizen and philosopher. Such persons the heavens will liberate from the prejudices of a usurper.

WE the People taking a standpoint of being anti-everything that you propose and maintaining American Patriotism against all enemies will expand OUR souls. Others will remain rogues and ask for trust, play golf, and be enthralled with their nothingness.

Frederick William Dame
Patriotic, Steadfast, and True
March 13, 2014

Frederick William Dame

The American Crisis

The Head Of Tyranny In America Must Expire

A Call To Take Action

Number Eleven

Beginning with the presidential election in 2008 and continuing throughout the years since, the United States of America has seen the wild establishment and unchecked advancement of tyranny in the person of Barack Hussein Obama and his regime. It is time for the tyrannical head to expire.

Had America pursued her advantages with half the spirit that she resisted her misfortunes, she would have now become a Barack-Hussein-Obama-free and peaceful, prosperous people. However, America was lulled on the lap of soft tranquility to the mantra of treasonous-infested, political propaganda supplied by the enemedia. America went to sleep on hope and change. Only within the past year has adversity convulsed her into action. Whether subtlety or sincerity at the close of the last year induced the enemy Obama regime to an appearance for pseudo-compassion for America is a point not material to know. It is sufficient that WE the People see the terrible effects it has had on America's politics, and that WE the People sternly rise to resent the delusion that the effects have been positive.

The domestic war on the part of the Obama regime has been a war of their natural hate feelings. Supposed leadership in distress; serenity in placating the masses, particularly the brain dead who are already placated with the pabulum of DemocRAT Party ranting; drowsiness while at rest with body servants; in every situation generously disposed to play golf; and a dangerous calm and a most heightened zeal against the American People have, as circumstances varied, succeeded and complemented each other. Every passion but that of despair has been called to a tour of duty; and so mistaken has been the enemy Obama regime of American Patriots'

123

abilities and disposition, that when Barack Hussein Obama supposed WE the People to have been conquered, WE the People have risen as the true conquerors for freedom.

The extensiveness of the United States of America and the variety of its resources; the universality of its cause as expounded by the *Declaration of Independence* and the *Constitution for the United States of America*; the quick operation of patriotic feelings, and the similarity of the patriotic sentiments, have, in every trying situation, produced a something, which, favored by providence and pursued with ardor, has accomplished in an instant the business of a nation-wide rise for patriotism and the defense of the American republic against the threats of Obama's socialism-communism. WE the People have snatched the opportunity for victory and have bravely begun in this historical hour to blot out the operations of an Obama dictatorship.

The present fate of America, like the misfortunes of 1776, has at last called forth a spirit and kindled up a flame which perhaps no other event could have produced. The Obama enemy has circulated falsehoods. They have unwisely aggravated WE the People into life. They have never told the truth. They have never intentionally done WE the People a service. With his dilettante diplomacy and rules of military engagement, Barack Hussein Obama has forced America to return with folded arms from the possible victories of war in Iraq and Afghanistan and brainwashed the nation to make it think that Islam is peaceful and that all America has to do is to sit leisurely down to enjoy repose.

The Obama regime attacks that have been put upon America have thrown drowsiness over the whole country. With the usurpation of political power by Barack Hussein Obama, the majority of Americans looked on the business as being done, the conflicts over, the matters settled, or that all which remained unfinished would follow of itself. In this state of dangerous relaxation, exposed to the poisonous infusions of the enemy Obama regime, and having no awareness of the common danger to attract the attention of Americans, the ardor that was established in 1776 has been extinguished by stages and Americans have surrendered by piece-meal the virtues that have always defended the United States of America. Afflicting as the attacks of the Obama regime on America may be, yet if they universally rouse Americans from the slumber of the past Obama years, and if they renew in Americans the spirit of former days, they will produce an advantage more important than a loss. America ever is what she thinks herself to be. Governed by sentiment, and acting her own mind, she becomes, as she pleases, the victor or the victim. Under the tyranny of Barack Hussein Obama, America has become the victim. It is time that she becomes the victor over the tyrannous head.

It is neither the Obama regime propaganda nor the accidental success of a round of golf that can support a country as extensive as this. The sufferings of one part can never be relieved by the exertions of another, and there is no situation the enemy Obama regime can be placed in that does not afford to WE the People the same advantages which Obama seeks himself. By claiming success, he leaves every policy attackable. It is a mode of confrontation that carries with it a confession of weakness and goes on the principle of distress rather than conquest. The decline of the enemy Obama regime is visible not only in their operations but in their original plans for the total control of American lives from the cradle to the grave. Hope and change was but a slimy con-phrase object in the system of attack. Total control is their principal goal via ObamaCare, because they have not been able to succeed elsewhere. It would have carried a cowardly appearance in the world had they publicly proclaimed their grand expedition of conducting a domestic war to institute socialism-communism against the country in which there was no social crisis. Therefore, the Obama regime created one by saying that it existed. Yet, year after year they have been failing in their impressions to the eastward and northward, to the westward and the southward. They have not deserted their capital design of socialist-communist dope and chains. At the same time, they are prudently contenting themselves with what they can get. Their modus operandi is to give a flourish of honor to conceal disgrace.

But this piece-meal work is not conquering the mass of American Patriots. It is a discredit in the Obama regime to attempt it, and in WE the People to suffer it. It is now full time to put an end to Obama's domestic war of aggravations, which, on one side, has no possible object, and on the other has every inducement which honor, interest, safety, and happiness can inspire. If WE the People suffer the Obama regime much longer to remain among US, WE the People shall become as bad as they. An association of vice will reduce US more than the sword. A nation hardened in the practice of iniquity knows better how to profit by it than a young country newly corrupted. WE the People are not a match for them in the line of advantageous guilt, nor are they a match for US on the God-given inalienable rights and the constitutional principles and laws of freedom which we bravely set out with. Our first days were our days of honor. They have marked the character of America wherever the story of her historical development is told; and convinced of this, WE the People have nothing to do but wisely and unitedly to tread the well known track.

The progress of a confrontation with the Obama regime is as ruinous to the individuals as the issue of it is to the nation; and it is not only necessary that our patriotic forces be such that WE be conquerors in the end of this domestic war, but that by timely exertions WE Patriots be secure until the final day of the Barack Hussein Obama regime has transpired. The present patriotic campaign will afford an opportunity which has never presented itself before, and the preparations for it are equally necessary whether free America stands or falls. Suppose the first, it is in that case only a failure of the enemy, not a defeat. All the conquest that a besieged society can hope for is not to be conquered; and compelling the enemy Obama regime to raise the siege, is to the besieged a victory. But there must be a probability amounting almost to a certainty that would justify an Obama retreat. Therefore should America not be taken into socialism-communism and should the enemy abandon the undertaking, every part of the American society should prepare to meet the results. Preparations are necessary to balance any losses. American Patriots must put themselves in a position to cooperate with all of WE the People.

WE the People are fighting against the Obama regime alone, as WE the People were fighting against England in 1776. Obama will continue to distress US. Obama will suffer US to be overrun by dictatorial decrees. Obama will steal as much from WE the People as he can, rather than quit the object that gratifies his revenge, truly a malicious disposition to America. This conduct on the part of Barack Hussein Obama has pointed out the propriety of subjected American society to socialism-communism on the spot. According to Barack Hussein Obama and his regime, the arrival of socialism-communism – what can only be called a curse! – cannot be very distant. Yet, WE the People know that the ravages of the pro-socialist-communist-enemy phase will not be long. The complete

126

refusal to accept the Barack Hussein Obama socialist-communist society will restore to America internal peace and prosperity.

At a crisis as big as the present, with expectation and events, the whole country is called to unanimity and exertion. Not an ability ought now to sleep that can produce but a mite to the general good, nor even a whisper to pass that militates against it. The necessity of the case and the importance of the consequences admit no delay from a friend, no apology from a once-upon-a-time Obama supporter. To spare now would be the height of extravagance and to consult present ease would be to sacrifice it perhaps forever. America is rich in patriotism and therefore neither persons nor supplies are wanting when a serious necessity calls them forth. The complete American Armed Services must begin a get-out-to-vote movement for the 2014 and 2016 elections to thwart the tyrant and rein in his tyranny. All active duty members, the National Guard units, the Military Reserve units, the retired servicemen and women are an interest group that can send the Obama regime into political oblivion. That is where this pseudo-commander-in-chief should be sent. In the present he only vacations, golfs, campaigns, ignores, and insults Americans who believe in the Republic that is the United States of America.

From this day until the tyrant head has expired, the following matters/questions must be raised and discussed every day and at every meeting of American Patriots regardless of how small or how large the group.

➢ Why does Barack Hussein Obama not prove that he is a natural born citizen according to Article II, Section 1, Paragraph 5 of the *Constitution* and therefore legitimize his being the occupant of the Oval Office?

➢ By what legal authorization did Barack Hussein Obama conduct war against Libya and it leader Muammar al-Gaddafi in 2011?

➢ What is the degree of involvement of Barack Hussein Obama in the coming to power of the evil Muslim Brotherhood in Egypt in 2012?

➤ Why has the Egyptian government implicated Barack Hussein Obama as a foreign force that is attempting to restore the Muslim Brotherhood to power in Egypt?

➤ To what degree were Barack Hussein Obama and the former Egyptian President Mohammed Morsi involved in the attack on the United States compound in Benghazi, Libya on September 11, 2012? Why did Barack Hussein Obama not undertake any initiative to save four Americans, including the American Ambassador to Libya, from being killed?

➤ Why has Barack Hussein Obama allowed, indeed, actively placed Muslim Brotherhood operatives at high, sensitive levels of the American government?

➤ Why has Barack Hussein Obama not undertaken any action against jihad training camps that have been established by Muslim organizations throughout the United States of America?

➤ Why does Barack Hussein Obama support Muslim jihadists, the enemies of the United States of America, in Syria?

➤ With what logic and diplomatic raison d'être can Barack Hussein Obama admonish Russia for annexing the Crimea and threaten President Vladimir Putin and Russians with major sanctions to teach them a lesson? Yet, at the same time his regime continues to provide Russia with the Multiple Integrated Laser Engagement System (MILES) that is used in training to simulate ground force-on-force combat. This is part of military grade technology that is used by the United States Marine Corps, the United States Army, and United States Special Forces Operations. The policy is schizophrenic! ... Or is it because regimes of a feather flock together?

➤ Why does the Obama regime support forces of an ultra-nationalist opposition government in Ukraine? These forces propagandize many aspects of Nazi philosophy.

➤ Why does Barack Hussein Obama want to sign on as a member to the United Nations International Criminal Court (ICC)? Becoming a member would mean that American troops could be arrested and tried for war crimes without redress to United States law and sovereignty. There would be no appeal process.

➢ What role did Barack Hussein Obama play in the Internal Revenue Service targeting of conservative groups to deny them tax exempt status?

The above aspects constitute acts of treason against the government and WE the People of the United States of America. Barack Hussein Obama is a hypocrite and tyrant!

The demand to tax the rich more and the extensiveness of the national deficit throw a double burden on Americans which has artfully been interpreted by foreign countries such as Russia and international organizations such as the United Nations as a general decline of America's economic power and military might. Yet this, inconvenient as it may at first appear, is not only remediable, but may be turned to an immediate advantage, particularly when the Obama regime and its call for the establishment of socialism-communism are defeated and at the direction of laws are executed or sent into political and physical banishment at their own expense. This is the cheapest and the best solution to Barack Hussein Obama's tyranny because it saves the expense which would be attended for by WE the People and brings the tyrants sooner to justice. Treason is the crime applied to traitors according to the *Constitution for the United States of America*. The law must be upheld and when executed, will add upwards respect to the force of the country.

The flame of anti-Obama patriotism which has broken forth not only does honor to America, but, like the blaze of 1776, will kindle into action the scattered sparks throughout America. The valor of a country may be learned by the bravery of its soldiery and the general cast of its inhabitants, but confidence of success is best discovered by the active measures pursued by its patriotic men and women. When the spirit of enterprise becomes so universal as to act at once on all ranks of men and women who are in action against the Obama regime, it will be styled truly popular.

In 1776, the ardor of the enterprising part was considerably checked by the real revolt of some, and the coolness of others. But in the present case, in the fight against Barack Hussein Obama and his regime there is a firmness in the substance and beliefs of the country to the public cause. There are American Patriots at all levels of society. They receive and support the undertaking and the active protest movement against the Obama regime, a measure which, while it does them honor, likewise contributes to their interest by rendering the operations of the American Patriots' campaign against the Obama regime convenient and effectual. The spirit of exertion has not stopped here. It has been the remark of the enemy Obama regime that everything in America has been done by the force of the regime government; but when the Obama regime sees individuals throwing in their voluntary aid, and facilitating the public measures in concert with the established WE-the People-powers of the country, it will convince them that the cause of America stands not on the will of a few but on the broad foundation of patriotism and massive desire to be governed responsibly in a democratic republic. Traitors must be accused, tried, found guilty, and executed! Thus aided and thus supported, disaffection will decline, and the withered head of tyranny will expire in America. The ravages of the enemy Obama regime will be short and limited, and like all former regimes, will produce a victory over themselves.

The American man and woman who does not now feel for the honor of the best and noblest cause that ever a country engaged in – the implementation of the principles of the *Declaration of Independence* and the rule of law established and guaranteed by the *Constitution for the United States of America* – and exert their personal strength accordingly, is no longer worthy of a peaceable residence among a people determined to be free.

★★★★★★★★★★★★

Frederick William Dame
Patriotic, Steadfast, and True
March 31, 2014

Frederick William Dame

The American Crisis

Taxed Enough And Controlled Enough Already

A Call To Take Action

Number Twelve

★★★★★★★★★★★★

Americans throughout their history have been taxed and controlled. Under the Barack Hussein Obama regime the taxes are increasing and the control over the individual American is daily violating the boundaries and limitations of all rationality and the guarantees of the *Constitution for the United States of America*. It is time for all Americans, those who are patriotic and those who are not – although non-patriotism is un-American – to sit down and think seriously on the affairs of America. The original principles upon which America resisted foreign control and taxes in 1776, and the glow and ardor which they inspired, will occur like the undefaced remembrance of a lovely scene. To trace over in imagination the purity of the cause, the voluntary sacrifices that were made to support it, and all the various turnings of the War for Independence in its defence, is at once both paying and receiving respect. The principles deserve to be remembered and to remember them rightly is repossessing them. In this indulgence of generous recollection, we become gainers by what we seem to give and the more we bestow the richer we become.

So extensively right was the ground on which America proceeded in 1776 that it not only took in every just and liberal sentiment which could impress the heart, but made it the direct interest of every class and order of men and women to defend the land. The war on the part of Great Britain was originally a war of covetousness. The sordid and not the splendid passions gave it being. The fertile fields and prosperous infancy of America appeared to Great Britain as mines for tributary wealth. She viewed the hive, and disregarding the industry that had enriched it, thirsted for the honey. The violence of temper was added to the rage of avarice; and therefore, that which at the first setting out proceeded from purity of principle and public interest was heightened by all the

131

obligations of necessity. It requires but little knowledge of human nature to discern what would be the consequence were America again reduced to subjection like that under Great Britain in 1776. Uncontrolled power in the hands of an incensed, imperious, and rapacious dictator is an engine of dreadful execution, and woe be to the United States of America over which it is now being exercised. The names of WE the People and American Patriot are now sunk in the general term of rebel, and the oppression, whatever form it takes, lights equally on all. Perhaps in such a season there is no better companion than a rifle!

Great Britain did not go to war with America in 1776 for the sake of dominion, because she was then in possession; neither was it for the extension of trade and commerce, because she had monopolized the whole, and the Colonies had yielded to it; neither was it to extinguish what she called rebellion, because before she began no resistance existed. It was then from no other motive than avarice, or a design of establishing, in the first instance, taxes in America; or, in the second instance, to confiscate the whole property of America, in case of resistance and conquest of the latter, of which America then had no doubt. This historical situation is now being repeated under the totalitarianism of Barack Hussein Obama and his dictatorial thug regime. The goal was and is to tax, tax, tax … in every form possible and to confiscate personal property ranging from firearms to private water springs. There is nothing safe from Barack Hussein Obama's grasp. The whole history of evil cannot be comprehended without him.

I mean to be open, candid, and sincere. I see a comprehensive American wish to expel the enemy Obama regime from government responsibility. There is more than a murmuring because the domestic war is carried on with a subtle vigor.

Beginning in January 2009, and for each year after, the United States of America under Barack Hussein Obama has borrowed about 40 percent of the money it spends. The latest official Congressional Budget Office figure from 2011 is that it was approximately 1,645,000,000,000 dollars. Now, this expense is being borrowed in the hopes of conquering or destroying America – there is no difference! As it is avarice which first induced Barack Hussein Obama to commence the domestic war, how truly wretched and deplorable the condition of OUR America has become. Americans by their own remissness suffer an enemy of such a disposition and so circumstanced who reduces America to subjection! The truth behind Obama's borrowing from future generations is that borrowers are nearly always ill-spenders, and it is with lent money that all evil is mainly done and all injustice protracted.

Now, throwing out of the question everything of honor, principle, happiness, freedom, and reputation in the world, and taking it up on the simple ground of patriotic interest, I present a straightforward analysis of the present situation concerning taxes and control.

The Tea Party movement which began in 2009 arose out of concern from a great many American people that government spending, and the taxes that pay for such spending, had grown wildly out of control. This movement was not particularly ideological, nor was it specifically partisan; members of the loosely-affiliated factions among the movement may be more likely to support the Republican Party than the DemocRAT Party, but at its core, the Tea Party movement was about nothing more than fiscal responsibility. Members of the movement may have had grave concerns about the policies of the newly-elected Oval Office occupier Barack Hussein Obama, but many members also voiced serious concerns about the spending habits of the administration of outgoing President George W. Bush. In short, members of the Tea Party movement did not care which party was spending too much of the people's money; they simply wanted such spending to be drastically reduced and confined to a realistic budget framework.

The Tea Party movement and those who support it are not the only members of the American public who have serious concerns about taxes, government spending, and the constant overreach of the federal government. Members of the Tea Party movement may be among the most visible or the most vocal protesters of the Obama-regime-out-of-control government spending and the bloated mess of government programs aimed at encroaching into every area of Americans' public and private lives. For every individual who voices support for the Tea Party, there are hundreds or even thousands more who are just as concerned about these issues. Since 2009, when Barack Hussein Obama moved into the White House, the problems rapidly worsened. One of the first things Obama did was to announce his intentions to have the federal government take control of the American health care system. Obama also supported increases in tax rates at all levels, grew the size of the federal government, and enacted countless new regulations aimed at restricting and controlling business and even the private lives of the American people. From rules about what we can and cannot eat to how we can and cannot conduct our own religious affairs, Obama has used the power of the usurped position to exert control over the public and personal affairs of the American people.

***

Let us forthwith examine the subject of Obama's taxes.

When Barack Hussein Obama illegally took office there was a massive global recession wreaking economic havoc in countries around the world. Liberals love to point to the policies of outgoing President George W. Bush – who admittedly spent more than many conservatives would have liked – and tried to blame him for the problems. Attempting to blame George W. Bush for the global recession would be like blaming Frosty the Snowman for a winter blizzard; yes, there were economic problems in the United States when Bush was President, but his Republican administration was able to stave off the worst effects. As he neared the end of his second term, many DemocRATS and even some Republicans pushed for the notion that the United States should spend its way out of the recession. As Obama and his regime were usurping control of the government offices, Congress did agree to spend billions of dollars on so-called *stimulus packages*, though the more sober-minded Republicans in office recognized the danger in these decisions, and were able to at least limit the size of such expenditures, even if they could not block them entirely.

The contrast between the inexperienced economic and fiscal policies of Barack Hussein Obama and those of the Republicans is stark. In the face of potential economic catastrophe, the Republicans – buoyed by the burgeoning Tea Party movement – understood that the federal government simply could not afford to keep spending money it did not have. Undaunted by the wisdom and experience of his opposition, Obama and his regime of thugs enacted a series of new programs, regulations, and spending initiatives that swelled the federal budget deficit and the national debt, raising both to historically high levels. Obama's budgets and spending simply could not be paid for with the amount of tax revenue the federal government was taking from the pockets of the American people, so the financial thief Obama simply borrowed trillions of dollars every year to pay for his extravagant policies. All the while, the Republican Party and the more responsible members of the American public argued that instead of spending more and more money we did not have, the federal government should do what everyone else has to do when there is not enough money: economize within the confines of a fiscally responsible, healthy budget.

Liberal DemocRATS like to refer to Republican ideas about fiscal responsibility as *austerity*, because they think *austerity* sounds like a bad word. Obama and his POLDS like to paint the Republicans as mean, Scrooge-like characters who want to take food from the poor and money from the middle class. Nothing could be further from the truth. Republicans simply stand for fiscal responsibility. They understand that the responsible handling of economic affairs is the only means by which America can successfully recover from the effects of the last recession. Ignoring the advice and wisdom of the Republican Party, Obama and his thug regime chose instead to supplement his borrowed trillions by enacting tax increases. Moreover, these tax increases have been aimed at those who are already shouldering the greatest economic load. Progressives love to wail and moan about the so-called *one percent*, while ignoring the fact that the top one percent of the American people are paying nearly 75 percent of all taxes. The remainder that is not covered by the economy's top earners is paid for by the middle class, who least can afford it.

Barack Hussein Obama's reckless spending habits have not gone unopposed by the Republican Party. Fiscally responsible Republicans have developed budget plans that clearly show how the United States could reel in spending and get the deficit and debt under control in just a few short years; indeed, possibly within a generation. Such fiscal responsibility would mean that some huge government-handout programs would have to be cut back to realistic and sustainable levels, or would have to be deleted, a move which is always met with howls from liberals who recognize that such programs are what sustain the obedience of their slave followers.

Every time cry-baby Obama has attempted to raise taxes or enact more spending increases, the adults in the room have done all they can to limit his extravagant choices. Despite Obama's best efforts to make deficit spending the cornerstone of his plan to keep the American people beholden to the federal government, the Republicans have managed to avoid allowing him to take everything he wants without paying for it. While thug Obama has increased spending far beyond the point of responsibility and good governance, the limited austerity measures the Republicans have successfully pushed are slowly having a too-small effect on the budget and spending habits of the federal government.

For every dollar Obama has raised taxes in ways that are clearly visible, he has matched it with taxes raised in ways that are not so immediately obvious. According to the figures presented by the non-partisan Congressional Budget Office, Obama raised taxes in the first five years of his dictatorship by three trillion dollars. Fully half of that figure is comprised of direct, overt tax increases, such as the increase in the payroll tax Obama demanded when he held the federal government hostage during the *fiscal cliff crisis* in 2012. The payroll tax increase hits the average hard-working American the most, because it increases payments to Social Security and other government programs, pulling more and more money out of the paychecks of the middle class. The spike in the payroll tax is just one example, however. Along with the increases Obama demanded in the payroll tax, he raised the top marginal tax rate from 35 percent to 38.6 percent while phasing out a number of exemptions for individuals earning over $250,000 and couples earning over a combined $300,000.

While 300,000 dollars may seem like a lot of money to most people, it must be recognized that a huge portion of the overall tax burden in America falls on the shoulders of those in that income bracket, while those earning only slightly smaller paychecks often pay no federal income taxes at all. Many of those people paying the highest marginal rates are the same individuals or families who have also seen their health insurance plans disappear because of ObamaCare. Moreover, they are now forced to pay higher premiums for the Obama-the-savior privilege of finding health insurance plans they did not want but are forced to purchase. The costs of ObamaCare are nothing short of hidden taxes that place an even more burdensome tax liability on those who can least afford to pay more. While everyone is now forced to purchase health insurance, it is really only those in the middle class and the top earners who actually have to pay for it; they also have to pay for the ObamaCare subsidies for those who earn less. Simply put, an estimated two thirds of the American people are paying not only for their own insurance, but also for the insurance of the other third of Americans, and these numbers are ever increasing.

Because the ObamaCare legislation is such a convoluted mess, it is often difficult for the American people to see or understand the true costs of this economic debacle. If a sober analysis breaks down some of these costs – which are nothing more than hidden taxes – one will find what is really in store for the American people. Publicly available figures from the Congressional Budget Office point out the fact that there are over twenty new taxes the American people will be forced to pay thanks to ObamaCare. These include everything from hikes in the Medicare payroll tax to increases in taxes on investment income that will be diverted to pay for Obama's socialized-communist-medicine program. All told, these increases amount to hundreds of billions of dollars over the coming decade. That estimate is on the low side, based on what we currently know about ObamaCare. In the event that the American people are faced with problems related to ObamaCare that have yet to be anticipated, the true costs of the program will surely climb much higher.

The thug-in-chief Barack Hussein Obama has hidden taxes in government regulations. Along with the onerous burden of direct taxation, the federal government extracts money and exerts control over the American people in less-direct ways. Among the most significant of these government activities are the command and control (CAC) regulations on American businesses and industries. In essence, command and control regulations are two sides of the same coin. The *command* side is comprised of the regulations, guidelines, and other demands the government places on industries to establish and enforce standards of quality, target outputs, safety rules, and other restrictions and limitations. To some degree, it is understandable why the federal government would establish and enforce policies of this nature; the biggest complaint from industries and businesses arise when the nature or the extent of such regulations exceed that which is necessary, fair, or reasonable. The *control* side of the CAC coin involves the costs of fees for doing business, and the sanctions levied against industries and businesses that fail to adhere to the often egregious government standards. These fees and sanctions can make it difficult or impossible for businesses to survive, especially in the current economic environment.

Just like private individuals, businesses also pay taxes on income, though for businesses *income* is profit. Also just like private individuals, businesses pay hidden taxes; often these hidden taxes are significantly greater than the overt, direct taxes levied against their profits. The full scope of CAC regulations is massive; the government establishes regulations and guidelines for virtually every aspect of conducting business in any industry, at any level. CAC regulations include, for example, standards about the levels of specific pollutants a business can generate. If the business exceeds those limits, it will be fined or face some other forms of sanctions. At first glance this might seem entirely reasonable; after all, no one likes pollution! Yet, at issue is the question of who establishes the guidelines related to pollutants, and on what basis do they do they establish such guidelines? There are undoubtedly some such regulations that are appropriate and necessary, but whenever government regulators are involved – as opposed to industry, business, and scientific experts who actually understand the relevant issues – problems are bound to arise. Simply put, the government has an economic incentive to establish regulations that ensure revenue for the government. When the federal government is involved, problems are part of the program involvement.

CAC regulations are not the only way to ensure that businesses or industry sectors engage in ethical and responsible behavior. As an alternative to the negative-reinforcement model on which CAC is based, the government can establish positive-reinforcement-based economic incentives that encourage responsible behavior rather than simply discouraging supposedly bad behavior. It is possible, for example, for the government to establish taxes that are direct and visible, that incentivize businesses and industries to avoid the production of so-called *negative externalities*. Finding the right balance in such incentivizing taxes can be difficult, but they are fairer and more manageable for businesses that can work with the fixed costs of such taxes rather than face fines or other costs that can be levied unfairly.

Since taking illegal control of the American government, Obama and his thug regime have chosen CAC as their weapon of choice against businesses. Acting through the overreaching power of federal bodies like the Environmental Protection Agency (EPA), Obama and his minions have extracted billions of dollars from American businesses for every conceivable violation of even the most ridiculous rules and standards. Whenever and wherever this qualification is present, it would by logic include Barack Hussein Obama's participation. Further, Obama has used the EPA to establish new regulations and standards for many different industries, often making such rules and standards virtually impossible to follow. By setting the regulatory bar too high, Obama can make it appear to his followers that he is taking a firm stance against the evil corporations that POLDS believe are ruining America, when in reality Obama is simply bleeding more and more money out of every possible industrial sector to increase government revenue. Rather than establish policies that incentivize good, corporate citizenship, Obama chooses to demonize businesses, simply because that plays well to his regime's brain-dead base support.

***

Let us now examine Obama's strategies of control.

The CAC regulations are not just a means of extracting hidden taxes from businesses and industry; they are also a means of exerting economic and political control. While the EPA and the other agencies that operate under Obama's dictatorship can set fines and fees against businesses, they can also establish regulations or offer tax breaks and other incentives as well. For an industry that may be politically popular with Obama's constituency, such as the so-called *green energy* sector, the government can and does offer huge economic incentives and advantages to companies in that sector, while fining and taxing other businesses in other sectors that may not share that same political popularity among liberals and progressives. One well-known example is that of Solyndra, a *green* solar company that was given hundreds of billions of dollars by Obama only to collapse into bankruptcy. In that instance, Obama spent enormous sums of the American people's money to curry favor with progressive voters. That money simply disappeared! One wonders as to whether or not that was the original intention!

The full scope of CAC regulations and how Obama and the federal government use them to exert control over the business sector and to extract billions, or even trillions in hidden taxes is far too massive to properly and adequately address in the context of this analysis. What is clear, after giving CAC the most cursory glance, is that they are just more examples of how massive the federal government has grown under the thug-in-chief Barack Hussein Obama, and the extent to which the federal government reaches into the pockets of every American to extract the ever possible dollar. When considering the issue of CAC regulations, it also becomes clear that the visible taxes and other costs exacted from all Americans by the government are just the tip of the economic iceberg; it is below the surface where the full scale of the Obama regime's reach and power are hidden from view.

Under Barack Hussein Obama there is a reality beyond taxation that shows the total implications of Obama's plans to control Americans' lives. Even with the briefest discussion of CAC regulations, and the ways they are used to restrict, control, and extract revenue from businesses, it is all but impossible not to consider the myriad ways that government uses similar tactics to control private citizens. Under the Obama regime, the reach of government into the lives of Americans has grown exponentially. It is not just in the obvious ways that huge, expensive programs like ObamaCare or the stupid government educational program Common Core force Americans to behave as the federal government sees fit, it is also in the small but innumerable ways that the government makes Americans comply with its demands on virtually every aspect of their lives. From voter-roll manipulation to unconstitutional gun regulations, the Obama administration seeks to exert command and control over all America and Americans.

Another CAC aspect that may not be immediately obvious to Obama's supporters – but which his political opponents recognize is one of its fundamental components – is in the way ObamaCare makes those who use it beholden to and reliant upon the federal government. For generations, Americans have typically acquired health insurance in one of several ways, including accessing health insurance as part of an employer-based program, or simply by purchasing private, individual health insurance. It is no accident that ObamaCare offers subsidies that make it extremely inexpensive or even supposedly free to millions of

140

Americans. Yet, somewhere someone is paying! Obama and the DemocRATS know that once these people become dependent on still another government program they will become even more beholden – they will become slaves to the federal government. More specifically, they will become – and, Obama hopes, they will remain – dependent upon the DemocRAT Party. The more handouts and freebies the DemocRATS can offer, the more those who take these handouts will become dependent on the largesse of the DemocRAT Party. The result is control!

The problem for the remainder of Americans, especially the hard-working and beleaguered middle class, is that someone has to pay the costs of ObamaCare for all of those who are getting it for free. Obama is putting the hidden taxes he is raising through ObamaCare to good use by spending those billions on millions of his supporters. For every dollar Obama takes from the middle class and gives to someone else, he and the DemocRATS are investing in their party's future. The analysis is simple: ObamaCare is not just a socialized-communist-medicine program; it is also an illegal voter mine. The group Voters Trust asserts that ObamaCare is nothing less than the "biggest voter registration fraud scheme in the history of the world." That is, of course, a pretty significant accusation; unfortunately for many Americans, there is plenty of evidence to back up such a claim.

A recent report funded by left-wing billionaire George Soros describes how simple it is to use ObamaCare as a scheme to drive up the number of registered DemocRAT voters. The National Voter Registration Act of 1993 mandated that virtually all government agencies must offer voter-registration services to the public in addition to providing the voters the agency's regular services. On the surface, this may appear to simply be a fair and positive use of government resources, until one considers that the majority of those who are likely to directly access government programs are also those who are likely to become or remain dependent on them. This establishes an unhealthy, and even unholy relationship between the DemocRAT Party – which loves nothing more than to give away money that does not belong to them – and those who take advantage of every government giveaway that comes along. If a potential voter knows that his or her free money is coming from the DemocRATS, and the same people giving away the free money are asking the potential voter to register, it is fairly obvious in which party this potential voter will become a member.

As if that is not enough of an unfair advantage for Obama and the DemocRATS, the applications for ObamaCare that were sent out to millions of Americans came with, in many cases, voter registration forms that were pre-marked *Democrat*, which should have read *DemocRAT*. The ObamaCare exchange named *Covered California*, for example, sent out millions of voter registration cards to California residents that were already marked for the DemocRAT Party. Groups such as the League of Women Voters and the American Civil Liberties Union have advocated for the inclusion of voter registration cards with ObamaCare signup forms, and ObamaCare phone representatives in many states are being told to ask every caller if he or she would like to register to vote at the same time as they sign up for the free insurance being handed out by Obama and the DemocRATS. There is simply no way to see such actions as anything less than unfair, and those who insist that ObamaCare registration is tantamount to voter registration fraud are making a true statement. There are simply no equivalent government programs that are similarly slanted towards the Republican Party which does not have a government program for registering its voters.

There are numerous other ways that Obama is using his usurped power of his office to exert and extend government control over the lives of the American people. One mandate enacted under Obama limits the amount of tax-free savings an individual can put into his or her Individual Retirement Agreement (IRA). This does not mean that an individual cannot save as much as he or she can afford to save; instead, it restricts the amount that can be saved and put into an IRA. Once that limit is reached, all remaining savings are subject to taxation. The cap on IRA savings is three million dollars. The cap on the amount that can be extracted tax-free is 250,000 dollars annually after retirement. This is an entirely new set of rules and regulations that Obama enacted, and these rules represent one more way that Obama and the DemocRATS are attempting to control the lives of the American people. These rules literally determine how much an individual can save without penalty, and how much an individual can spend. If it is an American's money, why can that American not save it or spend it as that American sees fit?

At a time in the economic life of the nation when people are saving their money at historically low levels, would it not make sense to establish laws and regulations that encourage, rather than discourage, the American people to save money? These Obama-regime regulations are established for the sole purpose of ensuring that the government has what it needs – or at least what it wants – while ensuring that the needs of the American people come second. This is just one example of a myriad of economic policies and laws that have been established by the Obama regime in the bygone years that are aimed at raising government revenue to the detriment of Americans and to the expansion of government handouts. The real problem with these sorts of regulations is that they do not just extract money from Americans – such as that which is acquired through direct taxation – they also police demands on the behavior, decisions, and choices made by individuals. That is the goal!

For anyone who believes that such restrictions or limitations on behavior are, at worst, incidental to the revenue-generating policies enacted by Obama, attention should be paid to the ways that the Obama thug regime offers direct consideration to the use of behavioral sciences in the development of public policies. Thug Obama and his cohorts are not just aware that their policies have a direct impact on the behavior and choices of the American people; their policies are *specifically and purposefully designed* to have such an impact. Beginning in 2010, the federal government adopted the recommendations of a Yale University study on behavioral sciences that offered advice and information on how public policy could be shaped to produce outcomes that the government finds favorable or beneficial. Agencies such as the Department of Health and Human Services and the Veterans Administration are developing policies that are designed to ensure that their constituencies behave in ways that are beneficial to and predictable by these agencies. In short, the federal government is using behavioral science to manipulate the ways that the public behaves.

Another behavior scheme that Barack Hussein Obama wishes to activate is to place the United States of America under the auspices of the United Nations Agenda 21 program – a global plan for the total control of the individual. It will eliminate personal property, terminate individual freedom and replace it with freedom within the collective. Agenda 21 will also control the distribution of wealth. Throughout their history

Progressives have made utmost contributions in making a Godless nation out of America. Coupled with the program Agenda 21 they will achieve in their Satanic goal of making America totally Godless. Agenda 21 is the opportunity of having Marxist dictates exercising brutal control over people. Free America will no longer be free! Americans will no longer be Americans!

Barack Hussein Obama has made no secret of his intention to use his power to accomplish whatever he would like to accomplish, even if that means going outside the bounds of constitutional limitations. He has, and will likely continue to use, executive orders to ram through rules or policies without congressional approval. All presidents have used executive orders, but they have traditionally been used to implement specific aspects of governmental policies once those policies have been developed and approved through the proper channels – namely, the United States Congress. Where Obama is breaking with the past and abusing the power of executive orders, is in using them to develop and implement public policy. There are innumerable examples of such misuse of executive orders. While Republicans in Congress have sounded the alarm over such abuses, many Americans seem completely oblivious to these actions by Barack Hussein Obama. Such obliviousness is the outcome when WE the People become brain dead with regard to politics.

One particularly egregious example of Barack Hussein Obama's misuse of executive orders was written in 2012, when he signed Executive Order 13603 on *National Defense Resources Preparedness*. This executive order mandates that his government regime can seize control of the following:
• All commodities and products that are capable of being ingested by either human beings or animals.
• All forms of energy.
• All forms of civil transportation.
• All usable water from all sources.
• Health resources – drugs, biological products, medical devices, materials, facilities, health supplies, services and equipment.

The above list includes just some of the resources and powers that the government can seize. This executive order also mandates that citizens

144

can be forcibly inducted into the military, and that the federal government and military leaders can, in essence, take control of any person, place, and resource they see fit. What this executive order amounts to is a declaration of the circumstances under which the federal government can declare martial law. The rules and guidelines contained in this executive order were all established without any input or oversight from Congress. It is impossible to view this executive order as anything less than a further gross usurpation of power by Barack Hussein Obama, and it is just one of the hundreds of rules and regulations the dictator has rammed into an Executive Order in the past few years.

One issue that may be more familiar to even casual observers of government is that of gun ownership. While there is certainly room for public debate on the issue of responsible gun ownership and ways that safety and security related to guns can be improved, what is not in question is that the Founding Fathers of this nation determined that the right to keep and bear arms was fundamental to the security of individuals and the nation itself. The authors of the *Constitution for the United States of America* were all too aware of the power of totalitarian governments like that under which WE the People lived during the reign of King George III of England. Had it not been it for their ability to fight back against the repressive British government, the Continental Army of OUR Forefathers would never have succeeded in their revolutionary quest to establish a free nation. The Founding Fathers understood that the power of government should rest with the people, not the leaders, and they further understood that the right to keep and bear arms was necessary for the people to protect their power against a tyrannical government like the Barack Hussein Obama regime.

Despite this constitutionally-guaranteed right, Obama and the DemocRAT Party have consistently and repeatedly pushed for broader and stricter gun control laws. By all available evidence, gun control laws are counter the reality. In cities such as Chicago and Washington D.C, where it is illegal to possess guns, the murder rates are higher than anywhere else in the United States. In regions where citizens are free to enjoy their Second Amendment rights, the number of people murdered by guns is lower by orders of magnitude. When citizens are able to protect themselves against criminals, the crime rates go down. It is simple and unassailable logic. In light of Obama's executive order about

145

martial law, however, it is easy to imagine why he and his party would prefer to have a populace that was already unarmed; such circumstances would make it that much easier to assume total control of the United States of America when and how the regime sees fit.

Taken in total, all of these different elements add up to create a reality that cannot be ignored. Barack Hussein Obama can be blamed for the massive further growth of the federal government. That growth actually began under an earlier DemocRAT, President Franklin Roosevelt, who used the excuse of World War II to enact massive new federal programs and explode the size and scope of presidential powers. That said, it must be acknowledged that Obama has used every level of government, every mechanism at his disposal to reach further and further into the lives of the American people. In addition to having the National Security Agency clandestinely record private data from unknowing Americans, the other primary means by which Obama has accomplished this intrusion into American lives is through taxes; he has developed a system of command and control of private citizens that rivals, or even exceeds the ways that CAC has long been used to control business and industry. Obama and the DemocRAT Party have also employed fraud and chicanery to grow the reach of their entire party and seek to ensure that an entire generation of Americans is dependent on the federal government. The full implications of Obama's actions are so significant as to be almost unfathomable, and it may be too late to turn back the clock on the advent of socialist-communist totalitarianism. If liberty is to be salvaged, it is first necessary to recognize that it is in danger. If Obama has his way, he will not only control Americans' ability to fight back against a repressive government; he will control Americans' ability to remember what freedom was like.

Suppose Barack Hussein Obama was to conquer America and as a conqueror was to lay America under no other conditions than towards America's annual revenue that amount which the Obama regime dictates or borrows on the international money market from international financiers who are involved in toxic derivative scandals that will destroy the American economy. This question must follow: Under these circumstances is it advisable to raise money on the international money market for a socialist-communist America? The patriotic answer is NO!

Can it be supposed that conquerors would choose to put themselves in a worse condition than what they granted to the conquered? Under the DemocRATS and the Obama regime there is scarcely a necessity of life that you can eat, drink, wear, or enjoy that is not loaded with a tax. Even the light from heaven would be taxed if Obama could do it, although there are enough taxes on environmental energy sources. Yet, light from the burning fires of Hell are free under Barack Hussein Obama. The humblest drink of life, a small beer, has a tax on it. In short, the condition of the United States of America, in point of taxation, is so oppressive, the numbers of America's poor who do not pay taxes so great, and the extravagance and rapaciousness of the Obama regime so enormous, that in the conquest of America, the distresses of America would further explode out of the economical framework. What Obama wants is clear: solid revenue! The modes which the Obama regime takes to procure solid revenue are not to operate alike on all, but only on the wealthy who work for their wealth. The Obama regime's manner of reasoning is short, because they would naturally infer that if WE the People are able to survive their domestic war that has been continuing for six years, WE the People, the successful people, particularly, should be taxed heavily for surviving the thug Obama regime.

Could I find a miser whose heart never felt the emotion of a spark of principle, even that man, uninfluenced by every love but the love of money, and capable of no attachment but to his interest, would and must, from the frugality which governs him, contribute to the defence of the nation, or he ceases to be a miser and becomes an idiot. But when Americans take in with it everything that can ornament mankind; when the line of American interest becomes the line of American happiness; when all that can cheer and animate the heart, when a sense of honor, fame, character, at home and abroad, are interwoven not only with the security but the increase of property, there exists not a man or woman in America, unless he or she be an hired emissary, who does not see that America's good is connected with keeping up a sufficient defence against the Obama regime.

I do not imagine that an instance can be produced in the world of a regime putting itself to such an amazing charge to conquer and enslave a free nation as Barack Hussein Obama has done. The sum of money is too great for Barack Hussein Obama to think of with any tolerable degree of temper. When we consider the burdens Barack Hussein Obama places on Americans, as well as the disposition Barack Hussein Obama has shown, it would be the height of folly to suppose that Barack Hussein Obama would not reimburse himself by the most rapid means, should Barack Hussein Obama have America once within his power. With such an oppression of expense, what would an empty conquest be to Barack Hussein Obama? What relief under such circumstances could Barack Hussein Obama derive from a victory without a prize? It is money, it is control of revenue that Barack Hussein Obama first went to domestic war for, and nothing but that will satisfy him. It is not the nature of avarice to be satisfied with anything else. Every passion that acts upon mankind has a peculiar mode of operation. Many of them are temporary and fluctuating; they admit of cessation and variety. But avarice is a fixed, uniform passion. It neither abates of its vigor nor changes its object; and the reason why it does not is founded in the nature of things, for wealth has not a rival where avarice is a ruling passion. One beauty may excel another, and extinguish from the mind of man the pictured remembrance of a former one; but wealth is the phoenix of avarice, and therefore it cannot seek a new object, because there is not another in the world.

There are two distinct items which make the payment of taxes difficult; the one is the large and real value of the sum to be paid, and the other is the scarcity of the currency in which the payment is to be made, which in itself is a form of control. Although these appear to be one and the same, they are in several instances not only different, but the difficulty springs from different causes. Hypothetically speaking, suppose a tax be laid equal to one half of what a person's yearly income is. Such a tax could not be paid, because the property behind the person's income could not always be spared; and on the other hand, suppose a very trifling tax was laid, to be collected in pearls, such a tax likewise could not be paid, because they could not always be had. Now any person may see that these are distinct cases, and the latter of them is a representation of the American taxpayers' predicament. That the difficulty cannot proceed from the former, that is, from the real value or weight of the tax, is evident at the first view to any person who will consider it. The convenience or inconvenience of paying a tax in money arises from the quantity of money that can be spared out of the person's economical status. It is not the want of property, but the scarcity of the medium by which the proportion of property for taxation is to be measured out that makes the embarrassment under which Americans suffer. There is not money enough, and, what is equally as true, the Obama regime will not let there be money enough!

Look at the destruction done by the Obama regime. All of the individual states are suffering the same fate: large deficits caused by the DemocRAT politics of the past and the present. Notwithstanding the weight of the domestic war, the ravages of the enemy Obama regime, and the obstructions it has thrown in the way of trade and commerce, so soon does a young nation outgrow misfortunes, that America has already surmounted many that heavily oppressed her. For the first year or two of the domestic war under Barack Hussein Obama, Americans were shut up within the envisioned wonderland of hope and change. Under the government of Barack Hussein Obama, the trade of this nation has been loaded with restrictions. Without Obama it would be otherwise. The case would show the vast advantage of an open trade, because America with the present quantity of trade under the Obama regime's restrictions cannot not support itself; from which I infer, that if half the quantity without the restrictions can bear itself up nearly, if not quite as well as the whole when subject to them, how prosperous would the condition of America be when the whole shall return open with all the world!?! By the trade I do not mean the employment of a merchant only, but the whole interest and business of the United States of America.

It is now appropriate for a salient remark. Fines like in ObamaCare are, of all modes of revenue, the most unsuited to the minds of a free nation. When a person pays a tax, that person knows that the public necessity requires it, and therefore feels a satisfaction in discharging his duty; but a fine – frequently levied with severity – seems to be atonement for neglect of duty, and of consequence is paid with discredit.

Everyone knows that I am not the flatterer of Congress. In most instances they are not right and if their measures are supported, Barack Hussein Obama will have his way and there will be no need for Congress.

I have now waded through a tedious course of difficult business, and over an untrodden path. The subject, on every point in which it could be viewed was entangled with perplexities, and enveloped in obscurity, yet

149

such are the resources of America, that she wants nothing but system to secure success.

***

The treachery of Barack Hussein Obama is well known and engrosses the attention and conversation of the public; and that, not so much on account of the traitor as the magnitude of the treason, and the providence evident in the discovery. The matter, as far as it is at present known, is thus briefly related:

The true character of Barack Hussein Obama is that of a desperado. His whole life has been a life of accomplished nothings; and where either plunder of government funds, or profit from a book he did not write was the object, no danger deterred, no principle restrained him. In his person he was criminally clever and active, somewhat diminutive, weak in his capacities and extremely trifling in his conversation; and because he is a gallant fake, he is defective in the talents necessary for command. The early convulsion of the times afforded Barack Hussein Obama an introduction into life, to the morality of which he was a stranger, and the eagerness to succeed by means of taking credit for other people's work, and to reward and encourage those who are not worth it, procured him at once both applause and promotion, because he always throws away those whom he uses once their usefulness has expired. His being a pseudo community organizer gave him fame in Chicago. The gaining of a seat in the Illinois state legislature put the first stamp to his public character. His behavior from this time, the true spring of his conduct being known, he is both disregarded and disesteemed. This last instance of his treachery – the usurpation of the Oval Office – has proved the judgment right.

When we take a review of the history of former times it will turn out to the honor of America that, notwithstanding the trying variety of her situation, Barack Hussein Obama is the prime example of a well-placed fraud. Even in this case, the unshaken honesty of those who detected him heightens their national patriotic character, to which Obama's apostasy serves as a foil. From the nature of his crimes, and his disposition to lie, it is reasonable to conclude that Barack Hussein Obama had direct accomplices. His sole object was to usurp a position and to destroy the United States of America and to be consistent with himself. He is a charlatan in that he would as readily betray the side he would desert to, as that he would desert from.

150

One reflection results from this black business that deserves notice, which is that it shows the declining power of the enemy Obama regime. Americans are a proud people. They ought to be above Barack Hussein Obama. They ought to despise Barack Hussein Obama. However they may feel on occasion, Americans will eventually despise Barack Hussein Obama and consider American Patriotism superior to his thug regime.

As of this writing Barack Hussein Obama is calling for more taxes, indeed, he is calling for the highest sustained taxes ever! What for? For socialism-communism? No, thank you!

To purgatory with you and your regime thugs Barack Hussein Obama! Americans are taxed enough and controlled enough already!

Frederick William Dame
Patriotic, Steadfast, and True
April 28, 2014

Frederick William Dame

The American Crisis

What Barack Hussein Obama Says Is Not What Is

A Call To Take Action

Number Thirteen

★★★★★★★★★★★★★

Of all the innocent passions which actuate the human mind there is none more universally prevalent than curiosity. It reaches all mankind and in matters which concern us, or concern us not, it alike provokes in us a desire to know the truth behind what is and what is not.

Although the situation of America, superior to every effort to enslave her, and daily rising to importance and opulence, has placed her above the region of anxiety, it has still left her within the circle of curiosity. In the beginnings, Americans fancied to see and hear the speeches of a man who had proudly threatened to bring America to his feet with the threats of hope and change. Such fancy was visibly marked with tranquil confidence at first, but now which cares nothing about their contents. The speeches are presently inquired after with a smile, read with a laugh, and dismissed with disdain. It surely has something to do with the fact that Barack Hussein Obama needs teleprompters to deliver simple sentence constructions. He, who would speak and cannot speak, can surely tell lies.

Yet, as justice is due, even to the enemy Obama regime, it is right to say that Barack Hussein Obama's speeches are as well managed as the embarrassed condition of their affairs could well admit of; and though hardly a line in them is true, except for the fact that lies are lies, they may serve to amuse the deluded POLDS and brain dead of America for whom they are calculated.

The job to change America, says the speeches, is still unhappily prolonged by that restless ambition which first excited the enemy Obama regime to commence it and which still continues to disappoint American

152

Patriots' earnest wishes and diligent exertions to restore the public tranquility.

How easy it is to abuse truth and language when the dictator, by habitual wickedness, has learned to set justice at defiance. That the very man who began the domestic war against WE the People; who with the most sullen insolence has refused to answer to WE the People, and even to hear the humblest of all petitions; who has encouraged his thugs in the most savage cruelties, and the most scandalous plundering; who has stirred up the socially weak on one side, and the African Americans on the other; and invoked every aid of Hell in his behalf, should now, with an affected air of pity, turn the tables from himself, and charge to the wickedness that is his own, can only be equaled by the baseness of the heart that spoke it. Of course, it is not his fault! In Obama's warped mind wickedness is the fault of the Republicans!

To be humbly wrong is manlier than to be meanly progressives who think they are always right. Humility is an attitude often encountered in many American Patriots and it is equally applicable now. American Patriots feel something like respect for consistency even in error. WE the People lament the virtue that is debauched into a vice, but the vice that affects a virtue becomes the more detestable: and amongst the various assumptions of character, which hypocrisy has taught, and men have practised, there is none that raises a higher relish of disgust than to see disappointed inveteracy twisting itself, by the most visible falsehoods, into an appearance of piety to which it has no pretensions.

Barack Hussein Obama says he should not have to answer to the trust committed to the sovereign of a free people, nor make a suitable return to his subjects for their constant, zealous, and affectionate attachment to his person, family, and regime. If Barack Hussein Obama consented to sacrifice, either to his own desire of domestic peace on his terms only, or to the temporary ease and relief of Americans on his terms only, those essential rights and permanent interests, upon the maintenance and preservation of which the future strength and security of the United States of America must principally depend, would cease to have meaning.

153

The man whose ignorance and obstinacy first involved and still continues to plunge the nation into the most hopeless and expensive of all presidential terms of office, now meanly flatters Americans by naming them a free people under his terms only and under the disguise of their essential rights and permanent interests, makes a merit of his regime's organized crimes against America. Barack Hussein Obama's behavior disgraces even the character of perverseness.

Is Barack Hussein Obama afraid Americans will send him into banishment, or what does he fear? Why is the sycophant thus added to the hypocrite and the charlatan who pretends to govern, sunk into the humiliation and submissiveness coming from foreign powers like Russia and China, and dwarf-rogue North Korea?

In his speeches Barack Hussein Obama talks about the vital rights and interests of America. Yet, what those essential rights and permanent interests are, on which the future strength and security of America must principally depend, are in fact not further alluded to. Indeed, American rights and interests coming from Barack Hussein Obama are nothing more than words that impress nothing but the ear and are calculated only for the sound.

If they have reference to America, then they amount to a disgraceful confession from Mr. Zero who once assumed he could lead. The dictator Barack Hussein Obama and his regime are constantly holding up the vast importance which America is in order to allure the nation to carry on his intent of instituting socialism-communism. Now, whatever ground there is for this idea, it ought to have operated as a reason for not beginning it; and, therefore, the Obama regime supports their present measures to their own disgrace, because the arguments which they now use, are a direct reflection on their former policy against productive, free market economies.

In his speeches Barack Hussein Obama is always of the opinion that the favorable appearance of affairs concerning the social safety net of ObamaCare for his subjects in his kingdom must have the satisfaction of the populace; that things are not quite so bad everywhere in America is the cause of some consolation, but can be none for triumph. One broken leg is better than two, but still it is not a source of joy. The same is with the appearance of affairs in the East, the West, the North, and the South be they ever so favorable! Yet, in reality, Barack Hussein Obama, you and your appearances are nevertheless worse than at first, without a prospect of either ever being better.

In the course of his kingly years in the Oval Office Barack Hussein Obama maintains that his assiduous endeavors to protect his fifty-seven domains have not only met with success, but that the result is equal to the justice and uprightness of his views. What justice and uprightness there was in the beginning of the war of hope and change with America the world will judge of, and the unequalled anti-social barbarity with which it has been conducted is not to be worn from the memory by the cant of sniveling hypocrisy.

Furthermore, it is with great concern that Barack Hussein Obama inform Americans that the events of his domestic and diplomatic policies have been very unfortunate, some having ended in the loss of American lives. The great concern of WE the People is that Barack Hussein Obama does not consider this important because he maintains that all served in the same manner, as if to say they knew they would die some day.

Obama claims that no endeavors have been wanted on his part to extinguish the social inequality that has always been a part of Americans' lives, and to give to his endeared subjects a happy and prosperous condition which will be found in his paradise of socialism-communism. In a republic the sovereignty of the political structure rests in each individual. In a democracy the sovereignty of the political structure is located in the group, in the mob. This is the reason Karl Marx said that the first step to socialism-communism is a democracy, rule by a political mob. "We have seen ... that the first step in the revolution by the working class is to raise the proletariat to the position of the ruling class, to establish democracy. The proletariat will use its political supremacy to wrest by degrees all capital from the bourgeoisie; to centralize all instruments of production in the hands of the state." Therefore, democracy will be used to establish certain socialist-communist policies so that the collective society will be directed toward communism. It must be stated that in a democratic republic the opportunity for a happy and prosperous condition of the citizens is guaranteed by laws and is derived from a due obedience to the laws. The Marx and Engels' ideology-revolutionary aspect places emphasis on the idea that people need to *actively change* the socioeconomic system to a better form. Interestingly enough, this is what capitalism and laissez-faire economics with moral and ethical principles does. Marxism-Communism does not change a socioeconomic system into a better form because it is neither moral nor ethical. This is the truth behind Marxism and its evil offshoot ideas.

One cannot help but believe that when Barack Hussein Obama says the term *democracy* he is using it in its classical sense: *democracy is mob rule*. The mob is his regime and the POLDS (Progressives, Obots, Liberals, Dumb-downers, Socialists-Communists) make up his regime. They are the more so contemptible when we see them licking up the drool that flows from the Obama regime in Washington, that the pride of not being laughed at would induce a man of common sense to leave it off. But the most offensive falsehood in Barack Hussein Obama's speeches is his attributing the prosperity of America to a wrong cause: Obama's social and environmental politics and unions. It was the unremitted industry of the workers without unions and their descendants, the hard labor and toil of persevering fortitude, that were the true causes of the prosperity of America. The former tyrannies of Europe served to people America, and the virtue of the adventurers served to improve the nation. Go back into American history and ask the man, who, with his axe, cleared a way in the wilderness to possess an estate, what made him rich, and he will tell you the labor of his hands, the sweat of his brow, and the blessing of heaven. It was not and never will be the handouts from the federal government. True American Patriots are not the parasites of society. The growth of America was a result of the aggregate efforts of a busy multitude. Every American toiled for himself. Each American gathered competence and wealth. The attempt of Barack Hussein Obama to control America is a gigantic Sisyphus ambition striving to take hold of a free, independent nation! It is a vain attempt!

Let Barack Hussein Obama but leave America to herself and America asks no more. The United States of America has risen into greatness without the knowledge and against the will of dictator Zero, and has a right to the unmolested enjoyment of her own created wealth.

Barack Hussein Obama will order the estimate wealth of the ensuing year to be laid before Americans. He says he will rely on America's wisdom and public spirit – wisdom and public spirit of the POLDS – for such solutions as the circumstances of the Obama regime's affairs shall be found to require. Among the many ill consequences which attend the continuation of the present policies, he says, he most sincerely regrets the additional burdens which it must unavoidably bring upon his faithful subjects. After such messages he departs for a round of golf!

It is strange that a nation must run through such a labyrinth of trouble and expend such a mass of wealth to gain the wisdom which an hour's reflection would have taught. The final superiority of America over every attempt that Barack Hussein Obama might make to destroy her, is as naturally marked in the constitution of things, as the future ability of a giant over a dwarf is delineated in his features while an infant. How far providence, to accomplish purposes which no human wisdom could foresee, permitted such extraordinary errors, is still a secret in the womb of time, and must remain so till futurity shall give it birth.

Barack Hussein Obama often claims that believing in change for America maintains a firm confidence in his being right in what he undertakes; that he has a special protection and conviction of his cause. Further, he has no doubt but that by the concurrence and support of his regime, by the begging of his pee-ons, and by a vigorous, animated, and united exertion of government handouts to his subjects, he will be enabled to establish the blessings of a socialist-communist paradise in all of his fifty-seven dominions.

King Obama is one of the readiest believers in the world of himself. In the beginning of the contest against WE the People he said he would sign a law to place America under the control of the United Nations, which would make the world safer and better. The truth of the matter is that the reverse would be more appropriate in providing for a safer and better world. Although providence, for the years together under Obama, has kept America out of his vision of United Nations protection, still the destroyer-in-chief has no doubt. Like Pharaoh on the edge of the Red Sea, he sees not the plunge he is making, and precipitately drives across the flood that is closing over his head. The tyranny of Barack Hussein Obama is worse than any other. His form of governing has become so oppressive that it must be thrown off.

157

I think it is a reasonable supposition that his speeches are composed before the arrival of the news which Barack Hussein Obama is addressing, because what he addresses in his speeches does not exist. Three examples provide the proof.

1. Obama claims that women must finally have the right to have their pay equal that of men. The truth behind the matter is that since the Equal Pay Act passed by Congress in 1963, it is a violation of federal law to monetarily compensate a woman less than a man for accomplishing the same work under the same conditions.

2. Obama falsely argues that comprehensive immigration reform would fix America's immigration system that is not functioning properly. The problem is not the lack of new immigration laws. The truth behind the matter is that Obama is not enforcing the already existing federal immigration laws.

3. Obama falsely argues that ownership of guns is responsible for the rise in the numbers of persons murdered or assaulted by criminals with guns. Therefore, he says, the freedom to possess a firearm that is guaranteed by the Second Amendment to the *Constitution* must be voided. The truth behind the matter is that in towns, cities, and regions where a state does not allow people to carry firearms, the murder rates and assaulted persons are always high because the people murdered and assaulted could not defend themselves.

If a crisis does not exist, Barack Hussein Obama will create one by claiming that there is a crisis! What Barack Hussein Obama says a situation is at the time he describes it certainly has no relation to the condition at the time the description was spoken. Truth is very scarce among politicians and Barack Hussein Obama's supply of it has always been in shortage of the demand. Barack Hussein Obama lies, not just sometimes, but always!

Be this as it may, it is nothing to American Patriots. Our line is fixed. Our lot is cast; and America, the child of fate, is arriving at maturity sans Obama. WE the People have nothing to do but by a spirited and quick exertion, to stand prepared for every evil undertaking the Obama regime comes up with. Too great to yield and too noble to insult; superior to misfortune, and generous in success, let WE the People untaintedly preserve the character which the United States of America has gained, and show to future ages an example of unequalled magnanimity. There is something in the cause and consequence of America that has drawn on her the attention of all humankind. The world has seen her brave. Her love of liberty; her ardor in supporting it; the justice of her claims, and the constancy of her fortitude have won her the esteem of the world, and attached to her interest the first power without Barack Hussein Obama.

America's situation now is such that to whatever point, past, present or to come, she casts her eyes and new matter rises to convince her that she is right. In her conduct towards the enemy Obama regime no reproachful sentiment lurks in secret. No sense of injustice is left upon the mind. Untainted with ambition, and a stranger to revenge, America's progress has been marked by providence, and providence, in every stage of the conflict, has blest her with success.

America! Do not wrap yourself up in delusive hope and change and suppose the business done! The least remissness in preparation and the least relaxation in execution, will only serve to prolong the struggle against Obama and his thug-regime-domestic war, and increase expenses. If the enemy Obama regime can draw consolation from misfortune, and exert themselves upon despair, how much more ought WE the People, who are to win back a country by the actions of American Patriotism, have an earnest of successful consolation. Patriotism gives the American the feeling of having glory over everything.

I shall now make my remarks on what Barack Hussein Obama's speeches do not contain.

There is not a syllable in them respecting alliances based upon reciprocal trust. Either the injustice of Barack Hussein Obama is too glaring, or his condition too desperate, or both, for no foreign power really comes to his support because they know that he is an illegal occupier of the Oval Office. This affects domestic and international relations because everything that Barack Hussein Obama signs as putative President of the United States of America is signed without legal authority. Should the United States Supreme Court uphold the legality of his signature, for example at any future instance on the ObamaCare legislation, the Court would continue its sanctioning of Obama's illegality. Likewise, if

Congress does nothing against Obama's illegality, WE the People can take it for granted that Congress is complicit in Obama's violations of the *Constitution*. The situation being such, Congress as the victim of Barack Hussein Obama's constitutional crimes is afraid of the political consequences. Furthermore, Americans then encounter an extremely important question: Does Congress believe in the *Constitution for the United States of America*?

In the beginning of the contest against America when he had only America to contend with, Obama seemed to be the savior of the world. Yet, what has he saved? Nothing! The remembrance of his nothingness ought to inspire us with confidence and greatness of mind, and carry us through every remaining difficulty with content and cheerfulness. What are the little sufferings of the present day compared with the hardships that are past? There was a time, in 1776, when WE the People had neither house nor home in safety; when every hour was the hour of alarm and danger; when the mind, tortured with anxiety, knew no repose, and everything, but hope and fortitude, was bidding us farewell.

It is of use to look back upon those situations; to call to mind the times of trouble and the scenes of complicated anguish that are past and gone. Then every expense was cheap, compared with the dread of conquest and the misery of submission. WE the People did not stand debating upon trifles, or contending about the necessary and unavoidable charges of one political party against the other. Every American Patriot bore their lot of suffering, and looked forward to happier days and scenes of rest.

Perhaps one of the greatest dangers which any country can be exposed to arises from a kind of trifling which sometimes steals upon the mind when it supposes the danger past; and this unsafe situation marks at this time the peculiar crisis of America. What would she once have given to have known that her condition at this day should be what it now is? Yet, Americans do not seem to place a proper value upon it, nor vigorously pursue the necessary measures to secure it. Yet, Americans know that they cannot be defeated by Barack Hussein Obama. WE the People have no right to expect it; neither ought WE to look for it. WE are a people, who, in OUR situation, differ positively from all the rest of world. WE form one common floor of public good, and, whatever is OUR charge, it is paid for OUR own interest and upon OUR own account.

Misfortune and experience have now taught us system and method; and the arrangements for carrying on the fight against Barack Hussein Obama. The positions of the several states are ascertained, and WE the People know what red states and blue states are, and the necessity as well as the advantages of vigorously providing for the right ones.

New information concerning the origin of Barack Hussein Obama is emerging every day. These revelations are truths, thus supporting the maxim that an error (Obama) is the more dangerous the more truth it contains. We all know that the Obama family does not have any legal certification of existence. Zero has succeeded Zeros. Barry, the adopted son of an Indonesian citizen was also an Indonesian citizen. While going to school in Hawaii and California (still an Indonesian citizen?), he was normally unacademically high on drugs, perhaps five or six shots a month, and made some attempts to be moderately successful. He gradually learned that success and power are the only situations in which cruelty – by throwing those he had used under the bus – can be transformed into being victorious, and those who are cruel, because they are victorious, can with the same facility act out any other degenerate character trait.

Immediately after Barry's arrival in Chicago, the true place of gangster education, Barry got to know the streets and how to *get over* without doing anything, except taking credit for positive outcomes to which he had no input. Going on to Colombia University – if he ever attended – and then to Harvard University where he became editor of the *Harvard Law Review*, again a position in which he did nothing, Barry *got over* on academics most likely as being part of the racial quotas. Returning to Illinois, he registered as a lawyer by lying on his application form. *Getting over* again by being dishonest! This was certainly not the first time! Barry then became a member of the Illinois state legislature where he did nothing but vote present and take credit for success that he did not accomplish. He then bought and bullied his way into being elected as United States Senator from Illinois in which position he continued to vote present and accomplish nothing, all the while taking credit for success he never had anything to do with and for being a chairman of a committee which he never held. Those who got in his way like Donald Young, Larry Bland, and others, were either shot in the head, like wild beasts, or put to death in cold blood – also methods of throwing someone under the bus!

161

Barack Hussein Obama presents the reader with one of the most shocking instances of successful cruelty ever practised. I leave it to rest on your mind that Barack Hussein Obama may be fully impressed with a sense of the destruction and likewise, that he may see and feel the necessity for his own personal safety as a result of those whom he obeys, as well as for the interest evil, to omit or delay no one preparation necessary to secure the ground which WE the People so happily stand upon.

Nothing is more anti-American than Barack Hussein Obama and his thug regime.

This is not what Barack Hussein Obama says. It is what is!

★★★★★★★★★★★★

Frederick William Dame
Patriotic, Steadfast, and True
April 30, 2014

Frederick William Dame

The American Crisis

Nothing Except Honesty Is Required

A Call To Take Action

Number Fourteen

‾Constitutional guarantees are only words! One either obeys them and the oath of office to the *Constitution,* or one does not. Barack Hussein Obama does not obey the *Constitution for the United States of America* and he does not uphold his oath to the *Constitution.* How can he? His oath is to Muhammad, the Koran, and to Islam! All other statements he makes are only words without meaning!

Money is only money! One either has it or one does not have it! The United States of America does not have it! It has only financial bookkeeping entries, inflation, and a national debt that will probably never be paid off ... at least as long as DemocRATS are in political power. Nevertheless, where constitutional guarantees for citizens and finances are concerned, all that is required is pure honesty.

When any necessity or occasion has pointed out the convenience of addressing the public, I have never made it a consideration whether the subject was popular or unpopular, but whether it was right or wrong; for that which is right will become popular, and that which is wrong, though by mistake it may obtain the cry or fashion of the day, will soon lose the power of delusion and sink into disesteem.

A remarkable instance of this happens in the case of Barack Hussein Obama. I mention this circumstance with the greater ease, because the poison of his hypocrisy has spread over the whole country, and every man and woman, almost without exception, has thought me wrong in opposing him. The majority of colleagues I had in academia in 2008/2009 and again in 2012/2013 stood at a distance. They deserve no tribute, no respect, and that is enough agreeable reflection. Such should be the fate of Barack Hussein Obama and his regime!

As he rises like a rocket, he will fall like a stick, is a metaphor which I have often applied to Barack Hussein Obama. He has exactly fulfilled the description. The credit he had so unjustly obtained from the public in 2008 and again in 2012, he has lost in almost as short a time. The rocket of delusion perished as it fell, and Barack Hussein Obama will soon see himself stripped of popular support. Many Americans have begun to doubt him. Many have deserted him. Many have decided to turn their backs on the DemocRAT Party, but not on America.

When Barack Hussein Obama looks in a mirror he sees himself as being perfect. Yet, if Americans look carefully in Obama's mirror they will observe cracks showing that he is really the object of general suspicion. When Barack Hussein Obama arrived in Washington, D. C., he thanked all of his thug supporters who did everything illegal that they could do to get him elected to office. They, in turn, fell upon their knees, paid reverence to Barack Hussein Obama, and then began to fall upon American citizens. Immediately, Barack Hussein Obama endeavored to continue by fraud what he had accomplished by treason. His plans, schemes and projects, together with his expectation of being the commander-in-chief have all miscarried. Barack Hussein Obama wants America to be a ruined country. He only meant to make a tool of America to get what profit he can out of her and then to leave her and accommodate with Islamic countries. To complete the character of a traitor, Barack Hussein Obama has used every expression and argument in his power to injure the reputation of America and to advise America to renounce her allegiance to the republic form of government and free market economy, and then surrender up her independence to his socialism-communism. Thus he abuses America and is endeavoring to create disunion among the different social and cultural classes of the American society by the same arts of double-dealing by which in the past he had already caused dissensions and distractions in America in whatever position he occupied.

Barack Hussein Obama's life has been a fraud. His character has been that of a plodding, plotting, cringing mercenary, capable of any disguise that suited his purpose. This final detection will very happily clear up

164

those mistakes and remove that uneasiness which his unprincipled conduct occasions. Everyone now sees Barack Hussein Obama in the same light; for towards friends and most enemies, Barack Hussein Obama has acted with the same deception and injustice, and his name, like that of America's famous traitor Benedict Arnold, ought never to be forgotten among WE the People. This is not the first time that I have mentioned Barack Hussein Obama as a traitor and it is my intention that it shall not be the last.

The domestic war against WE the People is not the domestic war of Congress, although they are doing nothing to stop it, but the domestic war of the Obama regime in any line whatever. At the same time, Barack Hussein Obama's domestic war on America has the accompanying quality that it can be used as a war of WE the People in OUR own behalf for the security of OUR natural rights, and the protection of OUR own property. First, by mutual compact WE the People have resolved to defend OUR rights and maintain OUR independence at the hazard of OUR lives and fortunes; WE have elected OUR representatives, by whom WE appointed OUR members of Congress, and said, act you for US, and WE the People will support you. This is the true ground and principle of the relationship of WE the People with the representatives on the part of America, and consequently, there remains nothing to do but for everyone to fulfill their obligation. It is the duty of the elected representatives to exercise the will of WE the People and not the will of Barack Hussein Obama, or any political party, especially the DemocRATS.

It is next to impossible that a relatively new country, engaged in a relatively new undertaking, can set off systematically right at first. WE the People have not seen the true extent of the struggle in which America is involved. Neither can WE the People avoid the beginning. WE the People supposed every step that is taken and every resolution formed would bring the enemy Obama regime to reason and close the contest. Those failing, WE the People have been forced into new measures; and these, like the former, being fitted to their expectations, and failing in their turn, have left WE the People initially unprovided and without system. Likewise, the enemy, Obama regime has been induced to prosecute the domestic war. WE the People have been continually expecting to see Obama's credit exhausted. The Obama regime has been looking to see our historic fight lose. Thus, between their watching US, and WE the People watching them, the hopes of both have been deceived, and the childishness of the expectation has served to increase the expense. WE the People are not interested in the possibilities of US being defeated. American Patriots will not take part in shielding Americans from the effects of Obama's folly, like the lamestream media does. To do so is to fill America with fools. Surely America has enough of them adoring the chief of fools Barack Hussein Obama!

Yet, who, through this wilderness of error, has been to blame? Where is the man or woman who can say the fault, in part, has not been his or hers? The faults are the Obama-caused errors of the election days. The faults are the errors of a whole country, which nothing but experience can detect and time remove. Neither can the circumstances of America admit of system till either those who committed election fraud in 2008 and 2012 have been tried, convicted, and sentenced, or the election system has been fixed. No calculation of an election could be made on a medium failing without reason and fluctuating without rule.

There is one error which might have been prevented and was not; and as it is not my custom to flatter, but to serve America, I will speak it freely. It certainly was the duty of every election body in America to have known, at all times, what the condition of its voting system is, and to have ascertained at every period of depreciation how much the real worth of the vote fell short of their nominal value: one person, one vote. This knowledge, which might have been easily gained, in the time of it, would have enabled the senators and representatives to have kept their constituents well informed. Instead the voters were brainwashed with the mantra of hope and change which has become American dopes in chains.

Keeping constituents informed is one of the greatest duties of representation. The same logic applies to government finances. They ought to have studied and calculated the expenses of the Obama regime, the quota of each state, and the consequent proportion that would fall on each person's income as a result of voting for Barack Hussein Obama; and this must have easily shown to them that an increase of 6.666 trillion dollars in six years cannot be repaid by this generation or the next generation. But instead of this, which would have been plain and upright dealing, the little line of temporary popularity, the feather of an hour's duration was too much pursued; and in this involved condition of things, every senator and representative, for the want of a little thinking, or a little information, supposed that it supported the whole expenses of the Obama regime, when in fact it has come to a point that can never be repaid. Obama's thinking and actions are destructive thinking and actions that have become incongruous with intelligence.

The reality of the comparison of the socialist-communist policies of Barack Hussein Obama with the free market policies of his predecessor George W. Bush yields the following facts respective the George W. Bush and the Barack Hussein Obama administrations:

- Full time workers: **120 million vs. 116 million**
- Workforce participation: **66% vs. 63.2%**
- Home ownership: **70% vs. 62%**
- Median income: **$55,484 vs. $52,098**
- Poverty rate: **13% vs. 15%**
- People on food stamps: **31.6 million vs. 47.8 million**
- Debt-to-GDP: **64.8% vs. 101.6%**

Such is the preview of socialism-communism: government handouts lead to deficits and negativism!

Impressed with a sense of the danger to which America has been exposed by this method of doing business, and the prevailing errors of the day, Barack Hussein Obama has nevertheless demanded a carte blanche for America's debt financing just as he has demanded carte blanche for the election process (one person, multiple votes), to say nothing of the amnesty legislation for illegal immigrants, who would automatically become DemocRAT Party members and vote multiple times.

Some say – most empathically the enemedia – that America cannot bear to change the ruling system of Barack Hussein Obama and the DemocRATS. This has been the most expensive doctrine that ever was held out and has cost America trillions of dollars for nothing. Can the United States of America bear to be overrun, ravaged, and ruined by the enemy Obama regime? This will immediately follow if an about-face is not undertaken in the 2014 and 2016 elections. Independence would be wanting and will ever be wanting when and where sufficient

167

constitutional freedoms are not guaranteed. But this is only one part of the folly. The second is, that when the danger comes and there is no political turn-around in 2014 and 2016, WE the People will be obliged by Obama and the DemocRATS, in a number of instances, to expend double the sums of money to do that which at first might have been done for half the money. But this is not all. A third mischief is the institutionalization of socialism-communism – the manifestation of fear on the American souls – under Barack Hussein Obama and the DemocRATS. This can be accomplished in 2014-2016 when Barack Hussein Obama's second term expires, or he will call out martial law by claiming a national emergency and remain longer to institute socialism-communism, which is the opposite of freeing markets from the chains of centralization.

Now, I ask, why was all this done, but from that extremely weak and expensive doctrine, as some say, that America could not bear to change the Obama system? That is, that America could not bear, in the first instance, that which would have saved her twice as much at last; or, in proverbial language, that America could not bear to pay a cent to save a dollar; the consequence of which has been, that she has paid a dollar for a cent. Why are there so many unpaid Federal Reserve certificates in almost every person's hands, provided they do not have credit cards? Why is there politically wanted socialist-communist parsimony of not providing sufficient revenues and incomes? Besides, the doctrine contradicts itself; because, if the whole country cannot bear to change the ruling system of Barack Hussein Obama, how is it possible that it should? Yet, this has been the case: for unsuccessful stimulus packages have been had; and they had to be had; but the misfortune is that they had been obtained and executed in a very unequal manner, and upon expensive credit, whereas, with ready money, they might have been successful for half the price, and nobody distressed.

The doctrine of Barack Hussein Obama and his supportive POLDS that America needs socialism-communism is false. Peoples in the free world have always tried to kill socialism-communism, but where it has taken hold, it has killed the people. There are not any large numbers of people in any part of the universe who live so well, or have such a fund of ability, as in the United States of America. The income of a common laborer, who is industrious, is equal to that, if not more, of the generality of tradesmen anywhere. In many professions and industries I have not

168

heard of one who could be said to be bankrupt without DemocRAT-supported union demands. In America almost every farmer/rancher still lives on his own lands. Everyone in America still has the opportunity to fulfill one's dreams without Obama's hope and change. Before ObamaCare arrived one could chose their doctor and there was no death-panel noose tightened around one's neck. These freedoms are disappearing and more freedoms are disappearing daily under the dictatorship of Barack Hussein Obama, for he occupies a position of unquestioned ascendancy and with every political undertaking he constitutes a system of plunder.

Yet, notwithstanding those advantages on the part of America, true it is that had it not been for the patriotism of Americans, the nation would have already sunk into a state of sloth and poverty. There is more wealth lost by neglecting to work and waiting for the government handout than by any bankruptcy. That which is lost by neglect of this kind, is lost forever: whereas that which is received for work without governmental interference, and remains in the country, returns to us again; and at the same time that it provides us with security, it operates not only as a spur, but as a premium to America's industry.

There was a time when America had no other bond of union than that of common interest and affection. In the 1770s the whole country marched to the relief of Boston, and, making Britain's cause America's own, participated in Boston's cares and administered to Boston's wants. The fate of the Revolutionary War is that the union became strengthened by a legal compact of the states, jointly and severally ratified, and that which before was choice, or the duty of affection, is now likewise the duty of legal obligation.

The union of America is the foundation stone of her independence; the rock on which it is built; and is something so sacred in her *Constitution*, that WE ought to watch every word WE speak, and every thought WE think, that WE injure it not, even by mistake. When a multitude, extended, or rather scattered, over a continent in the manner Americans are, mutually agree to form one common centre whereon the whole shall move to accomplish a particular purpose, all parts must act together and alike, or act not at all, and a stoppage in any one is a stoppage of the whole, at least for a time.

Before political parties – particularly the DemocRATS played to the whims of the people by making promises for their being elected – government in America was quite simple. Thus throughout America the several states have sent representatives to assemble together in Congress, and they have empowered that body, which thus becomes their centre, and are no other than themselves in representation, to conduct and manage politics, while their constituents at home attend to the domestic cares of the regions and states, their internal legislation, their farms/ranches, professions or employments, for it is only by reducing complicated things to method and orderly connection that they can be understood with advantage, or pursued with success. Congress, by virtue of this delegation, is supposed to estimate the expense, and apportion it out to the several parts of the country (and the federal departments) and according to their several economic abilities and necessities; and here the debate must end, because each state (and federal department) has already had its voice, and the matter has undergone its whole portion of argument, and can no more be altered by any particular state, than a law of any state, after it has passed, can be altered by any individual. For with respect to those things which immediately concern the union, and for which the union was purposely established by WE the People, and is intended to secure, each state is to the United States what each individual is to the state in which that person lives. It is on this grand point, this movement upon one centre, that our existence as a nation, our happiness as a people, and our safety as individuals, depend.

It may happen that some state or other may be somewhat over-rated or under-rated, but this cannot be much. The experience which has been had upon the matter has nearly ascertained their several abilities. Yet, even in this case it can only admit of an appeal to the United States, but cannot authorize any state to make the alteration itself, any more than our internal government can admit an individual to do so in the case of an act of assembly; for if one state can do it, then may another do the same, and the instant this is done the whole is undone. Furthermore, if an individual can make alterations in the law like Barack Hussein Obama has done with ObamaCare the whole is also undone. As of this writing there have been 40 changes by Obama single handedly! Ironic as it may appear, perhaps this is the solution to getting rid of Barack Hussein Obama! One state can start the getting-rid-of-Barack-Hussein-Obama avalanche!

170

Neither is it supposable that any single state can be a judge of all the comparative reasons which may influence the collective body in arranging the laws of the country. The circumstances of the several states are frequently varying, occasioned by the political accidents and commerce, and it will often fall upon some to help others, rather beyond what their exact proportion at another time might be; but even this assistance is as naturally and politically included in the idea of a union as that of any particular assigned proportion; because we know not whose turn it may be next to want assistance, for which reason that state is the wisest which sets the best example.

Though in matters of bound duty and reciprocal affection, it is rather degeneracy from the honesty and ardor of the heart to admit anything selfish to partake in the government of OUR conduct, yet in cases where OUR duty, OUR affections, and OUR interest all coincide, it may be of some use to observe their union. The United States of America will have become ever heir to an extensive quantity and quality of freedom ... believe it or not without Barack Hussein Obama and the DemocRATS!

It has been OUR error, as well as OUR misfortune, to blend the affairs of each state, especially in monetary matters, with those of the United States; whereas it is OUR case, convenience and interest, to keep them separate. The expenses of the United States of America for carrying on the federal business, and the expenses of each state for its own domestic government, are distinct matters, and to involve them is a source of perplexity and a cloak for fraud. I love method, because I see and am convinced of its beauty and advantage. It is that which makes all business easy and understood, and without which everything becomes embarrassed and difficult.

There are certain powers which the people of each state have delegated to their legislative and executive bodies, and there are other powers which the people of every state have delegated to Congress and, consequently, of managing the expenses attending it; for how else can that be managed, which concerns every state, but by a delegation from each? The individual states and WE the People have an undoubted right to know how the federal expenses have been applied, and it is as much the duty of Congress to inform the states and the individual, as it is the duty of the state and the individual to provide the other.

After the successful outcome in the 2014 congressional election it will be an agreeable matter to see a spirit of order and economy taking place, after such a series of errors and difficulties. A government or an administration that means and acts honestly, has nothing to fear, and consequently has nothing to conceal.

In the bygone years American Patriots have seen what a bitter, revengeful enemy regime we have to deal with and any expense is cheap compared to their merciless paw. WE the People have seen the unfortunate, conservative organizations and personalities hunted like partridges on the mountains by the Internal Revenue Service, and it is only by providing means for our patriotic defence, that WE the People shall be kept from the same condition.

When WE the People think or talk about Barack Hussein Obama, WE the People ought to recollect that at one time America sat down in peace and slept in safety; that Americans could follow their farms/ranches, or businesses, or other occupations, in prosperous tranquility without Obama's government regime involvement. These inestimable blessings were formerly procured to WE the People by the taxes that WE paid. In this view, OUR taxes were properly OUR insurance money; they were what WE paid to be made safe, and, in strict policy, were the best money WE could lay out. But nowadays taxes do not accomplish this. The payments are made by borrowing money from other nations, most of them unfriendly to the United States of America. It is time to reverse the situation. We must make America's system of politics and finance complete, and strictly just. The consequence is that it requires nothing but honesty to do it. There needs but little to be said upon it. According to Barack Hussein Obama, the guarantees of the *Constitution for the United States of America* are only words and money is only money, especially because they are not his constitutional guarantees that he does not observe and it is not his money that he steals.

★★★★★★★★★★★★★

Frederick William Dame
Patriotic, Steadfast, and True
May 2, 2014

Frederick William Dame

The American Crisis

Throw Shoes At Barack Hussein Obama!

A Call To Take Action

Number Fifteen

There is no historically documented record of when throwing a shoe or shoes at someone was used as a form of political criticism. In many cultures the shoe and the foot have a special symbolical meaning. When one walks barefoot, the soles of the feet get dirty. When wearing shoes, the shoes get dirty and the feet can become smelly. Although there is no mention in the Koran or the Hadith of Muhammad that throwing shoes at someone is condoned, throwing a shoe at someone is a behavior common in Islamic countries. Therefore, it is not prohibited. It is allowed. To throw a shoe or shoes at someone as a target indicates that the targeted person is no better than dirt! Regardless of how dirty it is, no shoe deserves to have Barack Hussein Obama for a target. However, Barack Hussein Obama deserves all of the shoes that can be thrown at him!

Since the arrival of Barack Hussein Obama from Hell in 2008/2009 and the reappearance in 2012/2013 at Washington, D. C., scandal news that has not been covered by the enemedia has circulated throughout the United States of America. These revelations have brought to the fore a great variety of speculation concerning Barack Hussein Obama's criminal involvement in at least 26 scandals, which are herewith listed chronologically. Detailed information concerning the contents of the scandals will be found in various non-enemedia reports and publications.

January 19, 2009 Barack Hussein Obama takes oath of office: On January 19, 2009, Barack Hussein Obama took his oath of office to uphold the laws of the *Constitution for the United States of America* after the fact that he knowingly broke the law of the natural born citizen clause (Article II.1.5) of the *Constitution*.

February 15, 2009 David Axelrod's AKPD Message and Media: The Obama regime gave $2 million to the firm of former-White House adviser David Axelrod in order to promote the passage of ObamaCare. Evidence exists that the money was used to pay David Axelrod $2 million that AKPD owed him. In other words, indications are that the Obama regime paid off a private debt of a non-government organization to David Axelrod.

June 6, 2009 Inspector General Gerald Walpin fired: Inspector General Gerald Walpin of the Corporation for National and Community Service was fired in 2009. He fought wasteful spending and investigated a friend of Obama's, Sacramento Mayor and former NBA player Kevin Johnson. The White House says Walpin was incompetent. Walpin says Kevin Johnson is a criminal. There are indications that Michelle Obama instigated Walpin's firing.

February 2010 Sestak (D-PA)-Specter (D-PA): At the request of former White House Chief of Staff Rahm Emanuel, former President Bill Clinton acted as an intermediary to find out whether or not former Representative Joe Sestak (D-Pa.) would accept a prominent, unpaid White House advisory position in exchange for dropping out of the 2010 primary against former Sen. Arlen Specter (D-PA.). Sestak lost the senatorial election to Republican Pat Toomey.

February 2010 Fast and Furious gun running scheme: The Justice Department's Office of Alcohol, Tobacco, Firearms and Explosives allowed weapons-trafficking from the United States into Mexico. The agency lost track of the firearms. Many of them landed in the hands of Mexican drug cartel dealers. They used the firearms to kill their opponents. One of the firearms was used in the killing of United States Border Patrol Agent Brian Terry on December 14, 2010.

Beginning in March 2010 Internal Revenue Service targets Obama's enemies: In the time period leading up to the 2012 election, conservative and pro-Israel groups seeking tax-exempt status were targeted and denied tax-exempt status.

July 2010 The New Black Panthers Racial Double Standard: The United States Department of Justice under Attorney General Eric Holder used a racial double standard and did not pursue a voter intimidation case against the Black Panthers who menaced voters at a polling place in Philadelphia in November 2008.

October 2010 General Services Administration: In October 2010, the General Services Administration held a training conference in Las Vegas that cost $823,000. A clown (not Obama) and a mind reader (not Valerie Jarrett) were part of the training show. The head of the GSA, Martha Johnson, Robert Peck, the chief of the Public Buildings Service, which is part of the agency, and Ms. Johnson's top adviser, Stephen Leeds had to resign their positions. Some minor officials were placed on forced leave.

March 19, 2011 Obama wages war without Congressional approval: Obama violated the *Constitution* as well as the War Powers Resolution (1973) by attacking Libya without the approval of Congress. The same can be argued for Obama's support of terrorists in Syria (October 2012).

May 2011 Perjury by Attorney General Eric Holder, Case I: The evidence is that Eric Holder knew about the gun running scheme Fast and Furious before he told Congress in May 2011 that he had not before heard about the Fast and Furious scheme.

July-August 2011 Veterans Affairs Conferences in Disney World: The Veterans Administration agency wasted more than $6 million with unauthorized expenditures on two conferences in Orlando, Florida.

August 31, 2011 Solyndra: The Obama regime funded and promoted its pet green energy company despite warning signs that Solyndra would go into bankruptcy. The Obama regime pressed Solyndra to delay the specific announcements of its layoffs and bankruptcy until after the 2010 midterm congressional elections.

February 25, 2012 Kathleen Sebelius violates the Hatch Act: Kathleen Sebelius made "extemporaneous partisan remarks" during an official speech on February 25, 2012. She called for the election of the DemocRAT candidate for governor of North Carolina. This was a violation of the Hatch Act, which prohibits employees of the executive branch from participation in partisan politics.

May 2012 Sussing Out the Associated Press: As part of a leak investigation The United States Department of Justice under Attorney

175

General Eric Holder performed a massive investigation of Associated Press reporters' telephone records.

September 11, 2012 Benghazi: On the eve of September 11, 2012, Islamic terrorists attacked the United States diplomatic mission in Benghazi, Libya. The result of the attack was the killing of Ambassador J. Christopher Stevens and United States Foreign Service Information Management Officer Sean Smith, as well as two CIA operatives Tyrone S. Woods and Glen Doherty. Ten others were wounded in the Islamic terrorist attack. The Benghazi scandal is really three-scandals-in-one scandal: 1.) official government talking points insinuated that the reason for the Benghazi terrorist attack was an anti-Muslim video; 2.) the Benghazi mission was not protected despite repeated demands by Ambassador Stevens for protection and security; 3.) members of the Obama regime refuse to say where Barack Hussein Obama was the night of the Benghazi terrorist attack.

September 2012   Anthony Rodman, Hillary Clinton's brother, obtains illegal visas: Alejandro Mayorkas, Director of the U.S. Citizenship and Immigration Services, is being investigated because he may have used his position to illegally obtain U.S. visas for foreign investors in Anthony Rodman's company Gulf Coast Funds Management.

November 7, 2012   Political Prisoner Nakoula Basseley Nakoula: "We're going to go out and we're going to prosecute the person that (sic: who) made that video," Hillary Clinton allegedly told the father of one of the ex-SEALS killed in Benghazi. Thereupon Nakoula Basseley Nakoula, the writer, producer, and promoter of the anti-Muslim video *Innocence of Muslims* was arrested and sentenced to prison. Mr. Nakoula was used as a scapegoat for the Obama regime's Benghazi crimes.

March 2013   Vice-President Joe Biden bullies the press: Vice-President Biden's office has repeatedly and actively interfered with news coverage of Joe Biden. They forced a reporter to wait in a closet. They made a University of Maryland student reporter delete photos, and they edited pool news reports.

March 2013 The Pigford Payment scandal: In 2013, the United States Department of Agriculture attempted to compensate black farmers who had been discriminated against by the Department of Agriculture. The agency gave several billion dollars in cash to thousands of minority and female farmers who were not discriminated against by the Department of Agriculture.

May 2013 Rosengate: The United States Department of Justice claimed that reporter James Rosen (Fox News) committed a crime because he reported about classified information. The Justice Department illegally monitored his phones and emails.

May 2013 Perjury by Attorney General Eric Holder, Case II: Eric Holder told Congress he had never been associated with "potential prosecution" of any journalist. The fact is that he signed the document that designated James Rosen, a Fox News reporter, as a potential criminal.

May 2013 Kathleen Sebelius demands payment: In May 2013, Secretary of Health and Human Services Kathleen Sebelius intentionally solicited donations from companies that she in her official position of Secretary would possibly regulate. This was payment money to help sign up uninsured Americans for ObamaCare, which is against the law.

June 2, 2013 Lisa Jackson is Richard Windsor: The former Environmental Protection Agency Administrator Lisa Jackson used the pseudonym *Richard Windsor* in email correspondence with other government officials. This was an attempt to evade scrutiny, transparency, and congressional control.

August 7, 2013 CBS Reporter Sharyl Attkinson's computer hacked: CBS reporter Sharyl Attkinson had her computer hacked during her investigation of the Benghazi scandal. Evidence and indications are that the hacking came from the Obama regime because they are the only hackers who have the capability of such complete hacking.

These are my laws: Dictator Barack Hussein Obama has repeatedly decided which laws to enforce and which laws not to enforce. Two prime examples are: 1.) his continuing personal goal since he was a United States Senator and his decision since he has been the illegal occupier of the Oval Office not to deport illegal immigrants; 2.) his personal changes to regulations in the ObamaCare (Affordable Care Act) legislation. Since

April 19, 2011 Obama has made 40 changes to the Affordable Care Act without congressional approval.

The Veterans Administration: Various Veteran Administration hospitals in Arizona, Colorado, Wyoming, Illinois, North Carolina, Florida, Mississippi, New Mexico, and Texas falsified secret lists of appointment data in order to conceal the fact that veterans had long waiting times and were being denied proper and prompt medical care. Obama does not call for the resignation of the Secretary of Veterans Affairs, four-star General Eric Ken Schinseki, but praises him instead.

These alone are justification enough for Americans to throw shoes at Barack Hussein Obama! The speculation of Barack Hussein Obama's criminality in these scandals has not been a subject of the enemedia, but a never-ending matter for American Patriots. In addition to the above scandals, Senator Ted Cruz (R-Texas) has thoroughly documented instances in which Barack Hussein has willingly broken the laws of the United States of America. The series of reports began in April 213. They are:

A. **The Legal Limit Report No. 1:** U.S. Supreme Court Rejects the Department of Justice's Expansive View of Federal Power. Nine times the Supreme Court of the United States rejected the Obama regime's positions on the expansion of federal power.

B. **The Legal Limit Report No. 2:** The Obama Administration's Lawless Acts on ObamaCare and Continued Court Challenges. The Obama regime has repeatedly ignored the law of ObamaCare and has changed the text of the law 40 times without the approval of Congress.

C. **The Legal Limit Report No. 3:** The Obama Administration's Assault on Texas. *The State of Texas has filed multiple lawsuits to prevent the Obama regime from assuming powers reserved for the individual states.*

D. **The Legal Limit Report No. 4:** The Obama Administration's Abuse of Power. This is a listing of attempts by the Obama regime to take control of *executive nominees, free speech, national security, ObamaCare, privacy, the economy, etc.*

These scandals and the documented reports of Barack Hussein Obama breaking the law are proof that more than just any *fauxpas* is at play in the enemy-Obama-thug regime. They are always under the water and it is certain that they have run their length of madness. That the thug regime is under the necessity of changing their measures may easily be seen into; but to what their change of measures may amount, or how far they may correspond with American interest, happiness, and duty, is yet uncertain; and from what Americans have hitherto experienced, WE the People have too much reason to suspect them in everything.

I address this writing so much to the brain-dead POLDS – the Progressives, Obots, Leftists, Dumbed-downers, Socialist-communists – for if it is their intention to promote any kind of good words for Barack Hussein Obama, it is proper they should know beforehand that the United States of America have as much honor as bravery; and that WE the People are no more to be seduced from OUR Patriotism alliance than that their allegiance to Obama is correct behavior. The American Patriots' line of politics is formed and not dependent, like that of OUR enemy, on chance and accident.

On OUR part, in order to know at any time what the Obama regime will do, WE have only to find out what they ought not to do, and this last will be their conduct. Forever changing and forever wrong; too distantly removed from patriotic, grass-roots America to improve in circumstances, and too unwise to foresee them; scheming without principle, and executing without probability; their whole line of management has hitherto been blunder and baseness. Every policy has added to their loss, and every year to their disgrace, till unable to go on, and ashamed to go back, their hope-and-change politics have come to a halt, and all their fine prospects to a halter. Barack Hussein Obama as failure-in-chief has prostrated himself to himself. Could OUR affections forgive, or humanity forget the wounds of an injured country, WE the People might, under the influence of a momentary oblivion, stand still and laugh. But the Obama regime is engraven where no amusement can conceal them, and is of a kind for which there is no recompense. Can the Obama regime restore to America the beloved dead? Can the Obama regime say to the grave, give up the murdered? Can the Obama regime obliterate from Americans' memories those who are no more? Barack Hussein Obama! Think not then to tamper with America's feelings by an

179

insidious contrivance, nor suffocate American humanity by seducing US to dishonor!

There has appeared some disposition in the Obama thug regime to cease the further prosecution of the domestic war. However, it would be accompanied by a dishonorable proposition to American citizens. By the speeches and statements which have appeared from the White House, it is easy to perceive to what impolitic and imprudent excesses the Obama regime's passions and prejudices have, in every instance, carried them during the domestic war. Provoked at the upright and honorable actions of American Patriots, the Obama regime imagined that nothing more was necessary to be done to prevent the final subjection than to promise, through the agency of their enemedia, a repeal of their offensive acts of bullying WE the People. The vanity of the conceit is as unpardonable as the experiment is impolitic.

I am so convinced of the wrong ideas of the Obama regime that I shall not wonder, if in their last stage of political frenzy, they propose to WE the People to accept Obama's socialism-communism as a sign of enduring reverence for The One. Such a proposition, should it ever be made (It has already been more than once hinted at in the regime and by the enemedia.) would discover such a disposition to perfidiousness, and such disregard of honor and morals, as would add the finishing vice to Obama's national corruption. I do not mention this to put America on the watch, but to put Barack Hussein Obama and his minions on their guard that they do not, in the looseness of their non-present hearts, envelop in disgrace every fragment of what remaining reputation they might possess.

By the complexion of some part of the news which has transpired through the enemedia, it seems probable that this insidious era in the Obama regime's politics is beginning to make its appearance. I wish it may not; for that which is a disgrace to human nature throws something of a shade over all the human character, and each individual feels his share of the wound that is given to the whole. The policy of the Obama regime has ever been to divide America in some way or other. In the beginning of the dispute, Obama practised every art to prevent or destroy the union of America, well knowing that could he once get them to stand singly, he could conquer them unconditionally. But this is not all. He will

180

uninterruptedly pour out all his regime's force and fury upon America, for it is evident that Barack Hussein Obama is to draw America from world-wide importance.

Failing domestically, Obama has placed his perspective on international relations and has apparently made concessions to Russia, China, Iran, and even North Korea in foreign policy, mainly by not taking any action against their power maneuvers. What is still more extraordinary, he at the same time made propositions to Islamic countries providing insurgents in Syria to further draw America into that conflict. Worry not American Patriots, for Barack Hussein Obama will be disappointed in the actions of his plans.

It is a thing very extraordinary and even ridiculous that the Obama regime which superficially says that America is independent, not only in acting, but of right, during the domestic war, should now have a repugnance to treat America as not being qualified to participate independently in individual rebellion.

WE the People answer that the Obama regime in the terms already mentioned are insulting themselves without knowing it. The Obama regime is making very great offers to American adversaries with the intent of submitting to their terms of politics. But there is yet more. Barack Hussein Obama is ruining the economic wealth of America by plunging the country into more debt, all the more to accommodate matters and interests with socialist-communist theory and Islamic positions.

From what has been observed, it evidently follows that the whole of the Obama regime politics is to disunite America by means of the false promises and offers which he separately made and still makes to the various politicians of the DemocRAT Party; and also to separate the states from consultations with each other and induce federal bureaucracies to arm against WE the People, or more probably to oppress US when they find US and OUR patriotic engagement so that WE might stand alone and without protection. Yet, dictator Obama and his regime forget that American Patriots can protect themselves and America.

This, therefore, is the net Barack Hussein Obama has laid for WE the People; that is to say, to tempt US with flattering and very magnificent

181

promises to come to an accommodation with his regime, exclusive of any intervention of American Patriots, conservative personalities, or organizations.

The Muslim King of the Oval Office in Washington, D. C. will make all the efforts in his power to obtain a solid and permanent peace according to wishes of world Islam, with full and satisfactory securities that America will accord to Islamic sharia law. Barack Hussein Obama is faithful on the one part of the engagements which bind him to his Muslim belief; unjust and anti-upright on the other to his own subjects whom he ought to protect and guard against so many dangers. Full of humanity and compassion for other nations except republics, he is determined to pursue and prosecute American success as well as individual Americans who according to him suffer under the free-market economic system.

What I have here given serve to show the various endeavors and contrivances of the enemy Obama regime to draw Americans from their connections with conservative, market-oriented America, and to prevail on Americans to make a separate accommodation with socialism-communism, leaving America totally out of the question, and at the mercy of a merciless, unprincipled, unethical and evil socialist-communist-Muslim enemy. Likewise, the opinion that has been formed by WE the People that Barack Hussein Obama's character for meanness and perfidiousness is becoming more exactly the opinion of America. The criticism eventually contains American Patriots' statements and language; for Americans, however remote, who think alike, will unavoidably speak alike. WE see the insidious use which Barack Hussein Obama has endeavored to make of the propositions facing America under socialism-communism in the framework of the Islamic world unity, the *Umma*.

I could wish the enemedia at liberty to make use of all the information which I am sure they possess or have access to on Mr. Fraud, Barack Hussein Obama, but as there is a delicacy in the matter, the enemedia do not conceive it prudent, at least at present, to make references and quotations in the same manner as I have done with respect to Barack Hussein Obama. Those in the enemedia fear for their lives, the lives of their families, and the loss of their positions. Therefore, what comes from me on this part of the business, must rest on my own credit with the

182

public, assuring them that when the whole proceedings relative to the exposure of all aspects of Barack Hussein Obama's life shall appear, they will find my account and the in-depth accounts of my colleagues in Patriotism not only true, but studiously important for the future concerning the greatest fraud in history.

WE know at this time that the expectation of the usurped Oval Office and the thug regime ran high with respect to the conquest of America. Filled with these high ideas, nothing could be more insolent towards America than the language and lies spewing forth from Obama in his blasts of verbal diarrhea. America is to be left to Obama's mercy, if she does not heed the writing on the wall of future history.

On the other hand, American Patriots with open, noble, manly determination, and a fidelity of good, patriotic brother-and-sister allies, will hear no proposition for a future pardoning of Barack Hussein Obama's treason against America. We insist that the presidential eligibility clause of the *Constitution* should be fully and unequivocally pounded into the brain-dead POLDS again and again in the style of American patriotic language.

Since the initial days of the Obama regime beginning in 2009, a reverse of fortune has overtaken pro-Obama political thoughts in Washington, D. C. and all the high expectations of the Obama regime are now crashing to the ground. Political opponents have read the Obama regime a loud lesson of disgraceful misfortune and necessity has called on the Obama regime to change their ground, for they are now criticizing the economic programs they themselves initiated.

In this situation of confusion and despair the present Obama regime politics have no fixed character. It is now the hurricane months of lame-duck politics. Every day seems to have a storm of its own, and they are scudding under the bared poles of hope and change. Beaten, but not humble; condemned, but not penitent, the POLDS act like men and women trembling at fate and catching at a straw. From this convulsion, in the entrails of their politics, it is more than probable that the mountain groaning in labor will bring forth a mouse as to its size, and a monster in its make. They will try on America the same insidious arts socialists-communists have always tried in every country they have attempted to conquer.

WE the People sometimes experience sensations to which language is not equal. The conception is too bulky to be born alive and in the torture of thinking WE stand dumbfounded. OUR patriotic feelings, imprisoned by their magnitude, find no way out. In the struggle of expression every finger and both hands try to be a tongue. The machinery of the body seems too little for the mind and WE look about for help to show OUR thoughts. Such must be the sensation of America whenever Barack Hussein Obama, teeming with corruption, shall propose to Americans that they sacrifice their faith in Christianity, traditions, ethics, and constitutional law.

Exclusive of the wickedness there is a personal offence contained in every such attempt. It is calling American Patriots villains: for no man asks the other to act the villain unless he believes him inclined to be one. No man attempts to seduce the truly honest woman. They argue it is the supposed looseness of her mind that starts the thoughts of seduction, and he who offers it calls her a prostitute. OUR pride is always hurt by the same propositions which offend OUR principles; for when WE are shocked at the crime, WE are wounded by the suspicion of OUR compliance. Could I convey a thought that might serve to regulate the public mind, I would make the interests of the Founding Fathers the basis of defending America. All the world is moved by interest, and it affords them nothing to boast of. But I would go a step further and defend America on the ground of honor and principle. That America's public affairs have flourished under the guidance of the Founding Fathers; that it was wisely made and has been nobly executed; that by their principles and foresight WE are enabled to preserve OUR country from conquest, and expel those who seek OUR destruction; that it is OUR true interest to maintain it unimpaired; and that while WE do so no enemy can conquer US, are matters which experience has taught US, and the common good of OURSELVES, abstracted from principles of faith and honor, would lead US to maintain the connection to the Founding Fathers

Over and above the mere letter of the Founding Fathers' logic, WE have been nobly and generously treated, and have had the same respect and attention paid to US, as if WE had been an old established country. To

184

oblige and be obliged is fair work among humankind, and WE want an opportunity of showing to the world that WE are a people sensible of kindness and worthy of confidence without Barack Hussein Obama. Character is to US, in OUR present circumstances, of more importance than interest. The United States of America is a young nation upon the stage of public life, and the eye of the world is upon US to see how WE act with the elected, cowardly, criminal Barack Hussein Obama. WE have an enemy who is watching to destroy OUR reputation, and who will go to any length to gain some evidence against US that may serve to render OUR conduct suspect and OUR character odious. Could the Obama regime accomplish this, wicked as it is, the world would withdraw from America, as from a people not to be trusted, and America's task of being a bulwark of freedom would then become difficult. The present example is the hatred the Egyptian people have for Barack Hussein Obama and his regime for their support of the former President of Egypt: Mohammed Morsi and his Muslim Brotherhood.

There is nothing which sets the character of a nation in a higher or lower light with others than the faithfully fulfilling their oaths of office, or perfidiously breaking their oaths of office. Oaths of office are not to be tampered with. Should Barack Hussein Obama, which seems very probable, propose that oath-taking for public office be done away with, it would merit from American patriotism a mark of detestation. It is one of those extraordinary instances in which WE ought not to be contented with the bare negativeness of Congress, because it is an affront on the multitude as well as on the government. It goes on the supposition that the public are not honest men and women, and that they may be managed by contrivance, though they cannot be conquered by arms. Let the world and Barack Hussein Obama know that WE American Patriots are neither to be bought nor sold; that OUR mind is great and fixed; OUR prospect clear; and that WE will support OUR character as firmly as OUR independence.

The Obama regime supposes they have many friends in America and that when all chance of conquest is over, they will be able to support DemocRAT Party politics *ad infinitum*. Now, if I have any conception of the human heart, the Obama regime will fail in this more than in anything that they have yet tried. This is not a question of policy only, but of honor and honesty; and the proposition will have in it something so visibly low and base that their partisans, if they have any, will be ashamed of it. Men are often hurt by a mean action who are not startled at a wicked one, and this will be such a confession of inability, such a declaration of servile thinking that the scandal of it will ruin all their hopes.

Of course, it is not practical to throw shoes at Barack Hussein Obama whenever he appears in public. Yet, there is one resort that Patriotic Americans have in this regard. WE can erect Barack Hussein Obama scarecrows in back yards, driveways, and fields and throw shoes at the scarecrows! Inform the local news media of this patriotic act.

In short, WE the People, American Patriots all, have nothing to do but to go on with vigor and determination, because the enemy is still in control of OUR country.

Barack Hussein Obama! I envision that in the elections of 2014, and 2016, and in history ever thereafter, you will always be thumped with more than shoes!

★★★★★★★★★★★★★★

Frederick William Dame
Patriotic, Steadfast, and True
May 14, 2014

Frederick William Dame

The American Crisis

Learn A Lesson Of Morality

A Call To Take Action

Number Sixteen

★★★★★★★★★★★★

As a matter of morality it is the nature of compassion to associate with misfortune; and I address this to you in behalf of a former United States Army Lieutenant Colonel. His name is Terrence Lakin. He challenged the eligibility of Barack Hussein Obama to be the President of the United States of America according to Article II, Section I, Paragraph 5 of the *Constitution for the United States of America.* This clause states that a candidate for the presidency must be born in the United States of America to two American citizen parents. As an American Army officer he was unfortunately doomed to imprisonment in Fort Leavenworth, Kansas. He was sentenced to loss of rank and dismissal from the United States Army for a crime that Barack Hussein Obama originally committed because he is not a natural born citizen.

LTC Lakin's sentence is so extraordinary and the execution so repugnant to every human sensation that it ought never be told without the circumstances which produced it. The victim was found guilty for disobeying an order from the Commander-in-Chief concerning deployment to Afghanistan. LTC Lakin questioned the legality of the order because Barack Hussein Obama cannot prove that he is a natural born citizen and is, therefore, an illegal president whose orders have no legal ground. Furthermore, LTC Lakin was not allowed to introduce evidence on his behalf because according to the presiding military judge Colonel Denise Lind, such evidence would have embarrassed Obama. Ask: How deep into Obama has Colonel Denise Lind crawled? What an anti-American, anti- patriotic standpoint! LTC Lakin still lives on as a true American Patriot! In the hands of the next presidential administration rests LTC Lakin's official rehabilitation and reinstatement into the United States Army with all entitlements thereto. Indeed, there

187

are other military personnel whose heads have rolled because there are peacock generals willing to lose their spine of courage because they refused to uphold their oaths to the American *Constitution*. The spineless peacock generals have willfully guillotined military careers to satisfy Barack Hussein Obama's wishes. For example, Lt. Col. Matthew Dooley, a United States War College instructor who taught military students about radical Islam (All Islam is radical!), was relieved of his teaching duties and his career was cut short because the Pentagon was urged by a collective action of Islamic groups in America to cease such instruction. Although three Army Command Review Board Generals and two Colonels defended LTC Dooley's teachings, the Sharia-compliant four-star General Martin E. Dempsey and the Army Vice-Chief of Staff General Lloyd J. Austin III had LTC Dooley's name removed from the Command List, thus guillotining LTC Doolley's chances of promotion to Colonel and possible later general after 19 years of military service.

A United States military officer takes the following oath of office:
I, (name), do solemnly swear that I will support and defend the Constitution of (sic: for) the United States against all enemies, foreign and domestic; that I will bear true faith and allegiance to the same; that I take this obligation freely, without any mental reservation or purpose of evasion; and that I will well and faithfully discharge the duties of the office on which I am about to enter. So help me God. (Note: for proper syntax and legal meaning, *of* should never be stated because it is a possessive preposition and the *Constitution* does not belong to the United States of America. It comes from WE the People *for* the United States of America.)
This lifetime oath binds military officers to disobey any order that violates the *Constitution*. This oath should apply to Generals Dempsey and Austin as well, or do they consider themselves to be above oath-taking to uphold the *Constitution* and place their emphasis on crawling into Barack Hussein Obama where the sun does not shine? As of this writing there have been over one hundred dismissals in the five branches of the United States Armed Forces. They were abruptly fired or relieved of their command on trumped charges, or it was decided that they were not qualified to command. Yet, another reason has been the Barack Hussein Obama regime's statement that these officers had to be released from active duty because of budget cuts. Even an idiot can see through the ruse. Military officers have been forced out of their careers because

they disagreed with Obama's ideology or position that one day the United States military must take action against domestic terrorists: WE the People – WE American Patriots! This is nothing more than a calculated shrinkage of military officers who disagree with the usurper-in-chief. In the eyes of American Patriots they are all heroes.

Also as of this writing, the Barack Hussein Obama regime is implementing a new defense policy that can be described as cutting the military fighting capacity and masquerading it as the Obama military strategy. This consists of measures to reduce the American Armed Forces by 8 to 10 percent in 2016. This will be the lowest American fighting force level since before World War II. Obama will eliminate the complete fleet of Air Force A-10 jets. There are eleven aircraft carriers that will have their operations reduced or halted. The *USS George Washington* will be mothballed in 2016. Obama is downsizing and Russia, China, North Korea, and Al-Qaeda are increasing their military fighting capacities. Furthermore, the Obama regime is planning to strip three-star and four-star generals of their commands so that they would not have any authority to oversee the management of their bases. This would undoubtedly cause a disaster in day-to-day operations like repair, training, and military preparedness, which would surely please the anti-defense-of-America-genius-of-nothingness Barack Hussein Obama. Every American patriotic human breast is filled with such patriotic outrage that American Patriots are determined to eventually punish the present illegal president. Indeed, he should be prevented from issuing further illegal orders and signing illegal laws. Barack Hussein Obama must be delivered up as a traitor and should suffer the constitutional consequences. The first reflection which arises on this black business is what sort of men and women must Obama, his peacock generals, and his thugs be, and what sort of order and discipline do they preserve in the United States Army, when in the immediate place of their headquarters, and under the eye and nose of the American public the commander-in-chief can take a Lieutenant Colonel at pleasure from his duty position or teaching position, and the guillotining of his career be made a matter of sport? The history of the most savage leaders always produces instances exactly of this kind. They never have a formality in their punishments. With them it is the horridness of revenge, but with Barack Hussein Obama as putative commander-in-chief of the Army it is a still greater crime: the horridness of installing fear and setting an example to officers who take their oaths to uphold the *Constitution for the United States of America* seriously and patriotically follow these oaths. The Army peacock generals who have succeeded each other have all affected to speak in language to which they have no right because they have failed to keep their oaths. In their proclamations, their addresses, their letters, and their supplications they talk of military honor and credibility; indeed, of constitutional law. WE the People and WE American Patriots whose eyes are open and ears not plugged, who speak the same constitutional language as military lawyers, many of whom were born on the same spot as they, and who can no more be mistaken in military jargon than in military actions, can declare to all the world that there is not a more detestable character, nor a meaner or more barbarous enemy, than the present Barack Hussein Obama. You straw soldiers have forfeited all pretensions to reputation, and it is only by holding you like a wild beast, afraid of your keepers, that you can be made manageable.

I can think no man innocent who has lent his hand to destroy the United States of America and to ruin those that he could not enslave, yet, abstracted from all ideas of right and wrong on the original question, Barack Hussein Obama in the present case, is the guilty man. The villain and the victim are here separated characters. The DemocRATS hold the one and WE the People hold the other. The DemocRATS disown, or affect to disown and reprobate the conduct of LTCs Lakin and Dooley. The DemocRATS give Barack Hussein Obama a sanctuary, and by so doing the DemocRATS effectually become the executioners of constitutionally responsible military officers, as if the DemocRATS had placed these officers' heads under a guillotine and dismissed them from the world. Whatever DemocRATS' and POLDS' feelings on this interesting occasion may be are best known to themselves. Within the graves of their own minds lies buried the fate of lifetime military oaths to the *Constitution for the United States of America*. Those who have elected allegiance to Barack Hussein Obama have killed their own oaths of office. These dead oaths become the corpses of DemocRATS' and POLDS' will, or the survivor of DemocRATS' and POLDS' injustice. Deliver up the one, and you ensure fright in the other. Keep those in fright to pay allegiance to Barack Hussein Obama and the others will die by choice. The case is exceedingly plain: officers have been taken from their careers and their patriotic services to the United States of America have been guillotined and the official killer is at the head of the chain of command. The saying goes that *the fish stinks from the head down*. This fish named Barack Hussein Obama *shines and stinks like rotten mackerel by moonlight*. Barack Hussein Obama is guilty of a thousand instances of cruelty, but they have been rendered equivocal, and sheltered from personal detection. Despite the propaganda of the enemedia, the crime is fixed. It is one of those extraordinary cases which can neither be denied nor palliated, and to which not even the custom of war applies; for it never could be supposed that such a brutal outrage against officers of the United States Army would ever be committed. It is an original in the history of civilized barbarians, and is truly Obamaesque. Yes, there are those who do lip service to Zero's derrière! WE American Patriots can have no idea of their honor, or their justice in any future transaction, of what nature it may be, while they shelter an outrageous criminal, and sacrifice respectable officers. If Barack Hussein Obama has no regard for WE the People, he should at least spare the blood which it is his duty to save. Whether the punishment will be greater on him, is, in the nicety of sensation, an undecided question! It rests with Congress to prevent the sufferings of more military officers. Congress has nothing to do but to impeach and try Barack Hussein Obama for treason and the matter ends. But to protect Barack Hussein Obama, be he who he may or may not, is to patronize his crimes. To trifle them off by frivolous and unmeaning inquiries is to promote them. There is only one declaration Congress can make. There is no promise Congress can give that will obtain credit. It is the man Barack Hussein Obama and not any clemency that is demanded.

DemocRATS and POLDS see themselves pressed on all sides to spare the life of Barack Hussein Obama, for to be executed he must if justice is done. The dismissal of highly decorated Army officers and further Obama crimes are offences not to be borne with, and there is no security which WE the People can have that such actions or similar ones shall not be repeated within the next two years, but by making the punishment of impeachment and treason fall upon Barack Hussein Obama. To destroy the last security of military officers and their oaths of office and to take the constitutional patriot and pass judgment with sportive career guillotining, is carrying barbarity too high for silence. Evil Barack Hussein Obama must be put to an end. The choice of representative persons rests with WE the People. But if the DemocRAT and POLD attachment to the person guilty of treason is stronger than to the innocent, then the DemocRATS and the POLDS have invented a crime that must destroy what character they have left. If the cause of your king needs to be so supported, forever cease to torture our remembrance with the wretched phrases of Obama honor, Obama generosity, and Obama clemency. The task before DemocRATS, POLDS and Republicans In Name Only (RINOS), though painful to them, is not difficult. Give up the criminal, and rehabilitate your military officers as the first outset of a necessary military reformation.

The POLDS are men and women whom predecessors in the DemocRAT Party have instructed in wickedness, the better to fit them to their master Obama's purpose. To make them useful, they have been made vile, and the consequence of their tutored villainy is now descending on the heads of their encouragers. They have been trained like hounds to the scent of blood, and cherished in every species of dissolute barbarity. Their ideas of right and wrong are worn away in the constant habitude of repeated infamy, till, like men practised in execution, they feel not the value of another's life. Likewise, it is their feeling towards a military officer's reputation and a patriotic concern for the United States of America!

DemocRATS and POLDS! Learn a lesson of morality from this melancholy, anti-American circumstance!

Frederick William Dame
Patriotic, Steadfast, and True
May 16, 2014.

Frederick William Dame

The American Crisis

The Limits Of The Tyrant

A Call To Take Action

Number Seventeen

A tyrant is an oppressive, despotic ruler who exercises governing power in a cruel, harsh manner over his subjects without paying regard to any constitutional or ethical restrictions. The term **tyrant** comes from the pre-Greek loanword Τύραννος *Týrannos* meaning *lord, master, sovereign*, which transferred into the Latin *tyrannus*, meaning *lord, master*. By 1300 it was spelled *tyraunt* and meant *absolute ruler*. The original Greek description of a **tyrant** was *a person who illegally claimed the control over the state* and *one who sets his will over and above that of the citizens of the state in a thuggish, violent manner*. There is no Indo-European word root of **tyrant**.

However, there are strong indications with probability bordering on certainty that the term **tyrant** has its roots in an Edenic language, i.e., it even pre-dates ancient Hebrew, or Semitic languages. It possibly and likely relates to the Edenic *RaDaH*, meaning *to take out, remove* – as used in *Judges14:9*: "... but he told not them he had taken honey (out) of the carcass of the lion." The same verb *RaDaH* appears in *Genesis1:26*. God charges man *to rule* and "*have dominion over* the fish of the sea", in the sense of domineering with the privilege of *raiding*. God allowed man to *raid*, *ride* (tyrannize, control) the seven seas to root out the inhabitants of the deep. In *Deuteronomy 20:20* there is another use of RaDaH when a war is waged upon a city "until it be subdued" and the enemy is routed. The Edenic [A]ReeYT(S) becomes **tyrant** by reversing the YT to obtain TYR[A](NT). Such reversals with omissions and additions are common in the constructional development of words in languages. The Edenic ROADahN is also a **tyrant** or **dictator**. The meaning of *tyrant* in Greek simply combines *being a sovereign with usurping*. This appears in the Nordic TYR, the Norse god of victory. Related to Barack Hussein

193

Obama the term **tyrant** tells exactly what Barack Hussein Obama is: *a sovereign who achieves control by usurpation and reduces his enemy until they are routed (out).*

Barack Hussein Obama! You are a tyrant! Yet, whether you accept it or not, there are limitations to you and your tyranny! Tyrant Obama's speeches that have been reprinted in several newspapers of the enemedia apparently contain expressions and opinions so new to Americans and so special, and are so enveloped in mysterious reasoning, that I address this publication concerning tyrant Barack Hussein Obama for the purpose of giving a free and candid examination. The tyrant's speeches are lies that show the spectrum of the tyrant's machinations against WE the People.

The tyrant in America is guilty of inconsistency. To clear himself of this guilt, Barack Hussein Obama asserts that he still holds the same principles respective American independence which he at first imbibed. But then tyrant Obama vomited out the principles of hope and change to socialism-communism. WE American Patriots are of the opinion that whenever Barack Hussein Obama is acknowledged in any manner, the sun of America's glory is set forever! Such are the sentiments WE the People possessed in a former time in 1776 and such are the sentiments WE continue to hold at this hour. It is the opinion of a multitude of American Patriots, as well as many able statesmen from foreign countries. As the majority of the American Patriots support this opinion, you, Barack Hussein Obama have somewhat acquiesced, dissenting from the idea of your infallibility. Thus, the point of your being a tyrant is settled for bringing the matter into the full discussion of Congress with the special investigative committee on Benghazi chaired by Representative Trey Gowdy (R-SC), where you will be candidly, fairly, and impartially investigated and debated ... as long as the DemocRAT members behave themselves properly and accept the truthful results of the investigations, and the enemedia does not spin the truthful outcome of the investigation according to their liking.

The independence of America from the tyrant Obama is at stake. Such independence would be the ruin of DemocRATS and their accommodations with their tyrant. It will be the end of giving the enemy the means of trampling on America. The sun of America's glory Obama wishes to see set forever. He is always looking for a spark which might in

194

time light US up to a new day so that he can extinguish it immediately. If American independence is maintained, if Congress deems that measure prudent, Obama will see in his own mind that his regime will be undone. He wishes to Satan that he will not be investigated by Congress, that he might plead the cause of his hope and change socialism-communism, and that he might exercise whatever powers he possesses as a ridiculous orator, to save both himself and his belief in a conviction to Allah, that, if fate was signed, America would be gone forever.

Domestic peace, the tyrant says, is a desirable object, but it must be a peace under his conditions, even if it is a humiliating one. Mr. Tyrant maintains that under previous American leaders who held his position that his American kingdom was not in a flourishing state, it was impoverished by false economic politics. Well, Mr. Zero, Americans were not exceedingly rich, but they were free and independent to pursue their dreams as they saw fit. Successful dreams were not the result of socialism-communism! They never will be! If successful dreams in America do not become reality, that is probably because the DemocRATS have always placed illogical, economic roadblocks in their ways. If WE the People are straitened in our finances, the enemy Obama regime will be exhausted in their resources.

America is a great nation without Barack Hussein Obama. It abounds with brave men and women who are able and willing to fight in a common cause. The tyrant Zero claims he is neither afraid nor ashamed of those expressions humiliating America and American Patriots. He maintains there are numbers, great numbers there, who are of the same way of thinking with respect to America needing to be humiliated, and who, with his lordship, perceive ruin and independence to be linked together. The language of humiliation is not the language of America. It is the language of Barack Hussein Obama and his minions. Barack Hussein Obama is a total stranger to the mind and sentiments of America. Barack Hussein Obama has wrapped himself up in fond delusion that nothing other than socialism-communism may, under his tyranny, be accepted; and he wishes himself sent to Hell to receive support for the most extraordinary of all doctrines, which is that America, the most sublime of all human conditions, is really the loss of liberty.

195

In answer to which WE the People may say that in order to know what the contrary word *dependence* means, WE have only to look back to those years of severe humiliation, before the War for Independence when the mildest of all petitions could obtain no other notice than the haughtiest of all insults; and when the base terms of unconditional submission were demanded, or undistinguishable destruction threatened. It is nothing to US that the rogues have been changed, for they may be changed again. The guilt of the Obama regime is the crime of a whole country full of DemocRATS; and the nation that can, though but for a moment, think and act as Barack Hussein Obama wishes, can never afterwards be believed or trusted.

There are cases in which it is as impossible to restore character to life, as it is to recover the dead. It is a phoenix that can expire but once, and from whose ashes there is no resurrection. Some offences are of such a slight composition that they reach no further than the temper and are created or cured by a thought. But the sin of Barack Hussein Obama has struck the heart of America and nature has not left it in OUR power to say WE can forgive. Tyrant Barack Hussein Obama wishes for an opportunity to plead before the enemedia the cause of his hope and change and the cause of the DemocRATS, and to save both from ruin.

That the regime that for too many years has sought America's destruction should now cringe to solicit OUR support, is adding the wretchedness of disgrace to the misery of disappointment; and if Barack Hussein Obama has the least spark of supposed honor left (If he ever had any!), that spark must be darkened by asking, and extinguished by receiving, the smallest favor from America; for the criminal who owes his life to the grace and mercy of the injured is more executed by living, than he who dies.

But a thousand pleadings, even from the tyrant Obama, can have no effect. Honor, interest, and every sensation of the heart, would plead against him. WE are a people who think not as the tyrant thinks; and what is equally true, the tyrant cannot feel as WE feel. The situations of these two beings are exceedingly different. OURS has been the seat of Patriotism; yours has seen nothing of it. The most wanton destruction has been committed in OUR sight; the most insolent barbarity has been acted on OUR feelings. WE can look round and see the remains of what happens when the tyrant throws people under bus and destroys careers, once the fair fruit of hard industry, and now the striking monuments of Obama's brutality. In every part of America WE walk over the dead whom we loved and remember by whom they fell. There is scarcely a village but brings to life some melancholy thought and reminds US of what we have suffered, and of those we have lost by the inhumanity of Barack Hussein Obama's illegality. A thousand images arise to US, which, from situation, tyrant Obama cannot see, and are accompanied by as many ideas which tyrant Obama cannot know; and therefore tyrant Obama's supposed system of reasoning would apply to nothing, and all of tyrant Obama's expectations die of themselves.

The question whether tyrant Barack Hussein Obama shall accede to the freedoms of America free from socialism-communism is a moot question. It scarcely needs a debate. Obama's wish to debate the future of American freedoms has no object except to placate. The sun of America will set whenever she acknowledges she is a socialist-communist nation, whereas the metaphor would be strictly just to leave the sun wholly out of the figure, and to ascribe America not acknowledging it to the influence of the moon, like Muslims with their lunatic Islam do.

But the expression, if true, is the greatest confession of disgrace that could be made, and furnishes America with the highest notions of sovereign, independent importance. Relinquish America to socialism-communism says Barack Hussein Obama. Well, what is it but to desire a giant to shrink spontaneously into a dwarf?

Those people who call themselves DemocRATS are of so little internal consequence that when America is gone, or shuts her eyes, their sun is set and they can shine no more. They will grope about in obscurity and contract into insignificant animals. America is still the giant of freedom and Obama only her dwarf in waiting! Is the case so strangely altered that those thugs and regime who once thought WE the People could not live without them, are now brought to declare that they can exist without former America? Will they tell to the world, and that from their first politicians of state, that America is their all in all; that it is by her importance only that they can live, and breathe, and have a being? Will they, who long since threatened to bring America to their feet, bow themselves to OURS, and own that without US they are not important? Are they become so unqualified to debate on independence that they have lost all idea of it themselves, and are calling to the rocks and mountains of America to cover their insignificance? Or, if America is lost, is it manly to sob over it like a child for its rattle, and invite the laughter of the world by declarations of disgrace? Surely, a more consistent line of conduct to the cancerous curse that is Barack Hussein Obama is to bear it without formal complaint; and to show that America without them can preserve her independence and obtain a suitable rank with other powers. Barack Hussein Obama, you were not contented while you had America. Your weeping as a result of your failures is childish!

Barack Hussein Obama still thinks something may yet be done. What that something is, or how it is to be accomplished, is a matter in obscurity. For the United States of America there is no Obama hope and change. The experience of nearly seven years, with the expense of trillions of dollars and the loss of respect must positively decide that point. Americans have lost their interest in Barack Hussein Obama with the disaffected. Every part of it has been tried. There is no new scene left for delusion: and the thousands who have been ruined by adhering to Barack Hussein Obama's policies have now become bankrupt and/or unemployed. They are conveyed like transports to cultivate the armchairs of doing nothingness and it has put an end to all further expectations of employment.

If you cast your eyes on the people of America, what have they to console themselves with for the billions or trillions expended? Or, what encouragement is there left to continue throwing good money after bad? What more evilness can WE the People expect from the tyrant? Are not the tyranny of the Affordable Care Act and its tyrannical ramifications on Americans and the American economy enough? Because of these reasons alone America can carry on the patriotic, domestic war against Barack Hussein Obama and his tyranny for years longer, and all the charges of government included for less than Barack Hussein Obama can defray the charges of domestic war and government for one year.

I, who know Barack Hussein Obama's non-positive character, know well that the people of America can afford to pay their share of the expense much better than the social dregs that follow Obama. Besides, it is OUR own estates and property, OUR own rights, liberties, and government that WE are defending; and were WE not to do it, WE would deserve to lose

198

all, and none would pity US. The fault would be OUR own and OUR punishment just.

The Obama regime in America cares not how long the domestic war lasts. They enjoy an easy and indolent life. They fatten on the political folly of the brain-dead Americans and the spoils of The One; and, between their plunder and their prey, may go home rich. But the case is very different with the laboring farmer, the working tradesman, and the necessitous poor in America, the sweat of whose brows goes day after day to feed, in prodigality and sloth, the regime that is robbing both them and US. Removed from the eye of the multitude that supports them and distant from the WE the People who employ them, they cut and carve for themselves, and there is none to call them to account.

The eventual truth, says the Obama regime, is that America will be ruined if America is free from socialism-communism. I say that the Obama regime is already ruined for America is already independent. If Obama will not comprehend this, he immediately denies the fact which he infers. Besides, to make America the mere creature of the Obama regime is paying too great a compliment to himself and too little a regard to WE the People.

But the declaration of hope and change is a rhapsody of inconsistency. For to say that the domestic war against America is ruinous, and yet to continue the prosecution of that ruinous domestic war for the purpose of avoiding ruin, is a language which cannot be understood. Neither is it possible to see how the continued independence of America is to accomplish the ruin of America after the domestic war is over. America can always be more independent and at the same time a great opponent to liberal, progressive, anti-humane politics hereafter than she now is. Obama and his fools will certainly derive fewer advantages than at present. Why then is ruin to follow in the best state of the case, and not in the worst? And if not in the worst, why is it to follow at all?

That a nation is to be ruined by Barack Hussein Obama with his hope and change to socialism-communism peace and billions-a-year more expenses than before, is the tyrant's doctrine in politics. WE have heard much clamor of national savings and economy; but surely the true economy would be to dispense with the whole charge of a silly, foolish, and headstrong regime; because, compared with this, all other retrenchments are baubles and trifles.

Is it possible that Barack Hussein Obama can be serious in supposing that the best advantage can be obtained by socialism-communism, or that any advantage can be equal to the expense or the danger of attempting it? Will not the capture of one free, independent American after another satisfy him? Must all become prisoners? Must America ever be the sport of hope and change and the victim of delusion? The United States of America is in the middle of the greatest delusion ever played upon the world. The patriotic hope for America will never fail.

At another time OUR will was to revolt. A General named George Washington commanded the revolution of moral right over immoral wrong. In General Washington's time 20,000 Russians and 20 Russian ships of the line were to come and fight for Great Britain. This did not happen and the Russian Empress, Catherine the Great, was abused without mercy or decency by Great Britain. Then the Emperor of Germany was to be bribed with a million of money, and the King of Prussia was to do wonderful things. At one time it was, Lo here! and then it was, Lo there! Sometimes this power is, and sometimes that power was to engage against American Patriots in the Revolutionary War, just as if the whole world was mad and foolish like Barack Hussein Obama is today. Thus, from year to year, has every straw been plucked at, and every will-with-a-wisp led them a new dance. Now Barack Hussein Obama is forced to dance to the dissonance of his own anti-American political music.

This year a still newer folly is to take place. Barack Hussein Obama wishes to let open the flood gates of illegal immigration: the king of illegal immigrants would be an illegal king with illegal subjects ... and he thinks that something more can be done! Are not the repeated declarations of American Patriots, which all Americans in their right minds support, that they will not even hear any proposals whatever until the unconditional and unequivocal freedom from tyranny political fact? Are not, I say, these declarations answer enough?

For the Obama regime to receive anything from Americans now after so many insults, injuries, and outrages have been acted towards US, would show such a spirit of dumbness in them, that WE the People could not but despise them for offering anything. It would be the greatest disgrace they could do to offer it. The Obama regime would appear as it is: a wretch indeed, at this time of day, to ask or owe anything to the bounty of America. Has not the name of America blots enough upon it without inventing more? Even Lucifer would scorn to reign in heaven by permission, and yet illegal immigrants can creep on their knees to the ever-feeling tyrant for an entrance into America and receive it at no restrictions. Has this land of liberty so many charms, that to be a doorkeeper in it is better than to be an American Patriot?

But more can be expected from Barack Hussein Obama. If obtained, what can it amount to but new disgraces, contentions, and quarrels? The people of America have for years accustomed themselves to think and speak so freely and contemptuously of the Barack Hussein Obama regime, and the inveteracy is so deeply rooted, that a person invested with any authority from the regime, and attempting to exercise it, should have the life of a toad under a harrow. Americans should look on that thug as an interloper, to whom their compassion would never be permitted a residence. He should be no more than the Mungo of a farce; and if he disliked that, he must set off. Emphatically, it should be a station of degradation, perhaps debased by OUR pity, and despised by OUR pride, and should place the tyrant Obama in a more contemptible situation than any he has yet been in. WE have too high an opinion of OURSELVES even to think of yielding again the least obedience to outlandish authority; and for a thousand reasons, America will be the last country in the world to yield to it. The Obama regime has been treacherous! WE know it! Its character is gone and WE will see the funeral!

Surely Barack Hussein Obama loves to fish in troubled waters and drink the cup of contention, or he would not now think of mingling his socialism-communism affairs with those of America. It would be like a foolish dotard taking to his arms the bride that despises him, or who perhaps already does and has placed on his head the ensigns of her disgust! It is kissing the hand that boxes his ears and proposing to renew the exchange. The thought is as servile as the domestic war is wicked and shows the last scene of the drama to be as inconsistent as the first.

As America is gone from Barack Hussein Obama and the DemocRATS, the only act of manhood is to let her go. Obama's tyranny had a large hand in the separation from independence in America to hope and change socialism-communism. Barack Hussein Obama will gain no honor by temporising politics. Besides, there is something so exceedingly whimsical, unsteady, and even insincere in the present conduct of Obama that he exhibits himself in the most dishonorable colors. American Patriots should have no direct communications with Barack Hussein Obama or his regime thugs. Ignore them with the positive actions of Patriotism!

Now, taking Obama's present measures into view and comparing them with his lies, pray what is the word of this tyrant, or his regime thugs, or the DemocRATS good for? Must WE not look upon them as a confederated body of faithless, treacherous men and women, whose assurances are fraud, and their language deceit? What opinion can WE possibly form of them, but that they are a lost, abandoned, profligate trash of humanity, who sport even with their own character, and are to be held by nothing but the patriotic firearms or the halter? To say, after this, that the sun of America will be set is not to acknowledge the independence of America, when the not doing it is the unqualified lie of the tyrant government and can be no other than the language of ridicule, the jargon of inconsistency. There were thousands in America who predicted the Barack-Hussein-Obama delusion and looked upon it as a trick of treachery to take US from OUR guard, and draw off OUR attention from the only system of financial market ideology by which WE can be called, or deserve to be called, a sovereign, independent people. Obama thought the fraud on the tyrant's part might be worth attempting. The sacrifice of WE the People to obtain freedom from tyranny is never too high. There are others who credited the assurance, because they thought it impossible that men and women who had their characters to establish, would begin with a lie.

The prosecution of the domestic war is savage and horrid; since which it has been mean, trickish, and delusive. The one went greedily into the passion of revenge, the other into the subtleties of low contrivance; till, between the crimes of both, there is scarcely left a patriotic man or woman in America, be they white, black, red, or yellow who does not despise or detest the tyrannical conduct of Barack Hussein Obama. The management of Barack Hussein Obama, whatever may be his views, is a caution to WE the People, and must be to the world, never to regard Obama's assurances. A perfidy so notorious cannot be hidden. It stands even in the public papers with his tyrannical proclamations that are not to be believed; that the spirit of lying is the governing principle of his person and his regime's politics. It is holding up the character of valued public offices to public infamy, and warning all men and women not to credit them. Such are the consequences which Obama's mismanagement has brought upon the United States of America.

The limits of your tyranny, Barack Hussein Obama are of two kinds. The first consists of limiting you by assassination, or capture and disposal via the Chicago concrete block style. The second consists of the constitutional measures: impeachment and trial for treason with the complete execution of the punishments according to the laws of the *Constitution for the United States of America*. The first method is illegal, although logical and ethical arguments for the assassination of a tyrant of the caliber Adolf Hitler, Josef Stalin, and Barack Hussein Obama can be termed a last-resort, patriotic action. The second method is fully legal.

WE the People, We American Patriots are your ultimate limit. Frederick Douglass once said profoundly that "The limits of tyrants are presented by the endurance of those whom they oppose." WE the People, WE American Patriots oppose you and are fed up with enduring you!

★★★★★★★★★★★★★★

Frederick William Dame
Patriotic, Steadfast, and True
May 22, 2014

Frederick William Dame

The American Crisis

Tyranny, Like Hell, Is Not Easily Conquered

A Call To Take Action

Number Eighteen

Since January 20, 2009, Americans have gone through hell under Barack Hussein Obama. When the present American Crisis comes to an end with the defeat of the DemocRATS in 2014, the impeachment of the tyrant Barack Hussein Obama and his trial for treason, and hopefully the defeat of the DemocRATS in the election of 2016, WE the People will truly learn what fetters have bound US since January 20, 2009.

With the surrender of the British Army under the command of General Charles Cornwallis to General George Washington, commander of the American Revolutionary Army, at Yorktown, Virginia on October 18, 1781, the times that tried men's souls for more than five years were over and the greatest and most complete revolution the world ever knew, gloriously and happily accomplished. Under the tyrannical regime of Barack Hussein Obama, America is in its second times that try men's souls. Sadly enough, there is no general in sight to defeat him. Therefore, it is the responsibility of WE the People, American Patriots all, and the few patriotic supporters in the United States Congress to defeat Barack Hussein Obama. Yet, Barack Hussein Obama's tentacle tyranny, like Hell, is not to be easily conquered.

To pass in the 1770s and 1780s from the extremes of danger to safety, from the tumult of war to the tranquility of peace, though sweet in contemplation, required a gradual composure of the senses to receive it. This is also the present situation. The same atmosphere will come upon the United States of America when Barack Hussein Obama and the DemocRATS are ousted from political power. Happiness will immediately ensue!

Even calmness has the power of stunning when it opens too instantly upon us. The long and raging hurricane that should cease in a moment would leave us in a condition rather of wonder than enjoyment; and some moments of recollection must pass before we could be capable of tasting the felicity of repose. There are but few instances in which the mind is fitted for sudden transitions. It takes in its pleasures by reflection and comparison and those must have time to act before the relish for new scenes is complete.

In the present case, the mighty magnitude of the object, the various uncertainties of fate it has undergone, the numerous and complicated dangers WE the People have suffered or escaped, the eminence WE now stand on, and the vast prospect before US, must all conspire to impress US with contemplation.

To see it in OUR power to make a world happy; to teach mankind the art of being so; to exhibit, on the theatre of the universe a rebirth of American character hitherto unknown; and to have, as it were, a new creation entrusted to OUR hands, are honors that command reflection and can neither be too highly estimated, nor too gratefully received. In this pause of recollection while the storm is ceasing, and the long agitated mind vibrating to a rest, let us look back on the scenes we have passed, and learn from experience what is yet to be done.

Never, I say, had a country so many openings to happiness as the United States of America. This nation's setting out in life, like the rising of a fair morning, was unclouded and promising. Her cause was good. Her principles just and liberal. Her temper serene and firm. Her conduct regulated by the nicest steps, and everything about her wore the mark of honor. It is not every country – perhaps there is not another in the world – that can boast so fair an origin. The first settlements of America corresponded with the character of the American Revolution. The present settlements, many of them controlled over generations by DemocRATS, have so far not repeated that colonial character. Nevertheless, America need never be ashamed to tell her birth, nor relate the stages by which she rose to greatness.

Rome, once the mistress of the universe, was originally a band of ruffians. Plunder and rapine made her rich, and her oppression of millions was the foundation of the empire. The Barack Hussein Obama regime is the Rome of today's American world.

The remembrance of what is past, if it operates rightly, must inspire America with the most laudable of all ambition: that of adding to the fair fame with which she began. The world has seen America great in adversity; struggling, without a thought of yielding, beneath accumulated difficulties, bravely, nay proudly, encountering distress, and rising in resolution as the Obama storm increased. All this is justly due to America, for her fortitude has merited her character. Let the world see that once again after Barack Hussein Obama America can produce and bear prosperity, and that her honest virtue in time of peace is equal to the bravest virtue in time of war.

The United States of America should begin a descending to the scenes of quiet and non-government-regulated domestic life. Not beneath the cypress shade of disappointment, but to enjoy in her own land, and under her own vine, the sweetness of her labors, and solving the evilness of government handouts. This will be the reward of her toil in building up America after the demise of Barack Hussein Obama and the DemocRATS. In this situation, may America never forget that a fair, national reputation is of as much importance as is independence; that this nation once again possesses a charm that wins upon the world and makes even enemies civil; that this nation once again gives a dignity which is often superior to power, and commands reverence where pomp and splendor fail.

It would be a circumstance ever to be lamented and never to be forgotten were a single blot, from any cause whatever, suffered to fall on this modern revolution, which to the end of time must be an honor to the age that accomplished it; and which will contribute more to enlighten the world, and diffuse a spirit of freedom and liberality among mankind, than any human event – if this may be called one – that ever preceded it.

It is not among the least of the calamities of a long-continued domestic war that it unhinges the mind from those nice sensations which at other times appear so amiable. The continual spectacle of woe blunts the finer feelings, and the necessity of bearing with the sight renders it familiar. In like manner, are many of the moral obligations of society weakened, till the custom of acting by necessity becomes an apology, where it is truly a crime. Yet, let but a nation conceive anew rightly of its character, and it will be chastely just in protecting it. None ever began with a fairer opportunity than a reborn America and none can be under a greater obligation to preserve it.

The debt which America will have contracted, compared with the cause she has gained, and the advantages to flow from it, ought scarcely to be mentioned. She has it in her choice to do and to live as happily as she pleases after Barack Hussein Obama. The world is in her hands once again. She will have no foreign power to influence her commerce, no usurper to perplex her legislation or control her prosperity. After Obama the struggle is over, which must one day have happened, and, perhaps, never could have happened at a better time. Instead of a domineering master, she will have gained exemplary greatness, and universal acclaim. A new America will exist!

With the blessings of peace, independence, and a universal commerce, the states, individually and collectively, will have leisure and opportunity to regulate and establish their domestic concerns, and to put it beyond the power of calumny to throw the least reflection on their honor. Character is much easier kept than recovered, and that man and woman if any such there be, who, from sinister views, or littleness of soul, lends unseen their hand to injure it, contrives a wound it will never be in their power to heal.

As we have established a new inheritance for posterity, let that inheritance descend with every mark of an honorable conveyance. The little it will cost, compared with the worth of the states, the greatness of the object, and the value of the national character, will be a profitable exchange.

That which must more forcibly strike a thoughtful, penetrating mind, and which includes and renders easy all inferior concerns, is the union of the states against a brutal tyrant and a socialist-communist. On this standpoint OUR great national character depends. It is this which must give US importance abroad and security at home. It is through this only that WE the People are, or can be, nationally highly regarded in the world; it is the determination, power, and exceptionalism of the United States of America that renders OUR ships and commerce safe on the seas, or in a foreign port. OUR passes must be obtained under the same style. All OUR treaties, whether of alliance, peace, or commerce, are formed under the sovereignty of the United States of America, not the United Nations of America or the Muslim States of America. Europe, the world, and Islam know OUR nation by no other name or title.

The division of the nation into states was and is for our own convenience. Abroad this distinction ceases. The affairs of each state are local. They can go no further than to each state. Were the whole worth of even the richest of them expended in revenue, it would not be sufficient to support sovereignty against a foreign attack. In short, WE the People have no other national sovereignty than the United States of America only. It would even be fatal for US if WE had, too expensive to be maintained, and impossible to be supported. Individuals, or individual states, may call themselves what they please; but the world, and especially the world of enemies, is not to be held in awe by the whistling of a name. Sovereignty must have power to protect all the parts that compose and constitute it. As the United States of America, responsible to no other organization, WE are equal to the importance of the title, but otherwise WE are not. OUR union, well and wisely regulated and cemented, is the cheapest way of being great, the easiest way of being continuously powerful, and the happiest invention in government of which the circumstances of America can admit, because it collects from each state, that which, by being inadequate, can be of no use to it, and forms an aggregate that serves for all.

For example, the states of the European Community are an unfortunate instance of the effects of individual sovereignty. Their disjointed condition exposes them to numerous intrigues, losses, calamities, and enemies; and the almost impossibility of bringing their measures to a decision, and that decision into execution, is to them, and would be to Americans, a source of endless misfortune.

It is with federated states as with individuals in society; something must be yielded up to make the whole secure. In this view of things WE the People gain by what WE give, and draw an annual interest greater than the capital.

I ever feel myself hurt when I hear the United States of America, that great palladium of our liberty and safety, the least irreverently spoken of. It is the most sacred aspect in the *Constitution for the United States of America*, and that which every man and woman should be most proud and tender of. OUR citizenship in the United States is OUR national character. OUR citizenship in any particular state is only OUR local distinction. By the latter WE are known at home, by the former to the world. OUR great title is **Americans**, legal citizens!

So far as my endeavors could go, they have all been directed to conciliate the affections, unite the interests, and draw and keep the mind of the nation together. The better to assist in this foundation work of the new revolution, I have avoided all places of profit or office, either in the state I live in, or in the United States; kept myself at a distance from all parties and party connections, and even disregarded all private and inferior concerns. When WE Patriots take into view the great work which WE have gone through and will continue, and feel, as WE ought to feel, the just importance of it, WE shall then see that the little wranglings and indecent contentions of personal parley are as dishonorable to OUR characters as they are injurious to OUR repose. The truth caries no injury because it sets US free!

It was the threat of the cancerous tyranny of Barack Hussein Obama and the DemocRATS that made me an author for political action. For those who have supported me, I thank them for their patriotic act. The force with which it struck my mind and the dangerous condition the country appeared to me in, by courting an impossible and an unnatural reconciliation with those who were determined to reduce her, instead of striking out into the only line that could cement and save her, a renewal, reassertion and legalization of the *Declaration of Independence*, made it impossible for me, feeling as I did, to be silent: and if, in the course of the past years I have rendered America any service, I have, I hope, likewise added something to the reputation of literature, by freely and disinterestedly employing it in the great cause of mankind, and showing that there may be genius in patriotism without prostitution.

Independence always appears to me practicable and probable, provided the sentiment of the country can be formed and held to the object. There is no instance in the world where a people so extended and wedded to former habits of thinking, and under such a variety of circumstances, are so instantly and effectually pervaded by a turn in politics, as in the case of independence from Barack Hussein Obama and the DemocRATS. The large portion of Americans support this opinion and will continue undiminished through such a succession of good and ill fortune till it is crowned with success.

That the present, patriotic revolution began at the exact period of time best fitted to the purpose, is sufficiently proved by the event. But the great hinge on which the whole machine turns, is the continuation of the United States of America as a federal structure in a free market economy.

Originally, in the Revolutionary War, this union was naturally produced by the inability of any one Colony to support itself against any foreign enemy without the assistance of the rest. Had the present individual states severally been less able than they were when the domestic war began, their united strength would not have been equal to the undertaking, and they must in all human probability have failed. On the other hand, had they severally been more able, they might not have seen, or, what is more, might not have felt, the necessity of uniting against Barack Hussein Obama and the DemocRATS, and, either by attempting to stand alone or in small confederacies, would have been separately defeated.

Now, as WE the People cannot see a future time (and many years must pass away before it can arrive) when the strength of any one state, or several united, can be equal to the whole of the present United States, and as WE have seen the extreme difficulty of collectively prosecuting the domestic war against Barack Hussein Obama to a successful issue, and preserving OUR national importance in the world, therefore, from the experience WE have had, and the knowledge WE have gained, WE must, unless WE make a waste of wisdom, be strongly impressed with the advantage, as well as the necessity of strengthening that happy union which has been OUR salvation, and without which WE would have become a ruined people.

I have never met with a man or woman who has confessed it as their opinion that a separation of the United States of America from its traditions and Judeo-Christian ethics would take place one time or other. There is no instance in which we have shown less judgment, than in endeavoring to describe what we call the ripeness or fitness of the nation for its continued independence based on the principles of Judeo-Christian teachings and traditions.

As all men and women allow the measure, and differ only in their opinion of the time, let US, in order to remove mistakes, take a general survey of things, and endeavor, if possible, to find out the very time. WE all must become revolters against socialism-communism hope and change. But we need not to go far. The inquiry ceases at once. The time has found us. There is general concurrence. The glorious union of all things proves the fact. It is not in numbers, but in a union, that our great strength lies. The nation is just arrived at that pitch of strength in which no single state is able to support itself, and the whole, when united, can accomplish the matter without Barack Hussein Obama, the anti-patriotic DemocRATS, and their pseudo hope and change. Accomplishing less than this would be fatal in its effects and consequently prove the statement by America's patriot par excellence, Thomas Paine: *Tyranny, like Hell, is not easily conquered.*

Frederick William Dame
Patriotic, Steadfast, and True
May 30, 2014

Frederick William Dame

The American Crisis

To All Patriotic Americans

A Call To Take Action

Number Nineteen

★★★★★★★★★★★★★

The American Crisis with Barack Hussein Obama as the cause is a subject that demands the attention of every patriotic United States citizen. Those who are not patriotic think Obama is God-like, although Satan-like is a better description. Therefore, these kinds of citizens could care less about patriotism and what happens to the existence of this free republic, the United States of America under Barack Hussein Obama.

The patriotic American public will remember that an illegal election of Barack Hussein Obama took place in November 2008 and again in November 2012. These elections were illegal because Barack Hussein Obama was an illegal candidate according to Article II, Section 1, Paragraph 5 of the *Constitution for the United States of America*. Until this said illegality of Barack Hussein Obama can be properly and legally prosecuted, it is necessary for American patriotic Republicans to gain political control of the United States Senate and keep control of the United States House of Representatives in the congressional election in November 2014. Furthermore, the enemedia must undergo a return to the responsibilities of a constitutionally guaranteed free press.

The Founding Fathers instituted and guaranteed a free press in the First Amendment to the *Constitution*. The press is the only profession stated in the *Bill of Rights*. The responsibility of the news media at the time of the Founding Fathers and now is to be a watchdog on government. The news media then and now has the responsibility of finding facts and reporting them with a perspective and sometimes contrarian views so that the informed citizen can better view the course of government. The enemedia has not done this since 2008 and in many cases since before that year. The facts concerning the vetting of Barack Hussein Obama and his

212

regime have neither been found, because the enemedia refused to find them, nor has the American citizenry ever been truthfully informed, because the enemedia has refused to inform them. Thus, the enemedia has broken itself off from its constitutional responsibility, in essence throwing aside the *Constitution for the United States of America*. In lieu thereof, the enemedia has established a selfish system of reporting Obama politics that can best be called going gaw-gaw over Obama, although there are other slang and vulgar expressions that can be used and which perhaps are better descriptions. The calculation of the enemedia is none other than to subtly fetter American opinion to Obama and his regime. In reality this fettering by the enemedia has two objectives: the one is to allure the American citizen to believe everything Obama says; and the other is to spirit up the Obama regime in placing the citizens of the United States under the total control of government for the eventual implementation of socialism-communism and sharia law. Viewed in this correct light, the Obama regime-enemedia interaction is an absurdity. It offends in the very act of endeavoring to ingratiate. The modus operandi and goals of the Obama regime and the enemedia are immoral.

Evidently, the enemedia thinks that America and its media have a right to be as foolish as they please, which has been proven by the practice of the majority of the American public and the enemedia throughout the past years. They forget that American Patriots are not sequestered from the happenings and revelations of the truth concerning Barack Hussein Obama. They forget that the truthful whispers are heard by other nations; that America's patriotic plans of politics and truth, which the Obama regime seems not to know, are necessary to return America to the right path of providence. America would be equally as foolish as any former tyranny were she to suffer a great degradation on her symbols the American flag and the founding documents, and a destructive stroke against the freedoms guaranteed by the *Bill of Rights*. Never forget that there is always a way to bring avarice and insolence to reason!

The ground of illegalities upon which the Obama regime has chosen to erect their policies is of a nature which ought, and I think must, awaken in every American a just and strong sense of national indignity. On the surface the policies appear to be sensible, but because they are based on

213

totalitarianism and rule of a mob, the Obama thugs are attempting measures which cannot succeed.

There is little time left for the politics of the United States to be properly directed to counteract the Obama regime's and enemedia's goals. The Obama thug regime exists for the sole purpose of wrecking havoc on the United States of America so that it will be ultimately destroyed. American society has been infiltrated and is being undermined by Progressives, Obots, Leftists, Dumbed-downers, Socialists-Communists (POLDS) who are a cancer that needs to be politically exterminated.

We are experiencing the day-to-day politics of political correctness. It is a behavior that is evil because it never tells the truth. WE the People have elected representatives in Washington who are not answering to WE the People. They are only intent at being asked to appear on political talk shows and interviews and to be o-so-politically correct. November, 2014 is the time and the opportunity to get rid of them so that America can return to act as a nation that is respected by its citizens and acclaimed by the world. The present situation of American politics discloses a truth too serious to be overlooked, and too mischievous not to be remedied.

The American citizen supporters of Barack Hussein Obama and the DemocRAT Party have committed treason against the United States of America, its traditions, and its patriotic Judeo-Christian values. The DemocRATS must be engaged head-on because they operate effectually as an injudicious, uncandid, and indecent mob made by sundry persons in a certain political nirvana who claim that only their recommendations to Congress are the answers to America's problems. It is because of the DemocRATS and the Obama regime that there is weakness in the national power of America. They are slowly but surely taking away a well-centered power in the United States with the goal of placing it under the auspices of the United Nations. There cannot be a doubt that if the idea of the diminished authority of America had occurred to them 100 years ago, they would have made the same grasp at socialism-communism as they are now making.

It is surprising that the process of honestly elected authority in the federal system, which can be supported with so much ease, and so little expense, and capable of such extensive advantages to the United States of

214

America, should be cavilled at by those DemocRATS and RINOS whose true duty – if they were ever responsible politicians with an ethical core to their spines – it is to watch over a freely elected authority, and whose existence as a free people depends upon it. But this illegal usurpation of government offices led by a charlatan-in-chief, perhaps, will ever be the case till some misfortune awakens us into reason. The instance now before America is but a gentle beginning of what America must expect, unless she guards her union with better care and stricter honor. United against Barack Hussein Obama and the DemocRATS the country is formidable, and that with the least possible charge a nation can be so. Separated in the fight against Barack Hussein Obama and the mob DemocRATS, America is a medley of individual nothings, subject to the whims of a usurper, and a DemocRAT Party fickle with itself, who have made America the sport of foreign nations.

The ingenuity of American Patriots has found out a simple method to counter and supersede the intentions of the Obama regime. That method is TRUTH! The Obama regime and the DemocRATS cannot carry on their policies without violating the truth. The most formidable truth is that America is sovereign and independent and ought to conduct her affairs in a regular style of character.

But it is only by the states acting in union against Barack Hussein Obama that the usurpations of his regime can be counteracted. Much is said about the implementation of the Obama regime's rules and regulations, and the chief thug's executive orders. There is no law in the United States of America that says a state or government body, whether it be local, regional, state, or nation-wide must implement illegal rules, regulations, and executive orders. The signature on such is based on the supposed fact that Obama occupies a legal position. But Obama is not occupying a legal position because he does not meet the legal qualifications of the presidential office as outlined and guaranteed by the *Constitution for the United States of America*. Therefore, there is no legal reason to enforce what the Obama regime passes as rules and regulations and what Obama signs off on as executive orders.

When WE the People view OUR flag, which to the eye is beautiful, and when WE the People contemplate its rise and origin, WE are inspired with a sensation of sublime delight. OUR national honor must unite with

215

OUR interest to prevent injury to the one, or insult to the other. WE the People must become ever more active in the political process. WE must communicate OUR thoughts to the enemedia and OUR elected representatives and senators in Congress, regardless of their wishy-washy political correctness. Bombard them with all kinds of mail. Perhaps the suggested formulation below will assist you.

Sources of form letters and petitions like the one below are to be found at

http://stop-obama-now.net/letter-to-congress/
http://act.theteaparty.net/10026/impeach-president-obama-remove-him-from-office/
http://www.petition2congress.com/6519/impeach-mr-obama/

You can modify, print, sign, and mail, e-mail, or fax the letter to your representative and two senators. You may edit the letter and personalize it and make it yours or send it as is. Do not forget to put the politician's name at the top and sign your name at the bottom. You can contact your representatives and senators via the information contained at http://www.contactingthecongress.org/ Send a copy of the letter to the enemedia of your choice or to all of them, as well.

Dear Congressman (So and So)

It is the duty of the Congress to impeach renegade Presidents and we certainly have one today. These past years, Obama has trampled on the *Constitution* and carried out multiple impeachable offenses against the citizens of this nation.

➤ He wages illegal wars, as in Libya, without the approval of Congress, as the *Constitution* requires.

➤ Four Americans died, because he did not adequately protect our ambassador in Libya due to his self-delusion about the war on terror being over and refusal to respond to the attack on our embassy there.

➤ Obama blatantly lied to the American public for weeks after the Benghazi attack as part of a political cover-up.

➢ He has intentionally assassinated American citizens abroad without due process in his illegal drone war.

➢ He has assassinated 5,000 other persons in illegal terroristic drone attacks in civilian areas of allied countries, such as Pakistan and Yemen, including hundreds of children and innocent bystanders.

➢ He has willingly sent thousands of military arms to the drug warlords, which will contribute to the death of hundreds of innocent Mexicans and Americans.

➢ He has performed unprecedented, massive surveillance on American citizens and used the Internal Revenue Service as a tool of revenge against his political enemies.

➢ He makes law by executive order, as with his self imposed Amnesty, rather than executing the laws as written. This is an obvious dictatorial violation of the *Constitution*.

➢ His fiscal policy is catastrophic, is bankrupting America and will make debt slaves out of all of us.

➢ His energy policies are a prescription to enslave us to foreign oil producers.

➢ He interferes in the internal affairs of the states, such as in Arizona and Texas.

➢ President Obama betrays some of our oldest and best allies and, while apologizing for and befriending some of our worst enemies. He even has the gall to shamefully bow to foreign dictators, such as the King of Saudi Arabia.

➢ Obama is not constitutionally eligible for the presidency in the first place as a non-natural born citizen, according to the Framers original intent.

➢ He has defrauded the American public with an obviously computer-fabricated image of his birth certificate posted on the White House website.

Barack Obama is the worst president the United States has ever had! He has some perverse, seditious personal agenda against the basic interests of the United States of America, whether it is an ethnic loyalty to radical Islam, due to his family origins, and/or the well-documented hateful religious mandate to destroy America and white society of Black Liberation Theology, the cult doctrine of his militant, pseudo-Christian "church" in Chicago.

I demand that you and the Congress impeach and remove him from office. If you do not, the continuing harm he does to this country will certainly impact your future as well as ours.

Sincerely,

(Your Name Here)

***

As the scenes of Obama's domestic war on America are very slowly drawing to a close and every man and woman is hopefully preparing for happier times with the 2014 and 2016 elections, I suggest that every American Patriot fly the American flag upside down. This is not a sign of disrespect. It is the official, federal recognition that the United States of America is in distress, a condition that will remain with US as long as Barack Hussein Obama and his thugs are still in office and have control of the United States Senate.

With this nineteenth *Call To Take Action* I take my leave of this present patriotic act against the tyrant Barack Hussein Obama. This does not mean that I will cease criticism of Barack Hussein Obama and refrain from placing him and the DemocRATS on the scaffold to be executed by truth. I will continue my patriotism with other subject matter at other times and at other places. I have most sincerely followed my course from beginning to end and through all its turns and windings. Wherever I may be in the future, I shall always feel an honest pride at the part I have taken and a sincere gratitude to my supporters, to Nature, and to

Providence for putting it in my power to be of some use to the present-day and the future United States of America.

Frederick William Dame
Patriotic, Steadfast, and True
June 4, 2014

POST SCRIPTUM

As used here, post scriptum means a carefully composed and concluding section of *The American Crisis* that contains afterthoughts.

★★★★★★★★★★★★★

Dear Reader!

There are two important subjects that reoccur in *The American Crisis* that you have just read. The first topic is the creeping threat of Islam and the fact that Barack Hussein Obama supports its institutionalization in the United States of America. The second topic is Barack Hussein Obama's goal of changing the United States of America with its capitalist, free market system into a socialism-communism state in which the control of everything from one's birth to one's death is in the hands of an all-powerful, centralized government. Both subjects are, like Barack Hussein Obama, inherently evil. It is of utmost importance that Americans understand why Islamization and socialism-communism are evil. Let us examine them closely and separately.

***

Islam

Contrary to what the propaganda claims and regardless of its source, Islam is not a religion. It is a political movement disguised in quasi-religious characteristics that at best can describe it as a destructive cult, a sinister, corrupt, and dangerous organization. Islam is a manipulative entity only bordering on the unstable fringe of being a religious movement. Islam has absolute control over its members. Islam is subversive. Islam claims to have a monopoly on all answers to questions of how to lead a true life, from going to the toilet, to having sexual acts with animals, adults, and minors. Islam claims that the believer can be saved from the evils of Satan by following Islam's own evil, anti-humane rules. Islam teaches that Muslims must follow their messianic, brainwashing, coercive, and bewitching, fear-evoking-leader-prophet Muhammad, if he ever lived, a postulation made by Robert Spencer in his book *Did Muhammad Exist? An Inquiry into Islam's Obscure Origin*s (ISI Books, Wilmington, Delaware: 2012).

220

Although there are some difficulties at describing Islam as a cult and not a religion, there are important characteristics that apply to Islam that do not apply to a religion such as Judaism or Christianity. Indeed, the following descriptions of Islam are completely the opposite in Judaism and Christianity, as well as other religions such as Hinduism or Buddhism. Aspects of Islam being a dangerous, political, pseudo-religious movement are:

➢ In Islam any criticism/questioning of the leader, the doctrines, and the teachings most often leads to death.

➢ In Islam the development of the individual is strongly limited with practically no emphasis on advancing one's potential. This is particularly true for females.

➢ In Islam the leader and follower both consider the leader to be beyond reproach. Therefore, leaders are not personally responsible for their actions.

➢ Islam demands the complete isolation of its members living in a non-Muslim country from the remainder of society.

➢ Islam exercises total control over its members, most often with brainwashing and mind-control techniques.

➢ Islam is not open to non-believers who want to keep their own religion.

➢ Islam's recruitment of followers is deceitful and based on fear.

➢ Islam's structure is totalitarian with no freedom of thought and speech.

➢ The commitment to Islam is a conversion process that a person undergoes without exercising a thought process.

At http://linkis.com/gatesofvienna.net/20/hqA12 there is an article by Bob Smith titled *Five Reasons Why Islam Is A Cult*. It explores the cultic core of Islam. Bob Smith lists five reasons with explanations as to why

Islam meets the criteria of being a cult. An abridgement with additional information is as follows:

1. A Muslim who quits Islam has to worry about being killed by another Muslim.

This is the first rule of Islam. This is why so few Muslims quit the faith. This simple fact – alone – makes Islam a cult. In Sahih Al-Bukhari Number 6922: Allah's apostle said, "if anyone changes his (Islamic) religion, then kill him." See also http://sheikyermami.com/apostasy-whoever-changes-his-islamic-religion-kill-him/. Muslims attempt to negate this fact by quoting the famous Islamic phrase *there is no compulsion in religion*. However, the Islamic doctrine of abrogation (repealing) negates this statement.

2. Muslims are encouraged to commit violence in the name of Islam.

There are 109 war verses in the Koran. They are:

Sura 2:178, 179, 190, 191, 193, 216, 217, 218, 244; **Sura 3**:12, 122, 123, 124, 125, 140, 155, 165, 166, 167, 169, 173, 195; **Sura 4**:71, 72, 74, 75, 76, 77, 84, 89, 91, 94, 95, 100, 102, 104; **Sura 5**:33, 35, 38; **Sura 8**:5, 7, 9, 12, 15, 16, 17, 39, 42, 45, 59, 65, 67, 69, 71, 72, 74, 75; **Sura 9**:5, 12, 13, 14, 16, 19, 20, 24, 25, 26, 29, 36, 38, 39, 41, 44, 52, 73, 81, 83, 86, 88, 92, 111, 120, 122, 123; **Sura 16**:110; **Sura 22**:39, 78; **Sura 29**:6, 69; **Sura 33**:7, 18, 20, 25, 26; **Sura 47**:20; **Sura 48**:16, 22; **Sura 59**:2, 5, 6, 7, 8, 14; **Sura 60**:9; **Sura 61**:4; **Sura 63**:4; **Sura 64**:14; **Sura 66**.9; **Sura 73**:20

There are 164 *Jihad* Verses in the Koran: Including some repetitions from the above listing they are presented in the following sourced table. (http://www.answering-islam.org/Quran/Themes/jihad_passages.html)

The *Koran*'s 164 *Jihad* Verses			
Chapter	**Verse**	**# per Sura**	**Running Count**
002	178-179, 190-191, 193-194, 216-218, 244	10	10

003	121-126, 140-143, 146, 152-158, 165-167, 169, 172-173, 195	25	35
004	071-072, 074-077, 084, 089-091, 094-095, 100-104, 144	18	53
005	033, 035, 082	3	56
008	001, 005, 007, 009-010, 012, 015-017, 039-048, 057-060, 065-075	34	90
009	005, 012-014, 016, 019-020, 024-026, 029, 036, 038-039, 041, 044, 052, 073, 081, 083, 086, 088, 092, 111, 120, 122-123	27	117
016	110	1	118
022	039, 058, 078	3	121
024	053, 055	2	123
025	052	1	124
029	006, 069	2	126
033	015, 018, 020, 023, 025-027, 050	8	134
042	039	1	135

047	004, 020, 035	3	138
048	015-024	10	148
049	015	1	149
059	002, 005-008, 014	6	155
060	009	1	156
061	004, 011, 013	3	159
063	004	1	160
064	014	1	161
066	009	1	162
073	020	1	163
076	008	1	164

Here are some selected examples from the war verses and those calling for killings:

➤ Slay the unbelievers wherever you find them. (2:191)

➤ Muslims must not take the infidels as friends. (3:28)

➤ Any religion other than Islam is not acceptable. (3:85)

➤ Maim and crucify the infidels if they criticize Islam. (5:33)

➤ Terrorize and behead those who believe in scriptures other than the Qur'an. (8:12)

➢ The unbelievers are stupid; urge the Muslims to fight them. (8:65)

➢ When opportunity arises, kill the infidels wherever you catch them. (9:5)

➢ The infidels are unclean; do not let them into a mosque. (9:28)

➢ Kill the Jews and the Christians if they do not convert to Islam or refuse to pay Jizya tax. (9:29)

➢ The Jews and the Christians are perverts; fight them. (9:3)

➢ Make war on the infidels living in your neighborhood. (9:123)

➢ Punish the unbelievers with garments of fire, hooked iron rods, boiling water; melt their skin and bellies. (22:19)

➢ Do not hanker for peace with the infidels; behead them when you catch them. (47:4)

Moreover, if a Muslim kills a Jew, that Muslim is guaranteed an honored place in the Islamic paradise, Jannah. As of this writing, the web site http://www.thereligionofpeace.com/ registers that Islamist terrorists have carried out 23,231 terror attacks in the name of Allah and Muhammad worldwide since 9/11. Of course, those who are politically correct will argue that Buddhists, Christians, Hindus, and Jews have carried out and still carry out such attacks. There are no historical facts to back up their claims.

3. Islam does not allow criticism or change.

Anyone who criticizes Islamic customs, beliefs, holy personages, religious artifacts, or tries to change Islam is guilty of blasphemy, because it is a matter of interpretation. Blasphemy is a capital crime under Sharia law, although no punishment of death is stated in the Koran.

Islam tells its devout believers to be *self-initiating* in the enforcement of Sharia law. This means *any* devout Muslim believer *anywhere* might commit violence spontaneously, if s/he finds anyone doing something s/he considers offensive to Islam.

4. Muslim ideology teaches hatred of non-Muslims.

This practice is widespread within Islamic society. It has been documented by numerous authors literally thousands of time. In Sura 2 there are 286 verses. One out of every 9.5 verses threatens non-Muslims and disobedient Muslims with eternal damnation.

5. Islam matches the *Characteristics Associated with Cultic Groups* according to the *International Cultic Studies Association* (*ICSA*).

Here are some of these characteristics that reinforce and support the listing according to the ICSA:

➢ Members are encouraged or required to live and/or socialize only with other group members.

➢ Members are expected to devote inordinate amounts of time to the group and group-related activities.

➢ Mind-altering practices (such as meditation, chanting, speaking in tongues, denunciation sessions, and debilitating work routines) are used in excess and serve to suppress doubts about the group and its leader(s).

➢ Questioning, doubt, and dissent are discouraged or even punished.

➢ Subservience to the leader or group requires members to cut ties with family and friends, and radically alter the personal goals and activities they had before joining the group.

➢ The group displays excessively zealous and unquestioning commitment to its leader and (whether he is alive or dead) regards his belief system, ideology, and practices as the truth, as law.

➢ The group has a polarized us-versus-them mentality, which may cause conflict with the wider society.

➢ The group is elitist, claiming a special, exalted status for itself, its leader(s) and members (for example, the leader is considered to be the messiah, a special being, an avatar – or the group and/or the leader is on a special mission to save humanity).

➢ The group is preoccupied with bringing in new members.

➢ The group teaches or implies that its supposedly exalted ends justify whatever means it deems necessary. This may result in members' participating in behaviors or activities they would have considered reprehensible or unethical before joining the group (for example, lying to family or friends, or collecting money for bogus charities).

➢ The leader is not accountable to any authorities.

➢ The leadership dictates, sometimes in great detail, how members should think, act, and feel: for example, members must get permission to date, change jobs, marry – or leaders prescribe what types of clothes to wear, where to live, whether or not to have children, how to discipline children, and so forth.

➢ The leadership induces feelings of shame and/or guilt in order to influence and/or control members. Often, this is done through peer pressure and subtle forms of persuasion.

➢ The most loyal members – *true believers* – feel there can be no life outside the context of the group. They believe there is no other way to be, and often fear reprisals to themselves or others if they leave or even consider leaving the group.

Islam is fear based on fear. Are these Islamic teachings questioned? No! Why not? Because Muslims and those who might question the doctrines fear for their lives!

Read the complementary information at:

http://gatesofvienna.net/211/11/islam-is-fear-part-i/
http://gatesofvienna.net/211/11/islam-is-fear-part-ii/
http://gatesofvienna.net/211/11/islam-is-fear-part-iii/

Supportive of the evidence that Islam is based on fear is the fact that in the 6,151 verses in the Koran, Muhammad threatens the reader with Hell, hellfire, wrath, and perdition in 783 verses. This is a ratio of 1 threat of Hell in every 7.9 verses.

***

Fear is the driving force behind the evilness that is Islam. It is also the driving force that is behind the evilness that is socialism-communism. Karl Marx called for all workers of the world to unite and that if they did not accept socialism-communism freely, it would be rammed down their throats.

The major problem with both Islam and socialism-communism is that it is constructed on falsehoods. We have seen some of the falsifications regarding Islam. Let us now look at the major falsifications of socialism-communism.

At the risk of being criticized with the argument of only scratching the surface of the subject matter, the false claims of socialism-communisms and the truthful facts concerning these claims are divided into sections below. Indeed, a complete book similar to *The Naked Communist* by W. Cleon Skousen, could be written on each aspect.

The INTERPRETATION OF HISTORY, SOCIETY and THE INDIVIDUAL

➤ Socialism-communism maintains that the course of history can only be defined by economics.

TRUTHFUL FACT COMMENT: A non-dumbed-down education teaches that the course of history is a mixture of climate, topography, geopolitics, inventions, scientific discoveries, religion, racial agreement and racial discrimination, patriotism, nationalism, regionalism, etc. There is nothing in the writings of Karl Marx or Friedrich Engels that comment on these influences. Marx and Engels claimed economic determinism determined everything. This is absurd.

➤ Human beings do not have the intellectual capacity of moral, free will and therefore cannot make a free choice in the developing course of history, which is determined by economics. Humans do not have the capacity to resist movement that is a predetermined direction. The human free will according to Marx and Engels is nothing more than the consciousness to realize that there are materialistic forces that determine

228

human actions in history. Human beings are only reacting to the dictates of materialism.

TRUTHFUL FACT COMMENT: Human behavior is more complex than just reacting to what materialism dictates. Humans have a desire for self-expression, want the implementation of religious beliefs, possess the desire to be a moral individual, and want to continue the quest to fulfill one's ambitions. These are not the dictates of materialism. Human beings not only react to the dictates of situations, they make decisions, moral decisions.

➢ The forms of past and future societies are pre-determined by economic situations.

TRUTHFUL FACT COMMENT: It is not true that the economic situation of a society demands that a certain type of society or government will or must exist. There is absolutely no relationship concerning the methods of production and the economic form the society will become. If any relationship exists, it is the feasibility of the productive process within the freedom of a society. Totalitarian societies will restrict the feasibility of everything that has to do with the production process. The restrictions will be mostly negative. People are free to choose the forms of governments they want, even if the process of choosing means revolting against tyranny.

THE STATE and the GOVERNMENT

➢ Socialists-Communists claim that the State (government) is created to preserve the interests of the ruling class and to exploit the workers.

TRUTHFUL FACT COMMENT: The State has to govern the society by some quality of authority because humans are social and political beings. A society without government would mean that the mob rules and there would no longer be any society.

➢ The coming into existence and the growth of the State is inevitable because of a particular economic circumstance.

TRUTHFUL FACT COMMENT: Let us allow that this is true. Therefore, the same mode of production in a State will always produce

229

the same form of government. However, we have to realize that this is not true. Slavery was the basic mode of production in Ancient Greece and Rome. Yet, Athens experienced successively hereditary monarchies, aristocracies, democratic republics, and despotism. Rome had successively an elected royalty, aristocracies, democratic republic, and absolutism of the Caesars. Slavery was and in many cases still is the mode of production in Islamic countries. The Gulf States are Islamic countries that have their economies based on oil. However, in the Middle Ages such economies were based on trade, although we must admit that the government form we can name Islamic despotism has not changed.

➢ Socialism-communism claims that the State develops laws to protect the ruling class in its exploitation of the workers. A change in the economic method of production requires a change in the laws of the State to govern the society in the new mode of production.

TRUTHFUL FACT COMMENT: The United States of America has had the *Constitution for the United States of America* as its fundamental governing law since 1790. Even when slavery ended after the Civil War the fundamental law of the nation and the states were not deleted for new legal codes. The articles in the *Constitution* dealing with slavery and citizenship of slaves were negated and re-written.

RELIGION and MORALS

➢ Socialism-communism claims that religion is a tool of the dominant classes to keep control of the exploited class by means of three functions:

• Advocates that the poor must have respect for the property rights of the rich.
• Tells the poor of their responsibilities to property and the ruling class.
• Destroys the revolutionary attitudes of the poor by allowing them to possess some commodities.

TRUTHFUL FACT COMMENT: Judeo-Christian teachings [Talmud (Jebamot 89b; Baba Batra 8b; Sanhedrin 17b), Old Testament (Isaiah 3:14-15), New Testament (James 5:1-6)] have always taught that the rich should pay the worker proper wages according to the worker's capability. Persons living according to Judeo-Christian rules will not steal property at the command of a leader and will not participate in destroying human life. Religion helps people to resist dominance by a political group and their ideology. Judeo-Christian teachings are for peace while socialism-communism, and Islam are for world revolution.

➢ The socialists-communists claim that Judeo-Christian laws (Ten Commandments and successive laws) exist to protect the propertied classes and private property. For example, children are the property of the mother and father as claimed by the commandment *Honor thy father and mother*; physical human bodies are private property as claimed by the commandment *Thou shalt not kill*; the man is the master of the house and the wife his property as claimed by the commandments *Thou shalt not commit adultery* and *Thou shalt not covet thy neighbor's wife*.

TRUTHFUL FACT COMMENT: Socialism-communism had to liberate people from these restrictions making women equal with men in the socialist-communist sense; by placing children in a state institution one month after the birth, where they were to remain until they were 17. Laws were passed that stated women were/are never violated by men. To say that they were violated would mean that women were property. Socialism-communism operates on the same moral formula as Islam: anything that furthers socialism-communism is good; everything else is bad. (Everything that promotes and furthers Islam is good; everything else is bad.) This is a formula with no morals.

CLASS STRUGGLE and WAGES

➢ The secret of human progress is the class struggle.

TRUTHFUL FACT COMMENT: The classes in ancient Egypt, Greece, and Rome did not struggle against each other respectively. The so-called progress that occurred in Greece and Rome were a result of the barbarian invasions. Egypt was invaded by the heathen Arabs under the guise of Islam. Egyptian culture was destroyed. In Greece and Rome a great majority of their cultures were allowed to survive.

➢ Class hatred and class struggle will develop and increase automatically, say Marx and Engels.

231

TRUTHFUL FACT COMMENT: This did not happen automatically. There had to be a ruse that did prove that class struggle happens automatically and that class struggle will increase. Therefore socialist-communist agitators have been used to fuel the fires of class struggle. However, workers have become an integral part of the free market system.

➢ Socialism-communism wants wealth to become monopolized. This is predominantly apparent under the politics of Barack Hussein Obama with his program to tax the rich in order to pay for the big-government handouts to the poor workers, if they have work. The propertyless class would increase under capitalism.

TRUTHFUL FACT COMMENT: The propertyless class has not increased under free market capitalism. In fact, more wealth has been very widely distributed under capitalism than under any socialist-communist system. However, the rules and regulations of Barack Hussein Obama governing America's economy have placed more proletarians on unemployment than there would ever be under a capitalist, free market system. Obama has created a greater crisis where before there was practically none.

➢ Marx claimed that technological development would mean that there would be more machines doing the work of the proletariat.

TRUTHFUL FACT COMMENT: It is economic fact that the technological advancements, at least in western democratic republics, have produced more jobs for workers and a better income because workers' unions and employers have consented to regulate their own business/industry wages. Business and industries that cannot compete on the open market are replaced with ones that can compete and possibly better compete and employ more workers.

➢ Marx and Engels believed that wages would ever decrease and therefore the only possibility of living would be left to those who owned property.

TRUTHFUL FACT COMMENT: The reality is that wages have always increased, regardless of a minimum wage level. Supply and demand of goods and services and available, qualified specialist worked influence

232

wages. Not all of these specialist workers have property. Some can live under very good conditions with a lower wage than one's neighbor. If my neighbor purchases a car every year, that does not mean that I have to purchase one, also. I may be satisfied with my car for five, ten, or even more years. Perhaps it will attain an age when it is an old timer and I can sell it for far more than what I paid. Nevertheless, I still live as well as my neighbor. I don't need steak and lobster and champagne every day like some people. Perhaps this is the real *from each according to his ability to each according to his needs*.

➢ The socialism-communism of Marx and Engels claims that the middle class would regress to the propertyless class under capitalism and unite with the proletariat to revolt and overthrow the capitalists.

TRUTHFUL FACT COMMENT: In every capitalist country since the age of Marx and Engels, the middle class has increased in numbers. Only in socialist-communist countries has the middle class decreased or become non-existent.

➢ The novice to political theory and political ideologies will often hear that the class struggle which is so necessary to socialism-communism will definitely lead to progress. The reasoning is the dialectic process of Karl Marx and Friedrich Engels: thesis ↔ antithesis → synthesis. The conflict and struggle between two opposing forces will yield a new advancement called the synthesis, which can then become a new thesis.

TRUTHFUL FACT COMMENT: Surely Arab countries, China, Egypt, Pakistan, India, Indonesia, and Moslem countries can be listed as quite unprogressive. Moreover, nations throughout the history of civilization have risen to become great powers only then to decline into intellectual, moral, and economic decay.

➢ Marx and Engels claimed that the class struggle mentioned above would predict what would happen to societies in the future and what kind of society a certain country would become and what type of government it would have. They said that socialism-communism would follow and grow as a result of the class struggle of capitalism. Marx said that socialism-communism would appear in Germany first. Then he changed his mind and said it would first appear in England.

TRUTHFUL FACT COMMENT: Socialism-communism first appeared in Zarist Russia which was a dictatorial monarchy in a feudal society. Communism in Russia did not result because of a class struggle. It was the result of a coup d'état by Lenin supported by Germany during the end phase of World War I. The famous dictatorship of the proletariat did not exist in the takeover of Russia. In fact it has never existed.

THE DICTATORSHIP OF THE PROLETARIAT and THE ECONOMY in REVERSE

➤ According to Marx and Engels, the goal of the dictatorship of the proletariat in socialism-communism was to destroy private property and place all modes of production under government control which would create an economic situation that would provide everyone with wealth.

TRUTHFUL FACT COMMENT: Whenever the dictatorship of the proletariat has attempted to accomplish the spreading of wealth to everyone by destroying private property and having the government decide on solutions to economic problems, there has always been a reverse of the country's economy. Marx and Engels failed to understand that there is a difference between private property rights and private property abuse. There is a not too famous saying in Latin, *proprietas obligat,* that is most famous in German as *Eigentum verpflichtet,* and hardly known in English as *property has its responsibilities.* In order for a socialist-communist state to destroy the abuse of property it always says it must abolish the right to property and place it under the control of government so that everyone has a right to its wealth. However, the state always becomes a monopolist and there is never a wider distribution of wealth that the populace can enjoy because this state monopoly makes the ultimate goal of socialism-communism to be never attainable and the populace becomes poorer than it was at first. Thus the economic goal of socialism-communism is reversed.

➤ Marx and Engels said that the dictatorship of the proletariat would pay each person for the work that said person accomplished, but it would never pay wages.

TRUTHFUL FACT COMMENT: Such an economic pricing for work accomplishment, often by means of work certificates or work stamps,

234

always forces such an economic system into a form of bartering. This is the reverse of economic advancement.

➢ The dictatorship of the proletariat is also responsible for the creation of a large defense army that will liberate the proletarians in other countries so that the dictatorship of the proletariat can control the world.

TRUTHFUL FACT COMMENT: This corresponds to the Islamic establishment of the world caliphate and the use of Islamic terrorists to liberate non-believers so that Muslims can control the world. The dictatorship of the proletariat defense armies are always defensive and their victims are always liberated into regressive economic slavery.

➢ The dictatorship of the proletariat will convince the mass population of the effectiveness of socialism-communism.

TRUTHFUL FACT COMMENT: The effectiveness of socialism-communism always ends in economic regression and a numbing of and dumbing down of mass consciousness. The goal is to have followers who will not question the leaders of the movement.

HURRAH for THE CLASSLESS SOCIETY and the ADMINISTRATION OF THINGS

➢ According to Marx, Engels, and Lenin people would learn how to live simply in the commune.

TRUTHFUL FACT COMMENT: The truth behind socialism-communism in this regard is that although a person can be conditioned by the environment, it cannot change a person's nature. Regardless of how forcefully one will be coerced into communal living, there will always be the quest for freedom and the wish to fulfill one's personal desires. What socialism-communism seeks to abolish are exactly those aspects of human life that bring success and progress. The same holds true for Islam. What Islam seeks to abolish are specifically those aspects of human life that make life worth living.

➢ Real socialism-communism is in the statement *from each according to his ability to each according to his needs.*

TRUTHFUL FACT COMMENT: Karl Marx summed up Communism with the words *from each according to his ability, to each according to his needs*. This is a good, pithy saying, which, in practice, has succeeded in bringing, upon those under its sway, misery, poverty, rape, torture, slavery, and death. Marx and Engels saw the communist utopia as being in the hands of the dictatorship of the proletariat led by the vanguard of the proletariat in the administration of things according to the principle *from each according to his abilities to each according to his needs*. This is based upon the perverted communist interpretation of human behavior. Marx and Engels saw the communist utopia in the future and claimed that it would be achieved by technology and industrialization. This is the core communist theory that class struggle will lead to necessary progress. This is a fallacy because as Jean-Jacques Rousseau argues, nations (societies) rise to power and then become immoral and decay, thus losing their culture and economic and technological predominance. In history this is called the retrogression of civilizations. *Chacun selon ses faculties, à chacun selon ses besoins* is from Étienne-Gabriel Morelly, in his *Code de la Natur ou la Vértitable Esprit des Ses Loix* (1755) It is not from Marx, Engels, Lenin, or Stalin. Hitler exploited a sub-thought (one's abilities and one's needs are freedom within the dictates of the system.) behind the statement with *Arbeit macht frei*! There is nothing but the destruction of work incentives in the maxim *from each according to his ability, to each according to his needs*. There is no incentive for self-improvement. Workers will never produce according to their ability. They will produce according to incentives.

➤ Marx, Engels, Lenin, and Stalin, even Mao Zedong contend that the masses will rule in a stateless society.

TRUTHFUL FACT COMMENT: Mass rule in any society is always rule by the mob.

➤ The condition of full socialism-communism in the administration of things will destroy ones desire to acquire property.

TRUTHFUL FACT COMMENT: Throughout the history of civilization it has never been possible for a government to destroy one's desire to acquire property.

➤ Marx and Engels contend that in a classless society and the administration of things the production process will produce more goods than in any other system.

TRUTHFUL FACT COMMENT: The classless society and the administration of things always requires more control mechanisms than in a free market or free-enterprise society because the workers are not producing to be paid in wages which they can use to acquire property of whatever kind, but are producing because the classless society and the administration of things is dictating to them to produce.
For those who want to understand socialism-communism in its naked evilness, this author recommends W. Cleon Skousen's book *The Naked Communist* (Salt Lake City, Utah: 1958), upon which many of the arguments presented in this Post Scriptum are founded.

***

To understand how the Obama regime functions, it is necessary to understand the Cloward-Piven strategy of social progress via big government handouts. In an article titled *The Weight of the Poor: A Strategy to End Poverty* in the May 1966 issue of the liberal magazine *The Nation*, a married couple who were sociology and political activist professors at the Columbia University, Richard Cloward (1926-21) and Francis Fox Piven (1932-), developed a social-political strategy that would cause an overloading crisis of the United States public welfare system so that the outcome would replace the welfare system with a national-government-backed system of guaranteed annual income which would result in ending poverty.

Cloward and Piven said that only the DemocRAT Party was able to execute this strategy because the party was made up of white, middle class, working class, ethnic groups, and minority poor, especially Blacks. To keep the DemocRAT Party alive it was necessary for the DemocRAT Party to provide a federal solution to poverty that would replace the failure of the present welfare system. A sideline effect would be the creation of a vast civilian army of full-time liberal activists who would help the poor and unemployed to file applications for government support. This army of liberal social workers would be paid by the money received from the taxation of conservative workers.

In 1975 New York City hovered on the edge of bankruptcy. Since then city bankruptcy, in cities with mostly DemocRAT Party administrations, has increased. According to the information at http://www.governing.com/gov-data/municipal-cities-counties-bankruptcies-and-defaults.html there have been 38 official city bankruptcy filings since January 2010. A high blame for these bankruptcies belongs to the Cloward–Piven strategy. The final phase of the Cloward-Piven strategy is the total collapse of the American economic system in order to make way for socialism-communism. There is good reason to argue that the Barack Hussein Obama regime has applied the Cloward-Piven strategy in several areas. The political author and researcher Don Fredrick in the June 2014 issue of *The Obama Timeline* at http://www.theobamatimeline.com/ notes that

➢ "With Operation Fast and Furious, the plan was to dramatically increase gun violence as a way to gin up public support for stricter gun control legislation. (The ultimate goal is to outlaw guns.)

➢ ObamaCare's taxes, rules, and regulations will drive private insurers out of business, encourage businesses to dump employees onto the federal exchange, and generally destabilize the entire health care system—with the intention of prompting Americans to eventually 'cry uncle' and say, 'Okay, I give up! Give us a fully socialized system!' (The ultimate goal is to have the government own and control all hospitals and make all doctors and nurses federal employees.)

➢ Flooding the nation with illegal immigrant children creates a 'humanitarian emergency' that provides Obama with an excuse to 'take action' that will likely conflict with the wishes of the American people. (The ultimate goal is to flood the United States with eventual Democrat voters.)

➢ The administration's 'global warming' scare tactics prompt non-thinking Americans to agree, 'Yes, the government must do something now!'—and suddenly the EPA is regulating coal-fired power plants out of existence. (The ultimate goal is to place all power production under direct government control.)

➢ The government makes it incredibly easy for students to borrow money for college loans they cannot afford to pay back, with the short-term goal of buying the votes of young people with loan-forgiveness schemes. (The ultimate goal is to eliminate all private universities and place all colleges under federal control.)

Don Fredrick continues, "The Cloward-Piven strategy is in the handbook of every community activist because it is an effective tool. The activists (or the White House or the Department of Justice) create a problem significant enough to make people willing to accept even greater government control over their lives. The process is simple: Do not ask people if they want more government; create a reason to demand it. Behind many crises is the hand of a local, state, or federal operative practicing the Cloward-Piven strategy." With the Cloward-Piven strategy and his other criminal and evil political schemes Barack Hussein Obama is undertaking political deconstruction by destroying the federal republic that is the United States of America and supplanting it with socialism-communism.

It would behoove all American citizens, even the POLDS, to impress in their brains the thoughts of three important Enlightenment thinkers. They are Thomas Jefferson, Henry David Thoreau, and Jean-Jacques Rousseau

In his *Notes on the State of Virginia*, Thomas Jefferson wrote that "Dependency begets subservience and venality, suffocates the germs of virtue, and prepares fit tools for the designs of ambition." American society under Barack Hussein Obama has no virtues because it condones such a collective evil as he and his regime. Thus America cannot advance forward. A stupid people will never be few. DemocRATS keep their hierarchical party that breeds itself by dependence on others. From that political party there emerged a powerful demagogue who plays on and panders to the passions of the mob, whom the DemocRATS have dumbed down in order to install their absolutist government. Only absolutist governments can maintain the absolutism status quo of absolutist inequality. The solution to the predicament is to remove them from public office and to reverse the dumbing-down process that the DemocRATS have conducted over the last 100 years. In a letter to George Wythe, Paris, dated August 13, 1786, Thomas Jefferson wrote: "Preach ... a crusade against ignorance; establish and improve the law for educating the common people. Let our countrymen know that the people alone can protect us against these evils of (dictatorial) government."

However, this can take place only if the people are not dumbed down and brainwashed by liberal illogical thought.

The American transcendental philosopher Henry David Thoreau was of the opinion that the individual who identifies with the class of DemocRAT politicians will eventually lose their self-esteem. In his essay *On Civil Disobedience*, Thoreau reasoned that "as most legislators, politicians, lawyers, ministers, and office holders, serve the state chiefly with their heads", and "as they rarely make any moral distinctions," ... "they are as likely to serve the Devil, without intending it, as God." Those few who "serve the state with their consciences", the "heroes, patriots, martyrs, and reformers in the great sense, and men ... are commonly treated as enemies by it" because the true, moral patriots, in their moral conscience, resist the state's collective evils. It is the true duty of the moral citizen to fight and protect against evil as it is practiced by the state. He should not only be prepared to face the country's foes, but, as Thoreau wrote in *A Plea For Captain John Brown*, the patriot must have "the courage to face his country herself when she (is) wrong." Thoreau proclaims in *On Civil Disobedience* that the American patriot cannot "for an instant recognize that political organization as (his) government which is the slave's government also." Indeed, "(t)he only government (the individual should) recognize – and it matters not how few are at the head of it, or how small its army – is that power that establishes justice in the land, never that which establishes injustice." Governments built upon injustice are immoral and deserve to be overthrown. The private citizen has a duty to resist all of the evils of the state, even if such resistance will demand disobedience, public or private, of its laws. The consequence is irrelevant.

We can compare this point with Jean-Jacques Rousseau's clear position in *Du Contrat Social*: "To renounce liberty ... is incompatible with man's nature; to remove all liberty from his will is to remove all morality from his acts." And "... it is an empty and contradictory convention that sets up, on the one side, absolute authority, and, on the other, unlimited obedience." Jefferson, Thoreau, and Rousseau were truly politicized citizen. The American Patriot must obey the dictates of his/her moral conscience, otherwise society is the equivalent of slavery. To paraphrase and quote Rousseau from *The Social Contract*, "(If WE the People) do not obey (OUR) moral conscience WE the People) put (OURSELVES) into a situation which will make US subject to evil, and obeying evil is not freedom. (People) who live in a society in which morality is removed from their acts (laws) must question their existence as *free* (persons)."

The majority of Americans are in a deplorable condition because they have allowed themselves to be duped and brainwashed by a regime of corrupt politicians. The Obama regime gives the people a false impression of participating, a feeling of being players. This hits at the heart of the American political and social psyche. If wisdom is maturity of outlook, then whatever virtues Americans may have, wisdom is not one of them. They have collectively, immature points of view; they have a typical youth's outlook on life. They are boys and girls playing games. They eat, work, sleep, and even think in terms of game and sport. American business and politics are games, for to be a *success* one has to follow the old dictum: *Play according to the rules of the game.*; whether the rules are moral or not.

These stated positions of Thomas Jefferson, Henry David Thoreau, and Jean-Jacques Rousseau, as well as the standpoints of this author in these essays must be an integral part of the American citizens' political undertaking.

The United States of America must remain a republic because democracies will always degenerate because demagogues will rise to power who will surely play on the vanities of the mob populace to secure their positions of political power. Once in political power DemocRATS will overstretch the rights of the government. They will despise government duties. They will put their trust in traitors and persecute American patriots. Would-be demagogues will dupe the public in order to achieve their long-sought goal of swallowing down American liberties. Such DemocRAT demagogues displace the superior men who are truly qualified to lead but will not pander to the vanity of the mob. The American republic must always be in the hands of WE the People.

***

Because practically no town, municipality, state, or national government agency will fly the flag upside down, a final suggestion this author has is for every patriotic American to fly the American flag upside down at

241

their homes, on their lawns, in their backyards, and even on their cars and trucks. Flying the flag upside down is a sign of distress. According to US Code:T36 Ch1.176 (a) "The flag should never be displayed with the union down, except as a signal of dire distress in instances of extreme danger to life or property." A flag flown upside down can indicate a mutiny, a piracy, a sinking, a coup, and particularly a rebellion of the people/government. A flag flown upside down under the regime of Barack Hussein Obama is a protest against the distress that is the anti-Americanism of the Barack Hussein Obama regime. Purchase a flag and fly it upside down!

The intent of *The American Crisis* is to wake up Americans to their dire situation under the Barack Hussein Obama regime and encourage them to take action against Barack Hussein Obama and his thug regime.

For those of you who are now awake, stay awake, and wake up other Americans!

★★★★★★★★★★★★★

Frederick William Dame
Patriotic, Steadfast, and True
In August, 2014.

INDEX

Like all indices, this index is selective. Names, words, and phrases such as Barack Hussein Obama, DemocRAT Party, DemocRAT, DemocRATS, WE the People, American Patriot, American Patriots, United Nations, etc., are not listed because they occur very often throughout the nineteen essays. However, the terminology *Obama regime* is listed in order to emphasize the fact that Barack Hussein Obama's government is in reality a regime.

247

www.ingramcontent.com/pod-product-compliance
Lightning Source LLC
Chambersburg PA
CBHW060240290526
45789CB00001B/126